A BRITISH ANARCHIST TRADITION

A BRITISH ANARCHIST TRADITION
HERBERT READ, ALEX COMFORT AND COLIN WARD

by

CARISSA HONEYWELL

BLOOMSBURY

NEW YORK · LONDON · NEW DELHI · SYDNEY

Bloomsbury Academic
An imprint of Bloomsbury Publishing Plc

175 Fifth Avenue
New York
NY 10010
USA

50 Bedford Square
London
WC1B 3DP
UK

www.bloomsbury.com

First published by Continuum International Publishing Group 2011
Paperback edition first published 2013

Library of Congress Cataloging-in-Publication Data
Honeywell, Carissa.
A British anarchist tradition : Herbert Read, Alex Comfort and Colin Ward /
Carissa Honeywell.
p. cm.
Includes bibliographical references and index.
ISBN-13: 978-1-4411-9017-8 (hbk. : alk. paper)
ISBN-10: 1-4411-9017-1 (hbk. : alk. paper) 1. Anarchism–Great Britain–History–
20th century. 2. Read, Herbert, 1893–1968. 3. Comfort, Alex, 1920–2000.
4. Ward, Colin. I. Title.
HX885.H66 2011
355'.83092241–dc22
2010051774

ISBN: HB: 978-1-4411-9017-8
PB: 978-1-4411-7689-9

Typeset by Newgen Imaging Systems Pvt Ltd, Chennai, India

Contents

List of Illustrations

1

A British Anarchist Tradition

Introduction

In June 2001, when British Prime Minister Tony Blair condemned what he referred to as an 'anarchists' travelling circus' for engaging in the violent protest that marred the EU Summit in Gothenburg that summer, he was not of course referring to the historic anarchist tradition. He was employing the notion of 'anarchy' in a manner that has been typical of mainstream debate in Britain, merely to designate a violent and unconsidered approach to political protest. It is a term which is of very little use when discussing the political theory of anarchism, which is marked by a tendency for careful and contextual debate around questions of social order and revolutionary tactics. The 'anarchy' of the Gothenburg protestors, identified according to its 'sole purpose of causing as much mayhem as possible', had, according to Blair, 'no place in a democracy'.[1] Rhetoric aside, the anti-globalization and anti-capitalist movements of the late twentieth and early twenty-first centuries have in fact exhibited some significant affinities with the anarchist ideological tradition. This can be identified in their rejection of both market economics and state-oriented social organization, and a commitment to means of social change that prefigure their non-hierarchical goals of autonomy, voluntary organization, direct action and mutual aid. These affinities have inspired research and scholarship into new movements by writers and academics concerned to take seriously the place of anarchist ideas in modern democracies.[2] This research suggests that there has been a marked utilization of anarchist themes in some new social movements, such as hostility to the state and to parliamentarianism, resistance to war, the use of direct action in practice and as a mode of analysis, organization through co-operative association and a commitment to bottom-up organization. As anarchist historian David Goodway remarks, 'It should therefore be immediately apparent that the current is of central contemporary pertinence.'[3] The scope of the new field of anarchist studies reflects a recognition of the value of research into the history of anarchist-inspired movement and struggle, political and social theories (and theorists) of anarchism, and new directions in anarchist thought.[4] This new field challenges some established assumptions about anarchism as they have been presented in mainstream literature on political history and ideas. In the majority of this literature anarchist theory and practice has been marginalized in comparison to other political ideologies as irrelevant, alien to familiar political traditions, amorphous, paradoxical, and anachronistic. However, Uri Gordon, drawing on activist research into radical social change movements, identifies contemporary anarchism as 'a mature and complex genre of political expression' which deserves 'serious attention from students of ideology'. Gordon identifies three defining elements to contemporary anarchism's stable ideological core: active opposition to systems of 'domination' or hierarchy, a commitment to strategies of direct action, whether 'destructive' or 'constructive' in nature, and an 'open-ended', 'experimental' approach to revolutionary goals and tactics, which is grounded in 'present tense action'.[5]

The wider field of anarchist studies that has emerged over the last decade or so directly challenges the dismissal of anarchism from the study of social and political theory, social movements and ideological tradition, and addresses the gaps in these fields generated by its absence. Little, however, has been written about British anarchism.[6] George Crowder has remarked that 'Anarchists are often presented by academic commentators as estranged mavericks among political thinkers, amusing eccentrics who, for reasons more psychologically than philosophically interesting, have rejected all precedents and traditions of political thought.'[7] This is particularly the case in the standard treatment of British anarchist writers. Even prominent anarchist historian George Woodcock dismissed the possibility of native anarchist currents with his claim that 'English anarchism has never been anything else than a chorus of voices crying in the wilderness.'[8] Yet, the relationship of British anarchist writing to native literary, cultural and political traditions and contexts belie established assumptions about the completely alien and imported nature of anarchist thinking in Britain. In particular, the work of the three British anarchist intellectuals to be addressed here, Herbert Read, Alex Comfort and Colin Ward, represents a lively domestic political and intellectual tradition, rather than a distant and polemic ideological outsider. These three writers shared methodologies, key concepts and modes of operation (and co-operation), and as such they form a coherent grouping within British radical thought. Focusing on their work helps to locate anarchism within the struggle of ideas in Britain, particularly concerning war and the state, and the limits of state intervention in light of the developing remit of its activity following World War Two. For example, many people are aware of Herbert Read as a historian of art, or of Alex Comfort as the author of *The Joy of Sex*, while having no idea that both of them were committed to anarchist thought in the particular context of the settlements being forged between government and the mainstream left in Britain in the mid-century era. The anarchist writers in question, Herbert Read, Alex Comfort and Colin Ward, drew on novel and embedded intellectual currents, and they were members of recognizable intellectual communities. They were not isolated eccentrics, but rather they were participants in public political debates and were engaged in political movements. These figures were clear about their commitment to anarchist political ideas. They were explicit about the anarchist themes and concepts that underpinned their intellectual endeavours and made public claims that their aim was to revive and apply anarchism to twentieth-century politics. They addressed their ideas to both anarchist and non-anarchist public audiences, and they took public positions in political controversies regarding war, democracy, pacifism and public policy. These three authors were prominent contributors to currents of thought relating to radical practice, housing, education and social policy, and, in one case, associated with a notorious challenge to conventional codes of morality in sexual behaviour. Anarchism underpinned their intellectual endeavours (and their notoriety) in these fields. Through their efforts they deployed and refined traditional anarchist themes and applied them to British social and political dilemmas. At the same time they asserted the presence and viability of an alternative libertarian breed of native British socialism. This book will examine the anarchist ideas of Herbert Read, Alex Comfort and Colin Ward in the contexts in which they were utilized in order to develop both a better understanding of modern deployments of the tradition and also demonstrate the distinct role which anarchism has played in recent ideas and movements. It will highlight in particular the fact that these thinkers deployed anarchism in response to features of the twentieth century in British contexts. These thinkers addressed British experiences, with parallel diagnoses of the problems and solutions facing modern British society, drawing on native literary, intellectual and political traditions, and with a clear line of influence linking them together. The book will present the work of these three twentieth-century British anarchist writers *as a tradition* for the first time, highlighting the consistency of their concerns and themes. This is not to suggest that the anarchism of these three figures constitutes the only British anarchist tradition. Other, related, strains of anarchist thought and practice in Britain include the more combative, class-focused challenge of figures like Stuart Christie and Albert Meltzer. These writers, associated with the paper *Black Flag*, adopted a more fiercely class-war form of anarchism. The anarchist Class War Federation of the 1980s took a similar stance, and the Direct Action Movement which reformed in 1979 focused on syndicalist traditions of anarchism. These other strands of British anarchism are not, however, the focus of this study, suffice to say that the distance between them and the subjects of this book have perhaps been overdrawn. Much of what can be said about the tradition of British anarchism that *is* being addressed could apply to these other parallel traditions of British anarchism.

State and Society in National Debate

Anarchism has been particularly overlooked in the study of twentieth-century British ideas and movements. This volume offers the reader a view of one seam of anarchist thinking that recognizes its distinct place in the twentieth-century history of Britain, a period in which most political history assumes the left in Britain to have been entirely dominated by collectivist, as opposed to libertarian, socialist traditions.

If we are going to take seriously a current of indigenous engagement with anarchism in British public debate in the twentieth century, we need to take account of embedded discussions and disagreement about the role and nature of the state in British political thought stretching back to the late nineteenth century, especially on the left. This national debate over the legitimate scope of public concern and state action engaged with some themes and concerns which have played central roles in the development of anarchist ideas, notably the distinction between society and the state. This distinction is an important component of the anarchist celebration of voluntary and egalitarian social order. However, the distinction is firmly embedded in classical traditions of political thought. The contrast between society and the state can be identified with ancient Greek distinctions between nature and convention, and traced through John Locke's contrast between 'the state of nature' and 'civil' or 'political' society by means of which he argued that the state is an artificial device, independent of the natural order, and devised to safeguard natural rights. Tom Paine relied on a similar distinction to argue, in *The Rights of Man*, published in 1792, that the 'great part of that order which reigns among mankind is not the effect of government. It has its origins in the principles of society and the natural constitution of man. It existed prior to government and would exist if the formality of government was abolished.'[9] From here, it is only a small shift in emphasis which led to Godwin's conclusion a year later, in *Political Justice*, that government can be dispensed with altogether, and Kropotkin's much fuller elaboration in *Mutual Aid*, published in 1902, of the social principle inherent in human nature, which removes the need for political regulation entirely. The belief in natural society is the basis for the anarchist rejection of the state, and of the attendant concentration and centralization of the organization of society in the hands of the few. The commitment to the idea of natural society runs through all anarchist rejections of hierarchy and political power, and it features particularly in Colin Ward's *Anarchy in Action*.[10] It underpins the anarchist conception of the positive relationship between the individual and society, which recognizes both the importance and interdependence of creative uniqueness and social cohesion. Importantly, this anarchist commitment undermines any state authority to engage civilian populations in warfare, which itself exposes the essentially coercive and violent nature of the state.

The dichotomy between natural society and the 'organized violence' of the state helps to explain the anarchist position on violence, which often advocates non-violent means of social change, yet does not always condemn episodes of violence as they occur in protests or movements against the actions of the state or in revolutionary circumstances. Most thinkers in the classic anarchist tradition from Michael Bakunin onwards have not rejected violence per se, celebrating left-wing causes in violent rebellions and civil wars in Russia and Spain for example, but they have opposed wars between states and adhered to anti-militarist agendas. Historically, while pacifism refers to opposition to war, and to positive efforts to create peace between nations, anti-militarism identifies war with the political and economic interests of elites. While pacifism tends to have a strong affinity with non-violent attitudes, anti-militarism is not necessarily associated with the rejection of all violence. American social critic Randolph Bourne is often quoted in anarchist explication of the view that 'War is the health of the State', an often repeated line from his 1919 essay 'The State'. Anarchists adhere closely to the socio-political analysis presented in this essay as the crux of their anti-militarist account of the social relationships underpinning the state's propensity to engage in warfare. War represents the full culmination of the collective identification and 'hierarchy of values' upon which the state depends, and which the anarchists in this volume make their particular enemy. 'At war,' Bourne wrote, 'the individual becomes almost identical with his society.'[11] In defending the social importance of individuality, and the pluralism underpinning co-operative and voluntary social relationships, anarchists seek to attack both the state and its ability to engage populations in war. In attacking war and the state together, the unity of this critique being represented in the concept of anti-militarism, anarchists seek to defend individuals and support the development of horizontal rather than hierarchical models of society. Bourne provided a concise account of the socio-political analysis underpinning this perspective: 'The State is intimately connected with war, for it is in the organization of the collective community when it acts in a political manner, and to act in a political manner towards a rival group has meant, throughout all history – war.'[12] As far as anarchists are concerned, this insidious political mobilization of individuals and communities as a collective national entity relies on the core elements of the nation–state, and reinforces their objection to these features. This highlights the identification anarchists make between war and the nation–state. These elements of statehood include its sovereign territoriality, with the maintenance of territorial borders; the exclusive jurisdiction over people and property within that territory; the monopoly over the means of force; the system of law which overrides all other codes and customs, outside of which no rights or obligation are seen to exist; and the idea of the nation as the principle political community.[13] The militarization of that political community was implied as soon as the state came to be seen as based on the nation and subjects were transformed into citizens. As Geoffrey Ostergaard remarks in this respect, highlighting the link between nationhood and military service, 'Bayonets were thrust into the hands of citizens often before they were given the ballot.'[14] The militarization of civilians that is implicit in the formulation of the nation–state clarifies for anarchists questions around the revolutionary use of violence. Against the oppressive state violence or the 'structural' or 'organized' violence of state institutions, including war, therefore, violence can be seen by anarchists as having an essentially liberatory role. This attitude highlights the extent, and the limits, of the affinities between anarchist and pacifist doctrines, overlapping in relation to war and diverging in relation to the state. Nonetheless, shared concerns about conscription drew anarchists and pacifists together in the Second World War, and anarchist and pacifist agendas began to merge from that point onwards. Many anarchists became convinced that the rejection of violence was an essential principle for the rejection of state forms of social organization, including war, and this line of argument was strengthened by the use of the atomic bomb at the end of the war. In 1947, Herbert Read listed non-violence as one of three fundamental anarchist beliefs, alongside personal freedom and mutual aid.[15] This was not the universal attitude of all anarchists in Britain, but it was a significant enough development of anarchist themes that Nicolas Walter felt able to suggest in 1963 that 'Pacifism is ultimately anarchism, just as anarchism is ultimately pacifism.'[16] Nonetheless, anarchism retains somewhere in its ideological makeup what April Carter refers to as its 'apocalyptic' strain and cult of 'heroic violence'.[17] This was revived to some extent in the 1970s with the activities of the Angry Brigade and the support offered in Colin Ward's journal *Anarchy* to the Red Army faction and the IRA, in which it was argued that 'Armed resistance is both possible and necessary in the advanced capitalist countries.'[18]

Colin Ward © Guardian Newspaper, London

The first half of the twentieth century saw a dramatic change in warfare and an increase in social intervention by the state. Concerns about war and conscription, and the limits of state jurisdiction over civilian individuals, have thus formed an important part of national debate in Britain in the twentieth century. Both Rodney Barker and W. H. Greenleaf rightly place anarchism in Britain within a wider struggle for ideas, Barker in terms of changing perceptions of the role and responsibilities of the state following World War One, and Greenleaf more specifically within tensions on the British left concerning the role of the state. Looked at in this way, and rather than being a cry in the wilderness, anarchism in Britain has been a unique voice in the national intellectual struggle between collectivism and individualism in political ideas and public policy. The examination of British intellectual contexts undertaken by writers like Barker and Greenleaf helps us to explore synergies and dialogues between anarchism and liberal, conservative and socialist traditions in Britain concerning pivotal dilemmas around individuality, the state and voluntary association, and, underpinning these dilemmas, fundamental concerns about freedom and equality. For Barker, the unprecedented extension of the functions and powers of the state from the end of the nineteenth century to the late twentieth century should be understood as the 'single most important event' in modern British history. In this period, more and more areas of social, economic, academic, and private life came to be understood in public and political terms, and wider sections of the population were included as citizens by means of the franchise and through conscription. From the late nineteenth century, and especially after the experiences of the First World War greatly expanded working assumptions about the scope of public policy, government became increasingly responsible for greater degrees of regulation and control, as well as new more directly interventionist roles and provision of services. Unemployment, poverty, and the condition of the people, for example, became viewed in terms of public order and the national interest, and the solution was increasingly perceived as resting in the hands of a state with extended responsibilities for direct public intervention.[19] The extension of what counted in the popular mind to be of 'political' concern generally went hand in hand with the widening expectations of what was considered to be the legitimate sphere of state intervention. Insofar as this concern envisaged a fairer distribution of advantage in society, this was a radical position, as in the case of socialists like H. M Hyndman, Fabian socialists like Beatrice and Sidney Webb, and New Liberals like T. H. Green. But it was not always the case that an increased public concern with hitherto private matters was associated with a desire for the increased competence of the state. Elements of both liberal and conservative thinking resisted the encroaching powers of the state, but the anarchist argument as represented by Kropotkin in particular hoped to defend the enlargement of legitimate public and political concern while setting limits on the extension of state action.

What Barker refers to as the 'wider state collectivist ambience' of the early twentieth century meant that the terms of the debate had dramatically altered such that the extended scope of state action was judged to be 'common sense' in dilemmas concerning manpower in war, control in industry, national fitness, and post-war social reconstruction. This meant that state collectivism looked less like 'contestable belief', and became instead the agreed 'starting point' for argument, rather than its 'disputed conclusion'.[20] Under these conditions there opened a distinct intellectual space for anarchism, reconfigured according to the dangers to freedom presented by large-scale political and economic administration. Greenleaf's identification of the developing anxieties among libertarian socialists in Britain applies to the more anarchist elements in particular: 'The moral concern was invariably focused on the question of how personal regeneration could be stimulated if individuals found their lives regimented, increasingly superintended by public authority.'[21] This is a concern that resonates through the work of British anarchist writers in the twentieth century, especially in relation to increasingly mechanized and bureaucratized forms of warfare. Greenleaf's work offers the historian of British ideas the opportunity to contextualize anarchist writing as part of the dialogue on the British left between state and non-state forms of socialism, arguing as he does that 'The dialectic between the growing pressures of collectivism and the opposing libertarian tendency is the one supreme fact of our domestic political life as this has developed over the past century and a half.'[22] Greenleaf argued that there was a basic antithesis in British socialism between a stress on the role of the state and a suspicion about its growth. This tension, he claimed, was a persistent one and had been particularly evident since the end of the Second World War, one manifestation of its persistence being the emergence of the New Left in the late 1950s and 1960s.[23] According to Greenleaf, British socialism could be divided according to two distinct and contrasting traditions. One tradition pursued the goal: '[T]o organise society properly, indeed scientifically, to eliminate all the wastes and defects that have hitherto disfigured the conduct of our industrial and technological affairs, our economic and social life generally.' This goal required supervision and control: 'It will necessarily mean a growth in governmental or some surrogate power and this may not be easily compatible with the continuation of extensive freedom of personal choice and action.' The other tradition, according to Greenleaf, was rooted in an ethical ideal orientated around the development of human potential. In this latter tradition: 'the restriction or even elimination of the state may be a condition of the achievement of the socialist ideal interpreted in this way.'[24] Colin Ward expressed the distinction between the centralizing, managerial socialist tradition and the libertarian, self-organized tradition most forcefully in his prolonged attacks on the dominance of the top-down Fabian approach to British social policy. He celebrates the following quote, from a tract called 'What Socialism Is', published in 1886, which highlights the once-evident but now submerged awareness of a viable anarchist alternative to collectivist socialism: 'when the unconscious socialists of England discover their position, they also will probably fall into two parties; a Collectivist party supporting a strong central administration and a counterbalancing Anarchist party defending individual initiative against that administration.' As Ward points out in relation to this quote, while it is difficult to imagine an anarchist political party, 'it was evident over a century ago that there were other paths to socialism beside the electoral struggle for power over the centralised state'.[25]

Anarchist Russian émigré Peter Kropotkin played a vital role in this national struggle for ideas, both intellectually and practically. Kropotkin was one of a number of political refugees living in London in the late nineteenth century, but unlike other anarchist writers within this community he wrote in English and directed his arguments to British readers. Much of his writing was undertaken for the attention of his acquaintances among British radicals, and serve as evidence of his interaction with them. This circle of radical influence included Kier Hardie, Cunningham Grahame, George Bernard Shaw, Edward Carpenter, William Morris, Patrick Geddes, Ben Tillett, Tom Mann and John Bruce Glasier. William Morris, for example, while distancing himself from uncompromising individualist positions, which is how he incorrectly interpreted anarchism, had much in common with Kropotkin's views as expressed in *Fields, factories and Workshops*. He approved particularly of Kropotkin's call for the reuniting of the communities and occupations of town and countryside, his belief in the social benefits of more access to nature via gardens and fields, and the agenda of small-scale production. Kropotkin's influence on a British anarchist seam of ideas runs through the work of the three anarchist writers that form the subject of this book. Also, his establishment of the anarchist Freedom Press in London with a group of British anarchists in 1886 has provided a focus for native anarchist ideas and campaigning in an almost uninterrupted publishing history up to the present. The two works for which Kropotkin is most well known, *Fields, Factories and Workshops* and *Mutual Aid*, were written as contributions to national debates, drawing on the British social and political context, and intended to be consumed by native audiences. In this sense, we can say that Kropotkin was part of British politics. *Mutual Aid* originated in a dispute between Kropotkin and T. H. Huxley over the meaning of Darwin's theory of evolution, specifically the individualist application of the notion of the 'survival of the fittest' in a human social context and Kropotkin's contrary assertion of the naturalness of social co-operation. This belief in the naturalness of human co-operation underpinned Kropotkin's objection to Huxley's views on the necessity of government. Quoting Darwin, Kropotkin defended his assertion of evolved human ethics and instincts for mutual aid, to be found 'in the social instincts which lead the animal to take pleasure in the society of its fellows, to feel a certain amount of sympathy with them, and to perform various services for them'.[26] Herbert Read said of Kropotkin's work in this respect that 'No better history of ethics has ever been written.'[27] Kropotkin's ideas had a significant impact on the tradition of town planning, initially via his influence on the work of pioneer urban planner Patrick Geddes. The attempt in urban design to utilize and rationalize already existing resources, and make improving rather than dismantling them the basis of urban transformation, is a major strand in the town planning tradition that rejects bulldozers and blueprints, and it can be traced through Geddes' deployment of Kropotkin's ideas. Elisée Réclus, the friend and editor of Kropotkin, was greatly interested in Geddes' work in Edinburgh, and this set of links highlights the anarchist roots of some radically qualitative piecemeal reformist movements. This relationship extends to the practical implications of the garden city proposals of Ebenezer Howard, whose *Tomorrow: a Peaceful Path to Real Reform* was published in 1898 and, in a modified form, underpinned the building of Letchworth. Influenced by the native reformism of early native town planning ideas, Howard proposed the garden city as a practical solution to urban problems.[28] There is a clear sense in which anarchism in Britain in the mid-twentieth-century period reclaims some of the themes and proposals which had been adopted from earlier anarchist thinkers and absorbed into more reformist traditions, like the Garden City movement. In the process, the reformist flavour of some of these themes is taken up in the work of anarchist writers as a kind of radical pragmatism, a revolution of everyday activity, and a piecemeal escape from the institutions of the collectivist state and the monopolies of privatized capital. If the subsequent tradition of anarchism in Britain shows us one thing, it is that it is a mistake to see reformist pragmatism or small-scale practical change as a dilution of anarchism. Rather, pragmatic activity and certain personal choices are conceptualized by these writers as a radical commitment to direct action and immediacy. We can also identify the specific contributions of these writers to the development of anarchist conceptions of freedom in the twentieth century. They contribute to an anarchist image of freedom as self-creation, which draws on inward and outward looking conceptions of human liberty. This is identifiable in the contributions of British anarchist intellectuals to important twentieth-century debates, reflecting and developing the modern anarchist concern with a vital and dynamic view of humanity.

Anarchism and the Collectivist Myths of Warfare

Anarchism in Britain is embedded in libertarian socialist sources as opposed to the collectivist, state-oriented sources of socialism that were dominant in the twentieth century. While placing significant emphasis on the importance of social relationships, the three authors examined here each took issue with any collectivist programme of social action that treated the social group as homogeneous or greater than the sum of its parts, especially as expressed in personifications of social groups such as 'the nation' or even 'the greater good'. A pivotal moment of anarchist engagement in Britain was the response of anarchist commentators to the Second World War and the political culture of the immediate post-war era. The anarchists in Britain during the Second World War were in a fairly unique position in Europe of relative freedom from censorship for their anti-state and anti-militarist publications, which enabled them to begin the revival and reapplication of anarchist ideas that continues to the present. As we have seen, war is an important focus in anarchist approaches to the state. The traditional anarchist depiction of the state is as an inherently militaristic body. For the anarchist, the war-making tendencies of states are closely related to their socially disintegrative characteristics, war is seen as one of the ways in which the institutions of the state corrode and inhibit spontaneous social cohesion. For the anarchist writers of the 1940s, the emergence of total war in the twentieth century was seen as closely related to the power-seeking, war-ready organizational and institutional nature of nation–states. In the pages of the wartime anarchist Freedom Press paper *War Commentary* the war was a 'symptom' of the state in all its 'newest' and 'most ghastly' implications.[29] The traditional anarchist position is that organic social order and hierarchical state authority are antithetical. It equates self-government and spontaneous order with equity and freedom, and state control with violence and injustice. It is from a distinct anti-militarist perspective that British anarchists challenged not only the social-democratic interpretation of the positive impact of the war on social welfare, but also the policies of the war itself, from conscription to bombing. Their challenges in the latter respect precipitated a pivotal set of events, culminating in the prosecution of the editors of the anarchist Freedom Press paper *War Commentary* in 1945 for seditious activities. The biography of each of the three thinkers examined in this book reveals the significance of this trial, and the underpinning political tensions regarding the war-making role of the state, in the development of British anarchist thought in the twentieth century.

Re-examining the anarchist position in ideological struggles surrounding the state and the post-war order adds insight to some important debates around the social-democratic interpretation of the impact of war on British social policy. As David Edgerton notes, 'Social democrats presented picture of Britain in which war was vitally important for the creation of a welfare state, but ignored the warfare state.'[30] Anarchists never shared the 'rosy view of war' depicted in these histories, which depicted the Second World War in particular as an important stimulus for positive social and political progress, assisting the rise of labour and the welfare state. As Edgerton notes of this approach, quoting key mainstream histories of the period: '*The people's war* put us on *The Road to 1945* and *The people's peace*'.[31] Edgerton concludes, 'the view that the war turned out to be good for Britain has been a historiographical staple since the Second World War'.[32] Despite some revisionist socialist interpretations of welfare policy in the 1950s and 1960s by figures such as Anthony Crosland and R. M. Titmuss, social-democratic history predominantly records the war as performing an important positive shift in the role of the British state towards predominantly social welfare functions. It is from their standpoint of hostility to centralized collectivism that the anarchists in this book raised a powerful challenge to the posited victories of socialism in the immediate post-war era, as evidenced by collectivist, state-managed welfare arrangements, which are said to have built on the successful collectivist solutions to social needs experienced during the Second World War. The anarchists stood outside the wider accommodation to state collectivism in public policy debates on both the left and right in Britain in the mid-century period, which focused on how the strength of the state might be employed *rather* than questioning the legitimate scope of its power. Anarchists were also unique during the war for the principled attacks they made on what Paul Addison has since termed the 'authoritarian side to wartime collectivism'.[33] The three anarchists addressed in this book challenged the mainstream accommodation to state collectivism that took place in Britain in the mid-twentieth century, but from within a native libertarian socialist tradition, not a free-market individualist one.

The anarchists recognized that planned control in the public interest was not a victory for socialism, and that economic demand management by the state was designed to sustain and cultivate capitalism, not to supersede it. It is from this perspective that the three anarchists discussed here raised alternative programmes of political action for social improvement, and exposed the social damage wrought by state-centred collectivist management and administration. In this respect these twentieth-century British anarchist authors highlight at least one of what Angus Calder has referred to as national 'myths' about the Second World War. It is worth quoting Calder in full in this context, because the point he makes about the conservatism of the mainstream left in Britain is key to understanding the unique place of anarchism in national socialist debate:

The war, and the mythical events of 1940, would become subjects for historical nostalgia on the Left as well as on the Right – perhaps more than on the Right – but the effect of the Myth would be conservative. For the left it would encapsulate a moment of retrenchment as a moment of rebirth; a moment of ideological conservatism as a moment of revolution. Because Blitz was held to have had near revolutionary consequences, to have somehow produced a 'welfare state', the Myth would divert attention from the continuing need for radical change in British society. The Left would think that in 1940 it had captured History. In fact, it had been captured by it.[34]

Twentieth-century anarchist thought in Britain is important for the historian of British ideas not least because the anarchists in Britain were not 'captured by history'. Their work stands as a challenge to conventional social-democratic interpretations of the era. However, this insight is not immediately obvious unless a wider account is made of the characteristics of the British state in the period in order to include the military dimensions of state policy. Anarchist challenges to the policies of the British state in the early and mid-twentieth century are not easy to contextualize unless proper account is made of the twentieth-century British 'warfare' state. Standard interpretations overlook the significance of 'readiness for international war' for the nature and activities of the British state, even during the period of the Second World War.[35] However, recent revisions of established historiographies of the twentieth-century British State focus on its anticipation of war, including the development, acceleration and entrenchment of military industries, technologies and infrastructure, as a defining characteristic. Edgerton highlights the 'military-industrial-scientific' complex underpinning the development of the British state in the twentieth century and depicts it as the 'pioneer' of modern, 'technologically focused' warfare and arms exporting, with a state machine operated by militarily oriented bureaucrats and technicians. Edgerton contrasts his image of a 'British military-industrial complex' with the dominant 'welfare state' image found in the majority of economic histories, social histories, labour histories and cultural histories. As he notes, 'In these histories the warfare state does not appear to exist, even in wartime.'[36] The overwhelmingly 'welfarist' image of the twentieth-century British state makes it difficult to reconstruct the stance of dedicated anti-militarist groups on the left in Britain during this period and explains the 'jarring effect that contemporary dissident views still have today'.[37] This is especially true of the challenge offered by the 1940s anarchist paper *War Commentary*, with which Read, Comfort and Ward were associated, and which focused on the military experience of conscripted civilians, the technologies of war, and the relationship between the social and military activities of government.

The revisions of writers like Edgerton give a greater scope for conceptualizing submerged or difficult to understand challenges to the militarist
policies of the wartime establishment, such as those raised by the *War
Commentary* anarchists. The fact that the warfare dimensions of the
British state have been overlooked or submerged by intellectuals and
commentators of both the right and left also highlights the singularity of
the anarchist anti-militarist challenge and its extension in relation to the
policies of the post-war British state. They not only recognized the extent to
which the Second World War was strengthening the warfare state, but they
were also acutely attuned to the warfare dimensions of the interventionist
and directive nationalistic economic policies pursued by the British state
after the war. Equipped with the more comprehensive account of the British
state of the period, as provided by writers like Edgerton, we can better understand that the prosecuted wartime dissidents behind the publication of *War
Commentary* were deploying the anarchist argument regarding spontaneous human order in critical responses to the twentieth-century war-making
state, as part of their challenge to conventional beliefs in the socially oriented
and democratic functions of World War Two. They were unique on the left
in their comprehensive criticism of the militaristic policies of the state. The
anarchist perception of the state as an inherently militaristic institution
rendered the *War Commentary* writers highly sensitive to the 'mechanised,
highly organised, technical' characteristics of the British state policy, under
which 'millions of men' were 'concentrated and drafted'.[38] In the event of
their trial, the case made by the prosecution was to connect a circular letter
sent to the members of the forces who were subscribers to *War Commentary*
with articles on the history of Soldiers' Councils in Germany and Russia in
1917 and 1918, and on the European resistance movements which, as the
Allied armies advancing in 1944, were being urged to hand over their arms
to the governments then being set up under military auspices. One of the
headlines in *War Commentary* urged resistance movements in Europe to
'Hang onto your arms!' and this was used by the prosecution to argue that
the paper was telling British soldiers to keep their rifles for revolutionary
action. On 26 April the editors Vernon Richards, John Hewetson and Philip
Sansom were found guilty and sentenced. The judge was Norman Birkett
and the prosecution was conducted by the Attorney General, Sir Donald
Somerville. A Freedom Press Defence Committee was organized to raise
funds for the defence and this won the support of many public figures including George Orwell, Herbert Read, Harold Laski, Kingsley Martin, Benjamin
Britten, Augustus John and Bertrand Russell. This signals the impact that
the Freedom Press Trial had, not only on an anarchist revival in Britain, but
also on political institutions and more mainstream intellectuals.

Sir Herbert Read by Howard Coster, half-plate film negative, 1934© National Portrait Gallery, London, NPG x19536

Anarchist historian George Woodcock argued that, despite the prosecution, the trial was in fact 'a great triumph for the anarchists'. This is not least because all the alleged 'seditious writings' on which the prosecution depended, including prose, poetry and works of art, were read in court and reported verbatim in the daily papers. As Woodcock noted, 'ideas that had previously reached only a few thousand people through *War Commentary* now reached several millions, courtesy Lord Beverbrook and Lord Rothermere.'[39] A letter condemning the impending charge and the police raids which preceded it was published in the *New Statesman* of 3 March 1945, and included the signatures of T. S. Eliot, E. M. Forster and Stephen Spender. On 31 March the *New Statesman* published a further letter which announced that the Freedom Defence Committee had been set up to organize and fund the defence of the anarchists. The officers of the Committee included Herbert Read and Fenner Brockway and the list of sponsors included Aneurin Bevan, Gerald Brenan, Vera Brittain, Alex Comfort, Cyril Connolly, Clifford Curzon, Victor Gollancz, Prof. H. J. Laski, J. Middleton Murry, George Orwell, J. B. Priestley, Reginald Reynolds, D. S. Savage and George Woodcock. The committee was also broadly concerned to guard free speech and went on to oppose the continuance of military and industrial conscription after the war. The anarchists found that their profile was raised from magazines of very low circulation to representation in the high distribution daily tabloids in which the case was publicized. In terms of British social history, the trial of the anarchists invites us to re-examine the impact of military experience on the civilian population in Britain and question the 'welfarist', 'consensus' paradigm, by which relations between society and government of the period has traditionally been viewed. This re-examination gives us a greater understanding of the period from the anarchist point of view, specifically in so far as it stimulated the renewal of anarchist thought in Britain which culminated in twentieth-century works of anarchist analysis and polemic that can be understood as parts of a British tradition of anarchism.

Three British Anarchists

Herbert Read had been professing his sympathies with anarchist political thought since the Spanish civil war. The events in Spain had become an external reference point for debate in Britain in the 1930s, reflecting a greater awareness in the period of the political dramas of other countries, especially in light of the retracting British dominion over territories beyond the British Isles. Rebellions, conflicts and revolutions overseas in particular stimulated the utopian imagination of those whose discontented speculations had previously been more hypothetical. External events provided practical demonstrations of political ideas in action, and their potential significance to British political life, most notably communism and fascism, but also to a less immediately prominent extent, anarchism. Pacifism was also a significant political reference point in national political debate in this period, especially following the end of the First World War. Read was one of a significant number of veterans of World War One who were moved by their participation in that conflict to reflect negatively on the experiences of warfare and, when the renewed possibility of war emerged again after 1933, profess pacifist inclinations. His background in this respect had a major influence on the manner in which he deployed anarchist themes in the British context. A movement in literature at the end of the 1920s expressed this veteran-pacifist trend including Richard Aldington's *Death of a Hero*, Seigfried Sassoon's *Memoirs of a Fox-Hunting Man* and *Memoirs of an Infantry Officer*, Edmund Blunden's *Undertones of War*, Robert Graves's *Goodbye to All That*, R. C. Sherriff's play, *Journey's End*, and Erich Maria Remarque's *All Quiet on the Western Front*.[40] In 1933 the Oxford Union voted by 275 to 153 votes that 'this house will in no circumstances fight for its King and Country'. The following year, a Peace Ballot conducted by the League of Nations Union from door to door collected votes against military action to counter aggression. In 1935 Dick Sheppard launched what became the Peace Pledge Union (PPU), a movement orientated around commitment to this 'pledge': 'I renounce war and never again will I support or sanction another, and I will do all in my power to persuade others to do the same.' PPU membership stood at 136,000 members in April 1940.[41] Alongside these debates, events in Spain affected and polarized political opinion, precipitating a revival of interest in anarchism. As Herbert Read expressed it, 'for a few breathless months it became possible to transfer our hopes to Spain, where anarchism, so long oppressed and obscured, emerged as a predominant force in constructive socialism'.[42] Despite the external stimulus for Read's declaration of his anarchist politics, he emphasized his affinities with the tradition of Kropotkin, Carpenter and Morris, and the cumulative, small-scale changes endorsed by that tradition as it developed in Britain. Read contributed his own scheme for such a programme of gentle, persuasive change in his educational treatise *Education through Art*, and in line with this he began to fortify the bridges spanning the gap between anarchist and pacifist traditions in Britain, which were to facilitate significant traffic between the two movements in the 1950s and 1960s.

In 1937 Auden and Spender published 'Authors Take Sides on the Spanish Civil War' in the *Left Review*, reflecting the national interest in Spanish events and their politically mobilizing effects. They sent out a questionnaire to virtually every leading British and Irish writer, asking if they were 'for' or 'against' the Spanish republic. Of the 149 authors who participated, only five were against (which is not to say that they necessarily supported Franco) including Evelyn Waugh and Edmund Blunden. Only three of the authors included expressions in support of the anarchists in Spain: Ethel Mannin, Aldous Huxley and Herbert Read. In 1938 Read published his *Poetry and Anarchism*, which he followed shortly afterward with *The Philosophy of Anarchism*, and for a period, which included the war years, anarchism became part of the British literary landscape. As a result, Emma Goldman contacted Read in 1938 and recruited him for her efforts to support Spanish anarchists. As part of his efforts in this regard, and in support of general anarchist causes, he raised funds, supported relevant literary endeavours, spoke on anarchist platforms and published regularly in the anarchist paper *Spain and the World*, forerunner to *War Commentary*. He was to be associated with the editorial group of the Freedom Press for the next 15 years, until his peerage in 1952.[43] In a de facto revival of Freedom Press publishing activities, *Spain and the World* had been founded in 1936 by Vernon Richards, whose father had been a friend of Malatesta, and his wife, Marie Louise Berneri, the daughter of Camillo Berneri. *Spain and the World* was succeeded by *Revolt!* in 1939, and during the war the Freedom Press group brought out *War Commentary*, resulting in 1944 in the arrest and imprisonment in 1945 of the editors. These publications drew contributions from younger radicals and also literary intellectuals, publishing work by Herbert Read, John Cowper Powys and Ethel Mannin, as well as Alex Comfort, and later, Colin Ward, who were all drawn to the defence of the editors in 1945.

Alexander Comfort by Howard Coster, half-plate film negative, 1943© National Portrait Gallery, London, NPG x10885

Anarchist and pacifist traditions converge when pacifists embrace anti-militarist conclusions, it is from within this overlap that anarchists emerged to develop the contributions that Herbert Read made to this tradition, most notably Alex Comfort, who, like Read, argued that a socio-political view of war necessarily entailed anarchist political conclusions. The moral underpinnings of the PPU, which drew largely on religious beliefs, could not sustain the interest of these newer radicals, who were developing anti-militarist understandings of war alongside their anarchist sympathies. As renewed warfare came to be publicly depicted in moral terms, justifying the allied cause according to the terms of Christian morality as they had been worked up within the Just War tradition, many PPU members rescinded their pacifism altogether in support of the allied cause. The alternative, socio-political, account of war, which underpinned anti-militarist pacifist objections to war as opposed to religious or moral ones, had a more robust following, generally atheist and anarchist, while never drawing the membership levels achieved by the PPU in the late 1930s. This perspective viewed war an intrinsic emanation of the political power of nation–states, rather than a redeemable aberration in inter-state relations. The shifting boundaries of pacifism in the early months of the Second World War between the moral and socio-political elements within the organization resulted in conflicts between the quietist approach of the PPU leadership and those PPU members who urged more radical attempts to stop the war. This 'Forward Movement' within the PPU developed close links with the Freedom Press group and many of these pacifist dissidents became anarchists, a notable example being John Hewetson, who became an editor of *War Commentary* and was charged with sedition alongside the other editors in 1945.[44] Hewetson was to be joined by energetic young anarchists Tony Gibson, George Woodcock, Philip Sansom and Colin Ward. The position taken up by the anarchists during the war was indicative of their anti-militarist stance. No where is this represented more forcefully than in the wartime anti-bombing campaigns of Alex Comfort.

Read saw anarchism in the twentieth century as a source of political and cultural renewal. The next chapter will highlight the relationship between anarchism in the twentieth century and embedded political, intellectual and national traditions of thought. This will emphasize the draw of the anarchist tradition for the mid-century intellectual concerned with individuality and solidarity. It will stress the use which anarchist intellectuals made of the tradition for their formulation of programmes of social change, in the case of Read this resulted in the influential work *Education through Art*. The chapter will explore the development within the anarchist tradition of a sophisticated range of thinking about the inner and outer qualities of the free and developed self. For Read, the creative capacities of the liberated individual agent were crucial to the renewal of British political culture. In his writing, part of the way that the war-creating activities of states betrayed both individuality and society was through the cultural debasement inherent in systems of mass administration. Thus, he looked to aesthetic and psychological sources for the renewal and re-individualization of culture. In a lecture to London Anarchist Group in 1947, entitled 'Anarchism: Past and Future', Read called for 'a sevenfold system of study and creative activity' in the fields of history, philosophy, education, anthropology, sociology, psychology and social psychology.[45] In this respect he anticipated the 'new' anarchism of figures like Alex Comfort, and, later, Colin Ward, which relied on 'evidence' to support anarchist conclusions drawn from disciplines such as sociology, psychology and biology.

The experience of the two World Wars had encouraged the convergence between anarchism and pacifism developed by Herbert Read. The proliferation of nuclear weapons, and particularly the dropping of the atomic bomb on Hiroshima on 6 August 1945 consolidated 'anarcho-pacifism' as a distinct and specific doctrine. This stance entwined reflections on 'the bomb' and on 'governmental society' in organizations such as the Campaign for Nuclear Disarmament and the Committee of 100. The task of eliminating nuclear weapons was seen from this viewpoint as dependent on a profound social re-ordering. As Colin Ward was to ask in relation to anti-nuclear movements, in an expression of the same anti-militarist alertness that Comfort deployed against the war-making capacities of the British state, 'What if we are driven to see war and the threat of war as implicit in the nature of government and the state?'[46] Comfort's campaign against the atomic bomb started in 1945, and, as part of his work through the 1940s and 1950s, he pioneered the 'new' social-scientific approach to anarchism. The wider nuclear disarmament movement began to mobilize in 1957 in response to the British government's plans to develop the hydrogen bomb. At the end of that year the Direct Action Committee (DAC) against nuclear war was formed and began direct action and industrial campaigns against the manufacture, testing and deployment of nuclear weapons. Read and Comfort acted as sponsors of this organization and of the Campaign for Nuclear Disarmament (CND) formed the following year. However, the direct action Committee of 100, formed in 1960 was to represent the current of anarchist or near-anarchist analysis and praxis within the anti-nuclear movement in Britain most conclusively. Read and Comfort were two of the approximately one hundred members or 'names' of the organization.[47] As Richard Taylor notes, 'Both the practice and ideology of the Committee in 1962–3 were strongly anarchist in flavour, and in underlying ideological assumptions.'[48]

The third chapter of this book will focus on the work and career of Alex Comfort. He is remembered as a critic of conventional sexual morality in the 1970s through his notorious publication *The Joy of Sex*, which he wrote after an illustrious and multifarious career in literature, science and politics. What is less well recognized is the much wider scope of his attack on war and post-war politics and society, and the anarchist political philosophy from which his challenge to politics and culture emerged. Comfort's anarchism was the key characteristic that bound together his social, scientific and political projects. His ideas also form an essential part of the story of the twentieth-century development of a British anarchist tradition and the role it has played in later twentieth-century dissonant political thought. The concerns and intellectual contributions of Comfort's anarchism are a key reflection of the breadth and complexity of British intellectual responses to the social and political changes of the twentieth century and his ideas are ripe for re-examination. This chapter will show how Comfort utilized anarchism to formulate a philosophy of autonomy and responsibility, which he turned against the mainstream political ideas of his age, particularly those regarding the notion of a democratic war. Comfort saw the pertinence of anarchism in the twentieth century in its powerful call for responsibility in an irresponsible age. He was particularly concerned to resist what he saw as the pathologies of mass culture and political authority engendered by war and the state. The discussion on Comfort will uncover some significant connections between anarchism, pacifism and anti-nuclear ideas and movements in the twentieth century. Focusing on Comfort's work will also highlight the ongoing draw of romantic currents of thought for anarchism in the twentieth century. Comfort's neo-romanticism was formulated in support of a politically activist anarchist agenda. He deployed the apocalyptic turn in British literature of the period to face the truths about the allied saturation bombing campaigns during the war. Most notably, early in 1944, Comfort drafted a declaration against the allied bombings and organized the signing of the petition by writers, artists, and musicians. This chapter will explore how Comfort utilized the anarchist tradition in order to launch his attack on the irresponsibility and hypocrisy of wartime democracies. It will also aim to highlight the connection between anarchist ideas and some notorious controversies of the era. These included the contentious attack on the allies in World War Two and the challenge to conventional sexual morality in the early 1970s. In this latter respect, he emphasized the socializing function of human sexual desire, focusing on biological instincts as representing the innate human predilection for freedom.

Anarchist influences on anti-war and anti-nuclear movements, and new thinking associated with sexual liberation were implicated in the earliest developments associated with the New Left in Britain, formed of radical socialists and former communists who had left the party after events in Hungary in 1956. By the end of the 1950s the conception of a stable consensus in British politics was being increasingly questioned, in fact the very notion of 'consensus' was increasingly challenged as ignoring important divergences of opinion and thus inherently ideological. Anarchist figures such as Colin Ward were well placed to capitalize on the heightened interest in anarchism generated by the associated ideas and movements in Britain in the late 1950 and 1960s. Like Colin Ward, E. P. Thompson celebrated the radial challenge to mainstream orthodoxies offered from within British political traditions of socialist humanism associated with labour movements and the arguments of William Morris. Raymond Williams contributed a call for more directly democratic forms of control in industry and in the management of public services, such as public housing. Their references to existing patterns of working-class co-operation as models of wider democratic social possibilities linked the ideas of the British New Left with the anarchist intellectual currents developing at the time. In the 1960s, as editor of *Anarchy*, Ward has some success in feeding anarchist ideas into this milieu and highlighting the anarchist elements of the new movements associated with the era.

The fourth chapter in this volume will focus on the work of Colin Ward. It will show that Ward's challenge to British post-war social policy and the influence of his ideas on new social movements framed anarchism as a viable alternative approach to political relationships in the twentieth century. Ward's work deploys and develops the relationship between anarchism, utopian and planning traditions. This chapter on Ward will illustrate his engagement with the impact of the modern state and capitalism on human freedom in the contemporary context and highlight his links with British radical currents of thought. The exploration of Ward's career and writing demonstrates the extent to which anarchism has had an impact on the new political movements of the later twentieth century, including urban based, direct action and DiY forms of political activity. Underpinning this influence is one of the most distinctive contributions of anarchism to twentieth-century ideas. This is a cluster of related concerns on the immediate environment, the congruity between means and ends in social change, the importance of direct engagement and the emphasis on proximate goals. This group of present-centred concerns developed out of distinctly anarchist challenges to the distant and abstract political goals which anarchist thinkers have traditionally associated with elitist and authoritarian political movements. Ward was committed to a notion of freedom as autonomy which entailed a high degree of personal and social responsibility and self-creation. He associated freedom with the type of personality fostered by engaged and dynamic activity rather than inertness, dependence and apathy. This view of freedom is a key theoretical connection which holds these three thinkers together as a tradition, alongside their overlapping contexts, deployment of British traditions of thought and the direct lines of influence between them.

Conclusions

This volume is chiefly an account of British anarchist *ideas* in the twentieth century, which focuses on the intellectual activity of written and spoken theorizing engaged in by key anarchist authors. This is distinct from the movement-driven approach of much recent groundbreaking research on anarchism, which identifies direct anarchist influence on social practices and modes of organization. Movement-driven approaches have played perhaps the more important role in reasserting the contemporary relevance of anarchism by helping to identify anarchism as a vital and dynamic influence on behaviour and social protest. However, writing and public debate are also important and interesting spheres of anarchist development and influence. In a wider sense, this is true of the relationship between political history and the history of ideas in general. Public intellectuals, polemists, ideologues and politically motivated writers advocate their ideas in the hope that such persuasion will inform public affairs, and often they do, even when those ideas have not traditionally formed an acknowledged part of mainstream debate. Also, we might make the further observation that, while the distinction between social movement and intellectual activity might indeed describe two different sorts of political activity, the separation between the two has perhaps been overdrawn, especially by anarchist activists themselves. While there is a clearly discernable difference between the activist and intellectual wings of anarchism in Britain, the distance between them is not as far as has been assumed. This can be seen in the cases of the three figures examined here, who each engaged in active and dynamic relationships with social movements, both shaping and being shaped by British responses to the civil war in Spain, movements against war and the allied bombing policies of the war, anti-nuclear movements, new direct action movements and the revival of mutualist practices in Britain. The tangible involvement of each of the three anarchists in the defence of the Freedom Press anarchists, arrested on charges of sedition during wartime in 1944, also blurs the distinction between active and intellectual anarchist engagement in Britain, as do the radical publishing activities of the prosecuted editors themselves. Further, the disappointment, disillusionment and anger within the anarchist movement in Britain when Herbert Read accepted a knighthood in 1952, a decision which is taken to indicate the distance between the active and intellectual tendencies, in fact, by the strength of feeling it raised, indicates the contact and connection between them.

The analysis and discussion offered in this book aims to support the perception of anarchism as a living tradition of political thought, utilized, developed and deployed by these British writers in the twentieth century, who draw it into dialogue with both novel and familiar intellectual traditions. Anarchism has contributed to twentieth-century political ideas in Britain and played a role in British political movements of the last century. These thinkers studied, utilized and developed the anarchist tradition for their defence of thorough and dynamic conceptions of human freedom in what they perceived to be an era of increasing encroachment into individual and community capacities for self-government. The analysis of British anarchist thinking offered here contributes elements to a potential framework for understanding the anarchist intellectual and ideological underpinnings of movements in Britain in the twenty-first century. These elements include the demonstrable centrality of concerns with state militarization. We also see elements of a biological conception of freedom, premised in various ways on an understanding of human psychology and physiology. Also, we have the privileging of temporally and spatially proximate values, an emphasis on agency and a theory of freedom that combines individual and social components. Also relevant are the philosophies of direct action, DiY politics and small-group organization which these anarchist concerns have helped to develop. This volume should offer potential avenues for exploring the anarchist influence that is taken to be implicit in some contemporary movements. The aim is to explore anarchism's place in the history of ideas in Britain in the twentieth century and, in so doing, to contribute to the emerging field of anarchist studies and challenge the interpretation of anarchism as firmly outside of the British political imagination.

Notes

1. BBC News online, 16 June 2001, 'Blair: Anarchists Will Not Stop Us' http://news.bbc.co.uk/1/hi/uk_politics/1392004.stm, viewed 11:34, 8 April 2010.

2. Leonard Williams 'Anarchism Revived', *New Political Science* 29 (3), 2007, pp. 297–312; and Uri Gordon, 'Anarchism Reloaded', *Journal of Political Ideologies* 12 (1), 2007, pp. 29–48.

3. David Goodway, *Anarchist Seeds beneath the Snow* (Liverpool: Liverpool University Press, 2006), p. 2.

4. Benedict Anderson, *Under Three Flags: Anarchism and the Anti-Colonial Imagination* (London: Verso, 2005); Uri Gordon, *Anarchy Alive: Anti-Authoritarian Politics from Practice to Theory* (London: Pluto Press, 2008); Simon Critchley, *Infinitely Demanding: Ethics of Commitment, Politics of Resistance* (London: Verso, 2007); Paul McLaughlin, *Anarchism and Authority : A Philosophical Introduction to Classical Anarchism* (Aldershot: Ashgate, 2007); Benjamin Franks, *Rebel Alliances: The Means and Ends of Contemporary British Anarchisms* (Edinburgh: AK, 2006); Samuel Clark, *Living without Domination : The Possibility of an Anarchist Utopia* (Aldershot: Ashgate, 2007); Ruth Kinna, *Anarchism: A Beginners Guide* (Oxford: Oneworld Publications, 2005); David Graeber, *Fragments of an Anarchist Anthropology* (Chicago: Prickly Paradigm Press, 2004); Todd May, *The Political Philosophy of Poststructuralist Anarchism* (Pennsylvania: Pennsylvania State University Press, 1994); Saul Newman, *From Bakunin to Lacan: Anti-Authoritarianism and the Dislocation of Power* (London: Lexington, 2001); Lewis Call, *Postmodern Anarchism* (Lanham: Oxford: Lexington, 2002).

5. Gordon, 'Anarchism Reloaded', pp. 29–48.

6. Recent works by Benjamin Franks and David Goodway are important exceptions to this oversight. See Goodway, *Anarchist Seeds Beneath the Snow;* and Franks, *Rebel Alliances : The Means and Ends of Contemporary British Anarchisms.*

7. George Crowder, *Classical Anarchism. The Political Thought of Godwin, Proudhon, Bakunin, and Kropotkin* (Oxford: Clarendon Press, 1991), p. 2.

8. George Woodcock, *Anarchism* (Harmondsworth: Penguin, 1962), p. 414.

9. T. Paine, *The Rights of Man* (1792; London: Watts, The Thinkers Library, 1939) Part 2, ch. 1, p. 134.

10. Geoffrey Ostergaard, 'Resisting the Nation-State: The Pacifist and Anarchist Traditions', pp. 171–96, in Leonard Tivey (ed.) *The Nation-State. The Formation of Modern Politics* (Oxford: Martin Robertson, 1981), pp. 183–4.

11. Randolph S. Bourne, 'The State' (1919), in *War and the Intellectual: Essays, 1915–1919* (New York: Harper Torchbooks, 1964), pp. 71–2.

12. Randolph S. Bourne, 'The State', pp. 71–2.

13. Ostergaard 'Resisting the Nation-State: The Pacifist and Anarchist Traditions', p. 172.

14. Ostergaard, 'Resisting the Nation-State: The Pacifist and Anarchist Traditions', p. 177.

15. *Freedom*, 17 May and 26 July 1947.

16. Nicolas Walter, 'Nonviolent Resistance: Men against War', *Nonviolence*, 63, 1963, p. 17.

17. April Carter, 'Anarchism and Violence', in J. Rowland Pennock and John W. Chapman (eds) *Anarchism (NOMOS XIX)* (New York: New York University Press 1978), p. 337.

18. See *Anarchy* 7, 1972, and 22, 1977, discussed in Martin Ceadel, *Thinking about Peace and War* (Oxford: Oxford University Press, 1987), p. 150.

19. Rodney Barker, *Political Ideas in Modern Britain* (London: Methuen and Co. Ltd., 1978), pp. 7–10.

20. Barker, *Political Ideas in Modern Britain*, pp. 48, 49.

21. W. H. Greenleaf, *The British Political Tradition Volume II. The Ideological Heritage* (London and New York: Methuen, 1983), p. 415.

22. Greenleaf, *The British Political Tradition Volume II*, p. 3.

23. Greenleaf, *The British Political Tradition Volume II*, p. 464.

24. Greenleaf, *The British Political Tradition Volume II*, pp. 350–1.

25. *What Socialism Is* (Fabian Tract No.4, 1886), quoted in Colin Ward, *Social Policy. An Anarchist Response* (London: Freedom Press, 2000, first published London School of Economics, 1996), pp. 10–11.

26. C. Darwin, *The Descent of Man* (Oxford: Oxford University Press, 1909), p. 150 quoted in P. Kropotkin, *Ethics: Origin and Development* (Dorchester: Prism Press, 1924), p. 33.

27. G. Woodcock and I. Avakumovic, *The Anarchist Prince* (New York: Schocken Books, 1971), p. 420.

28. Barker, *Political Ideas in Modern Britain*, p. 83.

29. Reg Reynolds, *War Commentary*, June 1941.

30. David Edgerton, *Warfare State: Britain, 1920–1970* (Cambridge: Cambridge University Press, 2006), p. 270.

31. Angus Calder, *The People's War* (London: Cape, 1969); Paul Addison, *The Road to 1945: British Politics and the Second World War* (London: Cape, 1975); Kenneth Morgan, *The People's Peace: British History 1945–1989* (Oxford: Oxford University Press, 1990), quoted in Edgerton, *Warfare State,* p. 287.

32. Edgerton, *Warfare State*, p. 290.

33. Paul Addison 'The Road from 1945', pp. 5–27 in Peter Hennessy and Anthony Seldon (eds), *Ruling Performance: British Governments from Attlee to Thatcher* (Oxford: Basil Blackwell, 1987), p. 24.

34. Angus Calder, *The Myth of the Blitz* (London: Jonathan Cape, 1991), p. 15.

35. Edgerton, *Warfare State*, p. 1.

36. Edgerton, *Warfare State*, pp. 292, 1, 13, 287, 13.

37. Edgerton, *Warfare State*, pp. 4, 290, 292.

38. Ridel, *War Commentary*, mid-January, 1942.

39. George Woodcock, *Letter to the Past: An Autobiography* (Canada: Fitzhenry and Whiteside Ltd, 1982), p. 267.

40. Goodway *Anarchist Seeds Beneath the Snow*, p. 202.

41. Goodway *Anarchist Seeds Beneath the Snow*, p. 203.

42. Herbert Read, *Poetry and Anarchism* (London: Faber and Faber, 1938), p. 57.

43. Goodway *Anarchist Seeds Beneath the Snow*, p. 182.

44. Goodway *Anarchist Seeds Beneath the Snow*, p. 207.

45. Freedom, 17 May 1947, quoted in Goodway *Anarchist Seeds Beneath the Snow*, p. 188.

46. Colin Ward, 'The Future of the Committee of 100: An Anarchist View', Peace News, 26 January 1962, quotes in Goodway *Anarchist Seeds beneath the Snow*, p. 260.

47. Goodway *Anarchist Seeds Beneath the Snow*, pp. 261–2.

48. Richard Taylor, *Against the Bomb: The British Movement 1958–1965* (Oxford: Clarendon Press, 1988), p. 247.

2

Herbert Read: Anarchism and Modernity

Sir Herbert Read by Howard Coster, half-plate film negative, 1934© National Portrait Gallery, London, NPG x19532

Introduction

In one late twentieth-century piece of artwork the authority of art criticism is challenged by the unceremonious display of the pulpy mess which has been made of Herbert Read's *A Concise History of Modern Painting* after having been 'Washed in a Washing Machine for Two Minutes'.[1] As a statement of challenge this artwork assumes an awareness of the significance of Read's contribution to art criticism. To date, no one has pulped any of Read's political commentary, which has mostly been treated as an eccentric quirk of his promotion of novelty. However, Herbert Read was more than an art critic. He succeeded in drawing anarchist and British intellectual sources into a unique set of insights about the transformative potential of human experience in one particular incorruptible sphere: the human perception of beauty. The singularity of this view reflects affinities between anarchism and some British intellectual sources, particularly romanticism, and the shared emphasis in these traditions on the dynamic verities embedded in organic orders. Read wrote, lectured and proselytized, not just for the sake of a public understanding of art and more widespread consumption of art, but in defence of his political conviction that there are biological drives at work in the production and consumption of art which have the potential to develop the foundations for a new social order. Perhaps most importantly, Read's anarchist commitments, particularly as expressed in works like *Poetry and Anarchism*, first published by Faber in 1938, and *The Philosophy of Anarchism*, published by Freedom Press in 1940, were, according to Colin Ward, 'among the vital books whose influence led people of my generation, as well as those a little older, to describe themselves as anarchists'.[2] If there is a place for thinking about the transformative significance of the individual and social consumption of art, or for investigating the continuities and developments in anarchist ideas, or for exploring the anarchist relationship to British intellectual traditions, then further study of the ideas of Herbert Read are overdue. This is not, however, to overlook the difficulties raised by his acceptance on a knighthood in 1952. His decision in this respect has made it very difficult for anarchists and later historians of anarchist ideas to recognize his contribution to anarchist ideas clearly or to present his political commitments neatly. While recognizing these tensions, the aim in this chapter is to contribute to an understanding of Read's intentions and impact that can feed into analyses of anarchist political thought and British intellectual tradition, and highlight the development of one particular twentieth-century seam of British anarchist thought and practice.

Read prominently declared his adherence to the anarchist political tradition following the Spanish Civil War. By the time he announced his privately long-held anarchism in 1937, he was a figure of considerable cultural authority. Read was involved in important cultural publications of the mid twentieth-century era including *Art and Letters, Criterion, New Criterion* and *The Burlington Magazine*. He lectured on art for the BBC and developed a close relationship with the cultural project of T. S. Eliot at Faber and Faber. In the 1930s and after, Read was the key promoter of significant British modernist artists Barbara Hepworth, Henry Moore and Ben Nicholson. He was also one of the most committed founders in 1946 of the Institute of Contemporary Arts. As a partner at Routledge he was influential in the development of its publishing identity. In 1952 he was knighted for services to literature and later in his career he was a trustee at the Tate Gallery. Read was also a published poet and novelist, a key signatory of the anti-militarist, anti-nuclear Committee of 100, and one of the first critics to use psychoanalytical methods. Read not only cultivated an audience in Britain for European and American modern art before and after the Second World War, but strived to conceptualize British contributions to modernism as dynamic developments of native cultural tradition. The unique appeal of his prose, alongside the stimulation offered by his insights, is now available to wider and more receptive audiences. What is less well recognized about this figure is the relationship between his conception of modernity in art and his view of the relevance of anarchism in the twentieth century. Both aspects of his thought rest on conceptions of renewal and the importance of utopian vision intimately tied to anarchist notions of freedom, individuality, community and spontaneous natural order. His persistent defence of modernism in the visual arts and his announcement in favour of an anarchist politics were parts of his search for sources of renewal in response to a civilization that he saw debasing itself by violence, war and homogeneity. His work mediated artistic and political conceptions of progress, presenting a uniquely political approach to aesthetic avant-gardism.

Read's politics drew on his interpretation of a variety of sources. These included Henry David Thoreau, Georges Sorel and Edward Carpenter. The individualist left in Britain, which included Guild Socialism and the Nietzscheanism of figures like A. R. Orage, nurtured Read's approach. Read was also conscious of the British literary tradition of socialism. As George Woodcock has noted, 'The artistic utopia is a peculiarly English vision.'[3] To this native tradition of socialism, which included John Ruskin, William

Morris and Oscar Wilde, Read added his modernism and his unequivocal anarchism, drawing on its innate suspicion of militarism, industrialization and mass production. To these influences he added Kropotkin's emphasis on natural and spontaneous order. Specifically, the natural order described by Kropotkin in his works *Mutual Aid*, of 1902 and *Ethics: Origin and Development*, of 1924. The order Kropotkin described was based on free association, mutual aid and the fundamental equality of rights, following the posited propensity of human beings to spontaneously associate according to their needs and sympathies. This was the crucial underpinning for the political significance Read attributed to the spontaneous forms and harmonies of art. He stated it in these terms: 'The most general law in nature is equity – the principle of balance and symmetry which guides the growth of forms along lines of the greatest structural efficiency. It is the law which gives the leaf as well as the tree, the human body and the universe itself, a harmonious and functional shape, which is at the same time objective beauty.'[4] Thus, he argued, making a political virtue out of an aesthetic one: 'If every citizen could be brought up to appreciate the beauty and harmony of the laws inherent in nature, he would be as incapable of establishing a tyranny as of enduring one.'[5] He also drew from the anarchist tradition a Proudhonian emphasis on the division and decentralization of political power and its dissolution in local and direct forms of social administration. Read was significantly influenced by the ideas of Max Stirner. He was deeply impressed by Stirner's defence of a rigorous individualist conception of freedom. Stirner's view of human uniqueness was important for Read's view of the relationship between art and politics. Also important was the traditional anarchist defence of individual judgement, discernible in figures like Stirner and also in the ideas of Godwin. Read added to these perspectives a psychological defence of the developmental importance of inner unconscious impulses and self-awareness to the mental health of the individual and his social role. Read contributed to the anarchist tradition of thinking about individual freedom a link between liberty, self-development and personality, and a parallel link between power, individual anxiety and psychosis.

For Read art was a concrete agent of political freedom, not through its subject matter but through an anarchist celebration of natural order and individual judgement that radicalized his view of the aesthetic appreciation of form. *Education through Art*, written as World War Two was drawing to a close, emphasized spontaneity and natural patterns of growth and order as pedagogical principles. Read's educational philosophy developed his emphasis on freedom as a condition of active and dynamic selfhood.

Also developed in Read's educational writing was the conceptual synthesis between individuality and sociability. This relied in part on his reading of Jung's notions of archetypal symbolism and collective unconscious. Through this reading Read emphasized the correlation between the insights of the individual imagination and the awareness of shared experience. The message of his philosophy of art was reiterated in his educational thought: the processes of social integration were, he argued, facilitated by the relationship of the individual to the forms and beauty of works of art. Also in his educational philosophy he drew on the insights of Gestalt psychology regarding perception to support his view of the natural order of form and extrapolated this to defend the distinctively anarchist concept of natural social order. *Education through Art* was an influential work; it formed the basis of a specific UNESCO project concerning art education. It has rarely been highlighted that it was primarily an integration of Read's thinking about art and politics and an anarchist programme which celebrated the inner life of the child as a source for the renewal of society along anarchist lines.

One of the first and most important things to emphasize regarding Read's revival of the concerns of anarchism in the British context is the importance of his experience in World War One for his intellectual development. For Read, the horror and brutality of the war was indicative of social, political and cultural crises in Britain. It highlighted the evils of state power, the loss of individuality and the rise of mass society, as well as the corrosion of social cohesion and responsibility. The dramatic barbarity and extent of human suffering led him to mount an extensive challenge to British political culture. The reactionary elitism of the British social order and the collectivism of its approach to government, as well as the profit-driven motivation of the ruling classes, were for Read enemies of liberty and justice. The experience of war highlighted the pernicious role of the state in undermining both human freedom and social solidarity. Read's contribution to the anarchist tradition crucially included this indictment of the state on the grounds of its propensity to undermine human freedom and solidarity via the waging of wars. Other British anarchist writers, Alex Comfort and Colin Ward in particular, followed Read in the close relationship they perceived between the growing domestic scope of the state, war, and the erosion of both vibrant individuality and social responsibility. According to Read, the war also highlighted the failures of mainstream socialism in Britain. The traditional left, Read noted, failed to mobilize in revulsion against the war. It failed to react and resist the war in defence of liberty and fraternity. The Spanish Civil War was also a key moment in the development of Read's anarchism. While World War One nurtured his anarchism, the Spanish Civil War prompted him to publicly declare in favour of it and to become associated with anarchist groups and the Freedom Press. He recognized the unfashionable and eccentric mainstream image of anarchism in Britain but sought to emphasize its urgent applicability. For Read, only anarchism, with its concern for the libertarian values of the socialist tradition, for diversity and individuality, and its challenge to authority, could respond to twentieth-century dangers of war and state totalitarianism. Read aimed to highlight the intellectual calibre of the tradition and emphasize its significance for the political problems of the contemporary era.

One of the most significant wartime catalysts for the revival and development of the anarchist tradition in Britain was the series of police raids on the offices of the Freedom Press in the closing years of the Second World War, and the subsequent sedition trial that followed. The trial drew the young writer Alex Comfort into the public campaign for the defence of the anarchists, and the young serviceman Colin Ward, who spoke up for the defendants during the trail despite being called as a witness for the prosecution. The case is thus an important historical moment in the emergence of a distinct trajectory of anarchist thinking in Britain. For British intellectuals, and for the anarchist ones in particular, the trial was direct evidence of the emergence of a more comprehensive and invasive model of British statehood. Read was directly involved in the attempts to defend the editors of the Freedom Press publication *War Commentary* against the charges of spreading disaffection in the military. It was significant to the defence that the editors were being charged under special wartime regulations in 1945 when it was clear that the war was nearing its end. This indicated to concerned intellectuals the effect of the experience of wartime administration on the scope of state ambition to regulate printed opinion. Another significant feature of the Freedom trial was the breadth of intellectual opinion it mobilized in support of the anarchists. This significantly raised the profile of the anarchist group. Importantly, Read defended the editors in terms of an idealized conception of traditional British liberties. This included freedom of the press and limited government. He argued for the acquittal of the editors in the name of a native civil libertarian sensibility, which he aimed to defend against the post-war British state. He equated his defence with the fight against fascism, which he saw as identifiable in any authoritarian style of government. He saw the fight for the freedom of the editors as an extension of the battle of resistance movements to repel fascist governments across Europe. Evidently, while

Read formulated a philosophy of anarchism which relied on the key figures of the eighteenth- and nineteenth-century tradition, it was also firmly rooted in British intellectual sources and contemporary debates.

Read's anarchism presented the anarchist tradition in a manner that made it more available to later twentieth-century British thinkers who picked up on its themes. In this sense, and satisfying his agenda on this count, he gave anarchism 'a place' in 'the political problems of our time'.[6] He did this by formulating a revised scope for anarchist insight, raising its profile by relating its principles to a number of political and cultural fields. His ideas were distinctly contemporary, concerned with the rise of the state, mass society and industrialization, and particularly critical of the declining concern for freedom in mainstream socialism. His ideas allied anarchism with non-violent philosophies and established a distinctive synthesis between subjectivity and social harmony. For this he drew on elements of communitarian and individualist traditions and reinforced his conclusions with his insights regarding art and psychoanalysis. Read's conception of developed selfhood, key to his conception of freedom, placed great emphasis on the social aspects of individuality. For Read the creative human self was an active, engaged being who participated with energy and vision alongside other creative selves in the transformation of the world. Read's ideas about the meaning of art and its significance to human experience still have the power to dramatically affect our readings of works of art and sculpture. This is because they are underwritten by a distinct and coherent social and political theory which indelibly connects individual human expression to collective social experience. For this underpinning, Read drew on classical anarchist insights about natural or organic order and by his work and example shaped and developed that tradition. The evidence of his intellectual and practical efforts to sponsor, develop and defend anarchism in Britain urges the historian of anarchist ideas and the student of British social and intellectual history to look past his paradoxical acceptance of a knighthood to recognize the even more surprising evidence of anarchist commitment in Britain among some persuasive and influential voices.

War and the Avant-Garde in the Early Twentieth Century

The First World War had a profound effect on Read's approach. He took part in some of the most horrific battles of the war, including the Second Battle of the Somme. The experience caused him to challenge the culture and politics that he considered had made such experience possible. Read's published war letters reveal the intensity of his experience and breadth of his reading during the war years. Reflecting on his experience from the perspective of the 1960s, he claimed that his war letters 'may help a later generation to understand how the world they now confront with such distrust came into being'.[7] This comment illustrated the extent to which he considered that war had shaped the twentieth century and exposed the debasement of British culture. The war saw the development of Read's radical sensibility move towards a fierce rejection of the state, mass society and conventional partisan political activity, and towards aesthetic sources of renewal. He was primed for the deep effect the experience of war would have on him by his involvement in the Leeds Art Club before the war. This was the intellectual and social institution founded by Alfred Orage and Holbrook Jackson in 1903 which continued until 1923, drawing a largely working class and lower middle-class audience and debating art, politics, society and philosophy. Read's intellectual roots in early twentieth-century British progressive thought and the impact of the First World War on his intellectual development led to his questioning of British political institutions and mainstream socialism and conditioned his turn to anarchism and aesthetics. His experiences in Leeds also furnished Read with a model of public engagement, politicized intellectual activity, and the creation of working class and middle-class audiences for avant-garde ideas that shaped his own publishing and institutional aims. The Leeds Arts Club celebrated the academy, artistic engagement and civic reform, fields which Read moved between comfortably throughout his career. This organization was an important and unique crucible of radical sensibilities, advocating the antibourgeois ideas of Nietzsche alongside the socialist and feminist politics of the early Labour Party and the Suffragette movement. Read's involvement in the Leeds Arts Club when he started University there in 1912 led him to an aestheticized Nietzschean individualism. Also important was Read's simultaneous exposure to some of the first modernist art to be collected in Britain.[8] It was here that Read first encountered Marx's *Capital*, Kropotkin's *Fields, Factories and Workshops* and pamphlets on anarchism, as well as works by Bakunin. Reading Edward Carpenter's *Non-Governmental Society* also had a decisive impact on Read at this time.

In 1914, Read claimed, he went to war 'with no better covering than the philosophy of Nietzsche'.[9] He ended the war with the beginnings of a more socially developed formulation of individualism. The war brought Read to an intense awareness of brotherhood and solidarity, which penetrated his Nietzschean notion of the significance of the individual. The most influential aspect of Read's war experience was his recognition of the bravery and suffering of 'English and German alike', who were forced to butcher each other 'simply because we are united into a callous inhuman association called a State'. By means of this association, he reflected while in the thick of the action at the front, 'life and hope are denied and sacrificed'.[10] Read hated the anti-democratic ethos of army life and found a deep sense of equality and harmony in the shared suffering of men and officers at the front in France. He described in his war letters the continuing evolution of his individualism alongside 'a growing sense of comradeship' and 'identity' with his fellow soldiers.[11] During the war he was influenced by his reading of the work of Thoreau, whose *Walden* he found to be 'full of wisdom'.[12] Of *Walden*, he stated that 'It all drives me to an individualism, an anarchy which is for each of us to realise.'[13] The influence of Georges Sorel's *Reflections on Violence*, published in a translation by T. E. Hulme in 1916, also strongly influenced Read. 'Few books have impressed me so deeply', Read wrote, 'his main function, in my case, was to supply to socialism the imaginative qualities which I found lacking in Marx.'[14] Sorel's emphasis on emotion, spontaneity and instinct over rational construction was to have a lasting influence on Read's aesthetic theory, the psychological aspects of his thought and his anarchism. This influence was the beginning of an alliance between rationalism and emotion that underpinned his system of thought. His experiences of war added to these influences an awareness of solidarity and human community. In essence, the elements of his anarchist mediation between unique individuality and social solidarity were in place by the close of war in 1918. The emphases on freedom, subjectivity, spontaneity and community that he drew from the anarchist tradition guided his aesthetic endeavour as a political project of renewal.

Read had become aware of anarchism, he claimed, in 1911 through reading Edward Carpenter's *Non-Governmental Society*, which opened up a new range of thought in which the ideas of anarchists Kropotkin, Bakunin and Proudhon ran alongside and were supported by the work of Nietzsche and Ibsen.[15] It has been noted that the influence of the Russian émigré Kropotkin on British radicals should be understood as a domestic rather than an imported influence. Kropotkin lived, wrote and established the Freedom Press in Britain, and he was in personal contact with British radicals of the era including Carpenter and Morris. Also, Kropotkin's work was addressed to British contexts and dilemmas, largely written for a British audience. Kropotkin's arguments in *Fields, Factories and Workshops* and *Mutual Aid* in particular were directed to English readers.[16] By the end of World War One, Read's turn towards these ideas was evident in the syntheses he began to attempt between the individual and his society, and impulse and rationality, and most of all in his feeling that the power of the state attacked natural human order. It was also his response to what he saw as the failures of socialism that had been highlighted as a result of the war. Before 1914 Read had expected that the war would be stopped by international working-class action, and the failure of socialist leaders in this respect was his 'first lesson in political disillusionment'.[17] Then, during the war he became convinced that the sense of comradeship and solidarity that he had experienced would lead to a new social order in peacetime. Instead: 'The war ended in despair in Germany, in silly jubilation in England, and in an ineffective spirit of retribution in France.'[18] For Read 'the political situation of 1919 offered no basis for allegiance or enthusiasm'.[19] The end of the war reinforced Read's alienation from state and society and added a profound disillusionment with traditional socialism. These disillusionments were for Read 'pointers to a political future in which he could find no place'.[20] At this stage Read became irrevocably suspicious of power and political systems and convinced of the 'rightness' and 'necessity' of anarchism represented by Kropotkin, Proudhon, Bakunin, Stirner and Tolstoy.[21] During the war Read had been struck by the contrast between the egalitarian model of community provided by the life at the front and the elitism of the society that had sent them there. Following this experience he could not reconcile himself to the notion that the 'war and collectivism' and 'plutocracy' of a British political order managed by 'a select club of old Wykehamists' could possibly embody ideals of individual liberty and social justice.[22] Read found that 'Political faith and action could not be invoked in England.'[23] His disillusionment was fuelled by 'the indifference which people in power felt for the opinion of the men who had fought' and the 'general spread of false sentiment and hypocrisy', 'greed', 'commercial profiteering', 'political reaction' and 'social retrenchment'.[24]

Read emerged from the war with a strong sense of pessimism about the state of society, but he claimed it was a pessimism in which was preserved a 'faith in the future of man' and a belief in the possibility of 'mental evolution'.[25] Read was keenly aware of the dire need for a source of renewal, a new source of ideas, and an outlook from which to regenerate a culture and society that had been debased by war and capitalism. He later described this outlook, in the words of Blake's poem 'The Clod and the Pebble', as the desire to 'build a Heaven in Hell's despair'.[26] The escape for human civilization from the indignity of war, he claimed, was the particular synthesis of dream and reality offered by art, in which the freedom of the mind and the necessity of experience could interact, 'I therefore sought the solution in art'.[27] In the preface to his collection of wartime poetry and prose, *Naked Warriors*, Read felt he spoke with the 'ethical rage' of the generation with whom he had been compelled to participate in 'ghastliness and horror' and 'inhumanity and negation' when he resolved to formulate a 'cleaner and more direct realization of natural values'. Then, he argued, 'may we strive to create a beauty where hitherto it has no absolute existence'.[28] While on leave from the front, Read had become drawn into the literary and artistic world of London figures Frank Rutter, Ezra Pound, Percy Wyndham Lewis, the Sitwells and T. S. Eliot, initially through the connections he had made at the Leeds Arts Club. After the war Read threw himself into the fray of contemporary cultural debate in Britain on the side of the aesthetic avant-garde. The ideas he developed in relation to the meaning of art, and the human significance of the creation and perception of art, were marked by his developing anarchist philosophy. His art criticism over the first half of the twentieth century was aimed at interpreting aesthetic modernism as a medium for radical and idealistic renewal.

Modernist Idealism

It was specifically within abstract modernist art that Read was to look for the source of a 'new culture on fresh perceptions'.[29] In 1921, taking on the editorship of the works of T. E. Hulme, who was killed in the First World War, Read was exposed to a distinctive modernist case which emphasized the aesthetics of rational geometric form. The ideas of Hulme were at the heart of the English avant-garde of the early twentieth century and an important influence on Read's contemporaries Wyndham Lewis, Ezra Pound and T. S. Eliot. Read was deeply influenced by Hulme's praise for abstraction in art as the creation of harmony, and escape from chaos, in the depiction of something essential. Wilhelm Worringer's emphasis on the significance of symbolism in the relationship between man and his environment was also highly important. Such was Read's enthusiasm that he learnt German in the early 1920s in order to read Worringer's work. The notion of abstraction rests on a cluster of theoretical ideas, including the idea that art should be like music insofar as its effects should be created by pure patterns of form. Also important is the Platonic ideal of ultimate forms of beauty, lying not in the forms of the real world but in objective, rational systems like geometry. From here develops the idea that abstract art represents virtues such as order and purity, rather than objects in the material world. There was a limit, however, to how far Read could develop his agenda of renewal and remain true to certain elements of Hulme's classicist perspective. Hulme advocated an understanding of man as limited and static, only achieving a level of civilization through adherence to tradition and organization. He attacked the contrary image of man as individual and dynamic on which he considered was based a harmful notion of progress that threatened to destroy the existing order. Hulme attacked romanticism in particular for propagating this dangerous conception of convention-breaking dynamic spontaneity.

Against Hulme's view, Read came to see the romantic emphasis on the emotional and intuitive content of art as crucial to the modernist regenerative task. His emphasis on the significance of the English romantic tradition of poetry was central to this challenge. Read's reassessment of the English romantic tradition in the course of his literary criticism led him to a unique synthesis of the romantic vision of the artist as the pioneer of society's forward direction and the classical emphasis on form as symbolizing essential verities. His sustained treatment of Wordsworth was a pivotal movement towards this reassessment. The significance of Wordsworth's poetry for Read was the emotional sincerity of its expression and its relationship to the poet's personality. The 'intense sensational awareness' of poetry created as a response to emotion 'elevates the human mind'.[30] Through the communication of the poet's emotional awareness the 'personal' became the 'universal'.[31] Through his reflection on the poetry of Wordsworth, Read came to the view that 'The very process of poetry involves the idealisation, or more exactly the universalisation, of individual experience'.[32] Similarly Blake's art represented the attempt 'to combine the greatest intensity of subjective thought and feeling with the greatest clarity of objective representation'.[33] Wordsworth, he argued, performed a revolutionary move by breaking with the convention driven and artificial style of poetry that had been dominant since the Restoration, and this act was a re-establishment of contact with the lost tradition of Chaucer, Milton and Shakespeare. For Read, Wordsworth showed that the English national character was not premised on the suppression of instinct and feeling. Following Worringer's distinction between Northern and Southern European characteristics as dynamic and static respectively, Read emphasized Wordsworth's Northern sensibility, in which he claimed 'the normal feelings of the human being are present in more than their normal force'.[34] Read used this conceptualization of the Northern identity as a defining characteristic of English culture. In this sense, as noted by Kevin Davey, 'He constructed and celebrated a transcendent, essentialized Englishness'.[35] For Read 'industrial prosperity' had stultified the atmosphere of England.[36] According to Read the English cultural tradition as represented by Wordsworth had been suppressed by Puritanism and capitalism: 'We in England have suffered the severest form of capitalist exploitation; we have paid for it, not only in physical horror and destitution, in appalling deserts of cinders and smoke, in whole cities of slums and rivers of filth – we have paid for it also in a death of the spirit.'[37]

Read's focus on the personality and emotionality of the artist played a large part in his claim for the value of the artist to society, and brought his growing interest in psychoanalysis into his critical analysis. Read applied Freud's and Adler's theories of personality and neurosis to claim that the artist was born of social dislocation and made a uniquely valuable contribution to society. Freud identified a similarity between the imaginations of neurotics and artists, Read observed, but noted that the objective form of the artists fantasy could be independently pleasurable. The explanation according to Read was that some quality in the work of art eased psychic tensions.[38] Read applied the idea of a 'lack of adaptation' derived from the psychoanalysis of Dr. Trigant Burrow to Shelley in particular.[39] According to this theory, Read concluded that 'Shelley lived in a state of heightened subjectivity' combined with a unity-complex, which determined the 'quality of imagery and verbal expression' of his verse.[40] Thus, as the concomitant of being a pathological neurotic, Shelley was a genius who could perceive more clearly a complete social order.[41] Shelley's psychological type, Read concluded, was of 'peculiar value to humanity'.[42] Read argued that this demonstrated the scientific basis of romanticism's insights that inspiration, individuality, and the breaking of social convention were the source of the regeneration of mankind.[43] As he claimed in a later, more explicitly political work, 'life depends on the agitation set up by a few eccentric individuals'.[44]

Read's emphasis on the visual arts was another important factor that helped to lead his thinking about modernism away from that of his anti-romantic contemporaries. Read worked as assistant keeper in the Department of Ceramics at the Victoria and Albert Museum from 1922. His 1928 work *Staffordshire Pottery Figures* emphasized the higher aesthetic worth of the home-produced figures made according to the spontaneity and direct impulses of the labouring craftsman, as measured against the mass-produced porcelain figures of the nineteenth century. The active visual sense awakened in Read by this experience with plastic arts was to form a significant role in his thinking. Aided by his interpretation of Henri Bergson's thesis, Read developed a view of evolution as inspired by a creative urge that led to deepening consciousness. Bergson was one of the key intellectual reference points for the early cubists. The reality that cubists were attempting to depict was matter in its various states of flux and novelty, suffused with transformative energy as Bergson had described it. According to Bergson, visual artists perceived the world immediately, intuitively and sympathetically rather than rationally and systematically. Bergson considered this emotional, as opposed to intellectual, understanding to be as important as rational and scientific thinking for understanding reality. For Bergson, reality was understood not through the intellect, which artificially divided and categorized observations, but through intuition, understood as an instinctual sort of consciousness which perceived reality in its continuous state. Intuition synthesized rather than analysed perceptions, and was thus able to penetrate the changing nature of reality. Intuition of this creative kind was also for Bergson, and for Read, the root of the creative process. Bergson argued that the creative energy he associated with the intuitive and emotional temperament of artists, a dynamic energy or vital force he termed *élan vital*, played an important role in the evolution of the species. For Read, both evolution and artistic perception entailed 'progress from chaos to form'.[45] Read was at pains to emphasize this perspective: 'The point I am trying to make, the whole point of my hypothesis, is that the work of art is not an analogy – it is the essential act of transformation; not merely the *pattern* of mental evolution, but the vital process itself.'[46] This view led him into deep conflict with his friend and rival cultural commentator T. S. Eliot over the possibility of rehabilitating British culture through art. Read argued, against Eliot, that modern artists were, in terms of cultural renewal, 'doing their job just as effectively as the artists of the Renaissance'.[47] This 'intimate and indivisible connection' that had existed between 'art and the origin of consciousness' since the earliest stages of human development, persisted as the mainspring of civilization and culture and the root, rather than the offspring, of philosophy.[48]

Read became the proponent of an interpretation of modernism which emphasized the feeling behind abstract art and its relationship to the indigenous romantic tradition. He came to see abstract art as both strongly emotive and capable of symbolizing ideals. Later theorists of avant-gardism, such as Renato Poggioli, have supported the idea that modernism owes a debt to the romantic view of the role of the artist. In his discussion Poggioli notes that, despite the assumed 'programmatic anti-romanticism of the avant-garde', there was in fact a 'parental bond between romanticism and the ideal of new art and poetry'. Romanticism was in this sense, he claims, a precedent for modernism and this relationship challenges the 'erroneous belief that modern art has completely overcome or liquidated romanticism'.[49] As Read managed the synthesis of classical and romantic impulses he defined art as 'emotion cultivating good form' with 'universal implications'.[50] The artist saw 'not only the object immediately before him, but . . . this object in its universal implications'.[51] Read posited the plays of Shakespeare as the literary analogy of this mediation of the subjective and the objective: 'The characters of Shakespeare's great plays are not merely individual characters, for all their realism and fidelity to life, but also prototypes of the passions and aspirations of humanity in general'.[52] Thus, Read maintained that the 'real distinction of the modern movement in art' was the creation of 'archetypal form'.[53]

The interpretation of modernism as the synthesis of reason and emotion that Read developed was most explicitly represented in his responses to the work of 1930s Hampstead modernists. The synthesis he performed, and its application to this group, was central to his political project. The modern artists for whom Read held out particular hope for cultural renewal were the abstract modernists with whom he became intimately connected, most notably the sculptors Henry Moore and Barbara Hepworth, but also the painter Ben Nicholson. These artists provided a key demonstration of his vision of modernism as pioneering idealism. Here, in the British abstract art of the 1930s, he perceived a subjective idealism striving for the higher realities and the 'pursuit of the inner essence of things'.[54] He celebrated the formal precision, harmony and proportion of their work, and also the emotional and intuitive content of their attempts to create works of absolute and permanent beauty. Modern art had taken this abstract turn, he claimed, because modern man had been made aware of chaos and ugliness by mechanization and war. Read found in the sculptor Henry Moore in particular the champion for his view of modern art. He was also, for Read, an exemplar of the unity of the English tradition and con-temporary movements in art. He praised Moore's 'persistent application of the senses in the pursuit of an ideal form' alongside the 'possession and projection into his work of certain insights which are universal'.[55] He considered that English sculpture had rediscovered itself in the work of Moore, who worked with primitive imagery, organic qualities observed from living processes, symbolism and abstraction to create ideal or universal forms. 'Under the guidance of this intuition', Read reflected with approval, 'the stone is slowly educated from an arbitrary to an ideal state of existence.'[56]

Read's response to the Spanish Civil War was consistent with his approach to the politics of art. He reaffirmed his view of the artist as the purveyor of a higher, renewing awareness that was beneficial to the whole society.

Read was deeply involved in the surrealist exhibition that was organized in London in 1936 as a protest against fascism, an attack on Chamberlain, and a move in support of Spanish Republicanism. Read's interest in surrealism was continuous with his claim that the political commitment of modernism was expressed in the construction of universal qualities upon which a new society could be built.[57] As a response to post-First-World-War conservatism and apathy, the role of surrealism in this project was in its active and dynamic dissolution of bourgeois values, preparing the way for the more constructive efforts of abstraction. He had strong artistic and anarchist sympathies with their project of protest and doubt. He endorsed their questioning of reason and their desire to expand awareness by exploring the recesses of the mind for dormant images. The surrealist view also fitted with the psychoanalytical perspective that Read had been developing concerning the secrets to which the artist had access by virtue of his neurotic personality. Read posited a marked continuity between romanticism and surrealism, particularly through the stress on the spontaneous impulse, the significance of dreams and myths in this context, and the passion to delve into the truths hidden to reason. Read argued that surrealism was thus an essentially English impulse, latent in the sensibilities of Coleridge, Blake, Lear and Lewis Carroll, and an affirmation of the romantic principle.[58] This was supported by the apparent influence of surrealism on Paul Nash, who saw it as a useful tool with which to deepen his understanding of the English landscape.[59] As the voice of surrealism in Britain, Read ensured that the British group were not only resolutely political, but also that the surrealist movement in Britain was marked by a very clear position on the indivisibility of their aesthetic and political commitments. Surrealist groups and initiatives were central to the efforts of British artists and intellectuals to rally support and funds for the Spanish struggle. Their political and fundraising agendas extended to wider challenges to totalitarianism, such as a retrospective of Max Ernst's works in 1938 to raise funds for Czech and Jewish refugees. The political aesthetics of British surrealism self-consciously combined the poetic and the social gesture. Under Read's influence, British surrealists saw the political role of art as more than just visual propaganda, they were committed to a belief in the fundamental power of art to shift human sensibilities and challenge established hierarchies.[60]

One key opponent of Read's view of art was the Marxist art historian and critic Anthony Blunt.[61] Blunt's was an alternative view of the relationship between art and radical politics, which advocated the necessity for art to have an overt political commitment. The contrary reactions of Read and Blunt to the display of Picasso's 'Guernica' in 1938 highlighted their relative positions.[62] Blunt's hostility to the painting was typical of Marxist commentators of the period, despite the fact that Picasso was a member of the French Communist Party at the time. They found the work to be too overtly individual and subjective, and as such, they argued, it threatened to fragment the shared consciousness which Marxism hoped to foster. Blunt attacked the picture as a private response with no political meaning. Read replied that 'Guernica' was a much wider and more emotional attempt to convey human suffering, and thus a true and artistic response.[63] Blunt's response to Read was that 'In art, as in morals, honesty is often unexciting at first sight. But the test comes not at the first, but at the fiftieth hour; and it is not obvious which will look duller then – a Picasso or a Coldstream.'[64] Blunt's reference was to William Coldstream, one of the founders in 1937 of the Euston Road School of painting. This group of artists were engaged in a conscious reaction against avant-garde styles. Instead, combining radical politics with conservative art techniques, they asserted the importance of painting politically charged subject matter in a realist manner. A number of people in the group were members of the Communist Party and their attitude, like Blunt's, was based on a political agenda to create a widely understandable and socially relevant art. Read disliked the realism of the Euston Road School, he balked at the social realist agenda of communicating clearly discernible social or political comment at the expense of an idealized aesthetic conception of form. While Blunt disliked the failure of modern surrealism and abstraction to depict a real proletarian world, Read denounced the realist approach as a confusion of art and propaganda. This highlighted the uniquely utopian vision which Read attributed to the modernist movement, a vision intrinsic to the aesthetics of the work of art itself.

Read was not opposed to a Marxist view of cultural production: 'Personally', he stated, 'I can travel a long way with the Marxists in their analysis of the social origin of the forms and uses of art.'[65] He shared the Marxist concern that the cultural values imposed by dominant political elites supported their economic and political power. But Read was anxious to identify art as something distinct and uniquely liberatory in a concrete biological sense, as distinct from culture, which could be debased and manipulated. Read was concerned that the Marxian materialist dialectic sacrificed artistic consciousness and its capacity for 'irrational and irregular irruptions of light in the midst of a universal darkness.'[66] In failing to recognize the distinction between art and culture, Marxism sought to do nothing more than replace one cultural dogma with another. As distinct from the possibilities for the political manipulation of culture, for Read, art was 'an unpolitical manifestation of the human spirit, and though politicians may use it or abuse it for their ends, they can neither create it nor control it – nor destroy it'.[67] In a general response to the Marxist notion of political art, Read lamented that:

> What in the attitude of our between-war socialists probably repelled me most directly was their incapacity to appreciate the significance of the artist's approach. To me it seemed elementary that a belief in Marx should be accompanied by a belief in, say, Cézanne; and that the development of art since Cézanne should interest the completely revolutionary mind as much as the development of socialist theory since Proudhon. I wanted to discuss, not only Sorel and Lenin, but also Picasso and Joyce. But no one saw the connection . . . No-one could see that it was the same force that was transforming the whole of reality.[68]

For Read, anarchism was the only political theory which could support his politicized view of creative activity, or of 'art as a primary factor in human experience'.[69] Vital for Read's approach was Stirner's emphasis on the unique experience of the human self and its inviolate subjectivity. As Read's philosophy developed, the influence of Kropotkin's ideas became marked. Kropotkin's philosophy supplied the idea of natural and spontane-ous order, against which Read's emphasis on objective form and harmony in art assumed a political significance. Kropotkin's ideas supplied Read with an optimistic view of the socially cohesive possibilities of an un-coerced community of individuals. Read's utilization and development of anarchism provided him with the view of the mind and the person as inviolable, the psychological and social value of subjectivity, and the concrete biological uniqueness of human selves. It also supplied him with a view of the importance of their communication with other unique selves. As Read claimed, 'the poet must be an anarchist. He has no other choice. He may temporize with liberalism, with democratic socialism, with state socialism . . . But they cannot guarantee the creative activity of the poet.'[70]

Anarchism and Art

In modern art Read saw the potential for a reviving and renewing utopianism. He put significant emphasis on the emotional and intuitive content of art as crucial to the modernist regenerative task. For this he relied heavily on his rehabilitation of the reputation of the English romantic tradition in poetry. Read added to this tradition his identification of art as something distinctly and uniquely liberatory in a concrete biological sense. This view of art rested absolutely on an anarchist political philosophy. In drawing specific anarchist insights from contemporary movements in art, Read contributed theoretical structure and further inspiration to a relationship between artistic production and the anarchist perspective that preceded his writings, and that has continued to flourish after his death. Acknowledging that 'the arts have been an integral part of the movement' Alan Antliff has provided a wider survey of the relationship between anarchism and art that can help contextualize Read's intellectual contribution to the broader dynamic of the politics of art. As Antliff shows, positive perceptions of the importance of art recur in anarchist sources from anarchism's beginnings in the nineteenth century to the attitudes evinced by anarchist writers and activists in the present. Examples include Proudhon's defence of the artist Gustave Courbet, Kropotkin's assertion of artists as important players in the social revolution, and Emma Goldman's acknowledgement of the inspirational power of creative work as propaganda.[71] The particular affinities between the practice of art and the anarchist tradition lie in the shared emphasis on the individual in anarchist theory and artistic endeavour, in the wider definition shared by the anarchist and the artist of what counts as 'political' action, and in the anarchist model of the free society as one marked by creativity, variety and differentiation.[72] Read's reflections on art and anarchism revisit these themes, which were already embedded in debates around art and politics, particularly as they were carried on by artists and writers, such as Proudhon and Emile Zola, the neo-impressionists in France and the Dadaists in New York.

Read's reflections on art and politics, particularly as they were expressed in his public disagreements with his Marxist contemporaries, revisit themes raised by the debate between Proudhon and Emile Zola. The contrast between locating the political in art in *subject matter* versus the location of the political in art in *form* was inherent in the tension between Proudhon and Zola, and reflects Read's own disagreement with Anthony Blunt. Proudhon argued that the political import of art was in the degree to which it confronted us with 'a mirror of our own conscience' for the moral improvement of society.[73] Zola argued against this perspective with a radical subjectivism, claiming that Proudhon failed to celebrate the autonomous individuality of the artist and the importance of originality in art. According to Proudhon, argued Zola, the artist 'is not to be himself, he must be me, he must think only as I do and work only for me'. And he continued: 'The artist himself is nothing . . . In a word, individual feeling, the free expression of a personality, are forbidden.'[74] 'A work of art', argued Zola, against Proudhon, 'exists only through its originality.'[75] Proudhon's position presented the political role of art as the depiction of socially significant subject matter, whereas Zola understood the importance of art to be in the originality and uniqueness of the style of the individual artist. Like Zola, Read emphasized the significance of the temperament of the artist, and in this way collapsed artistic creation itself into a politics of art. But in Read's formulation the social significance of art and the celebration of the subjectivity of the artist are reconciled. The tension between individual freedom and social cohesion is often revisited in anarchist thinking and practice, making Read's resolution of this dialogue consistently pertinent. In another example of overlapping political and aesthetic ideas, the technique of the neo-impressionists of the late nineteenth century has been interpreted as an anarchist metaphor expressed through artistic form. According to both Antliff and Robyn Roslak, the relationship of the individual spots of colour to the harmonious synergy of the whole image was understood by the neo-impressionists themselves as 'akin to the human individuals in anarcho-communist social theory'.[76] This depiction of technique itself as imbued with anarchist politics is parallel to the Read's treatment of the organic and spontaneously harmonious products of artists like Henry Moore. In Read's treatment, however, significant anarchist importance is attached to the transformative experience of the *perception* of the harmony in works of art, and this develops the harmony engendered by works of art beyond the allegorical level to that of concrete social experience. The utopian elements in certain works of art have a transformative impact on the sensibilities of the observer and change his social relationships.

As well as revisiting themes raised by anarchists and artists in the nineteenth and early twentieth centuries, Read's reflections on art and anarchism also develop these themes and look ahead to more contemporary examples of explicitly political works of art. Read's work contributes an important development to the distinctive intellectual history of anarchist engagement with the politics of art. His invaluable intervention in these debates concerns the social significance of the subjectivity of art. Read developed a theoretical position which removed the distinction between the social and the aesthetic via a philosophy of the aesthetics of good form and the human perceptive machinery. Through this philosophy we can trace a direct line of influence from Read's aesthetic anarchism to concrete and controversial challenges to militarism and the state in the recent past. Read aimed to show that great art builds social relationships, and this significantly social dimension to individual creativity can be seen in the anti-militarist linocuts of Richard Mock in their focus on the harm done to others, both human and non-human, through the behaviour of the state, especially in the military sphere. Richard Mock's socially critical linocuts, such as the 'Gulf War' series (1991), have featured regularly in the New York Times. He claims to have been decisively influenced by reading Herbert Read's collection of explicitly political essays *Anarchy and Order* while at college in the mid-1960s.[77] In line with Read's influence on the critical themes and ideas behind Mock's art, as well as his perception of the role of the artist in political change, Read's voice is also discernible in Mock's identification of anarchism as a philosophy of harmony, social awareness, and expanded sensibilities.[78]

Despite significant contributions to key debates in social theory and art and the ongoing inspiration they have provided for political artists, the centrality of Read's anarchist framework to his view of art may help explain the lack of a unified political view of his ideas since his death. According to Michael Paraskos, the dominance of Marxist forms of cultural criticism since the 1970s, particularly in England and America, have created an audience deeply hostile to Read's ideas and 'perpetuated the absence of Read'.[79] Jerald Zaslove supports this explanation: 'It might be argued that cultural studies as a displaced form of social theory has eviscerated any relic of historical, anarcho-communism from theory.'[80] These authors agree that the marginalization of Read's ideas in cultural debate should be understood in the context of the absorption of Marxist cultural theory into the academic establishment after the war. According to Paraskos, the importance of the pioneering university-Marxism of figures like Raymond Williams led to what Paraskos terms a *'pattern of marginalisation'* which excluded Read from academic discourse. Particularly striking is the omission of Read from Williams's influential *Culture and Society*, published in 1958 when Read's was still a prominent and influential cultural commentator.[81] Once this gap was established, the fundamental difference between Read's ideas and the Marxist view distanced him from mainstream debate. Admittedly, the acceptance of a knighthood would have certainly reinforced this distance. In the terms of Marxist cultural theory, art and the appreciation of art merely reflects and reproduces social stratifications as they already exist, bolstering the existing socio-economic order with class signifiers based on cultural symbols of dominance. Read's writings presented a utopian view of art as a mechanism by which the body created reality in a shared social context. It could appear that he had little concern for the differential possibilities for social action within social structures imposed by elites in a capitalist society. But, as Read stated, economic and social factors were fundamentally important, and he was alive to the manipulation of cultural values by powerful vested interests. As an anarchist, he shared the Marxist analysis of dominant and subordinate socio-economic relations between classes. But, like anarchists, and deeply influenced by romantic sources, psychological insights and more contemporary existentialist influences, he was committed to the idea of a dynamically creative and self-aware human mind. Further, he maintained, consciousness is not passive but active, not received or given but created and designed and part of the human engagement with his environment, particularly through the sensations of the body. Individuality, far from being merely a bourgeois construct, was a factor in evolution. It was this difference between Marxism and the anarchist perspective, as he developed it, that Read was referring to when he wrote 'Marxism is based on economics, anarchism on biology'.[82] It is also these ideas that link Read and his anarchist project so firmly to the pioneering avant-gardism of the modernist revolution in literature, aesthetics and ideas in Britain. Anarchism and modernism are both conceptually and historically linked, and the absence of a clearly identifiable field of anarchist cultural studies reflects the Herbert-Read-shaped gaps in the intellectual history of these movements.

Paraskos argues that, by excluding Read's pluralistic, subjective and radical anarcho-modernism from debates about art and culture in the later twentieth century, and by ignoring the fact that Read's anarchism was 'simultaneous with the main period of modernism', the Marxist cultural writers 'stole modernism from the anarchists'.[83] For the Marxists, art can only reflect existing hierarchies, it cannot extend human knowledge or consciousness. Because of this, argues Paraskos, the Marxist-dominated field of cultural studies excluded the work of Herbert Read, colonizing and misrepresenting 'a cultural phenomenon that was inherently anarchist'.[84] The problem was that the anarchists ostracized Read after 1952, as a result of his opting into the British peerage, just at the time that the field was being annexed by Marxist influence in the universities. By doing so, adds Paraskos, they 'hamstrung' the intellectual development of an anarchist school of cultural studies, for which Read's work should have been a starting point.[85]

Reviving Anarchism

Read's adherence to anarchist ideas extended beyond his interpretations of aesthetic activity. It was the Spanish Civil War that prompted Read to publicly declare himself in favour of the political perspective of anarchism in 1937. The Civil War had quickly become the test of the political commitment of British intellectuals of the 1930s. The defence of the Republic was seen as the battlefield for the defence of liberal and progressive values both in Spain and at home. The effect of the Spanish Civil War on Read was compounded by the news of the Moscow trials, which prompted his desire to publicly declare against Soviet Marxism. During and after the war, Read became associated with anarchist groups in Britain, notably the group oriented around the Freedom Press in London, and he served on committees to aid refugees and organized and addressed numerous meetings. Read announced his anarchism in the *Left Review* survey, 'Authors Takes Sides on the Spanish War', and in 'The Necessity of Anarchism', a three-part article in *Adelphi*.[86] Aware of the negative reception which would greet such a move, he nevertheless saw his attachment to this unfashionable 'remote' movement as a statement of a rigorous intellect honestly confronting 'essentials':

> To declare for a doctrine so remote as anarchism at this stage of history will be regarded by some critics as a sign of intellectual bankruptcy; by others as a sort of treason, a desertion of the democratic front at the most acute moment of its crisis; by still others as merely poetic non-sense. For myself it is not only a return to Proudhon, Tolstoy, and Kropotkin, who were the predilections of my youth, but a mature realisation of their essential rightness, and a realisation, moreover, of the necessity, of the probity, of an intellectual confining himself to essentials.[87]

Read was fully aware of the neglect from which he was retrieving the anarchist tradition in Britain, 'I begin with this challenge: no fundamental thought has been devoted to the principles of anarchism for half a century.'[88] He was also aware of how far such a philosophy removed him from political acceptability: 'In the parochial atmosphere of England, to profess a belief in anarchism is to commit political suicide.'[89] Nonetheless, Read claimed that the combination of new fields of knowledge and a number of significant developments in the first half of the twentieth century made the era and the intellectual milieu strikingly ripe for a revival of anarchist philosophy.

One field of knowledge particularly pertinent to anarchist restatement and revival and 'significant for the rise of anarchism' was psychology. Also pertinent to the revival of anarchism were 'certain historical events of the past fifty years which have fundamentally affected all systems of thought'. These included wars, which were 'symptomatic of some deep social disorder'. Also important for the revival of anarchism in Read's view were the fascist victory in the Spanish Civil War, the Russian revolution and the rise of America as a world power. Further, anarchism was relevant to the changes in production and communication 'which have transformed the economic basis of society', and the invention of the atom bomb 'which has decisive implications for revolutionary strategy'.[90]

After World War Two Read had again hoped that the impact of war would generate the impetus for political renewal but again the rights and responsibilities of the state were permitted to expand even further. Witnessing the stability of British political institutions for the second time, Read wrote:

> Though anarchism as a political doctrine has a respectable ancestry, and has numbered great poets and philosophers like Godwin and Shelley, Tolstoy and Kropotkin among its adherents . . . though, that is to say, it is one of the fundamental political doctrines of all time, it has never been given a place in our insular discussions of the political problems of our time.[91]

Read saw his work as contributing to a revival of the values and meanings associated with a vital and humanist ethic. It is highly significant that a public figure such as Read, deeply concerned about war and civilization in the mid-twentieth-century era, should have grappled with modernity by a turn to the anti-authoritarian intellectual perspectives of the anarchist tradition. He argued that anarchism was the true application of the socialist principle, and, as the century wore on, the lone defender of the individualist tradition. But he added a wide range of sources and absorbed a number of influences during this period which all contributed to the distinctive position he defended. Thus, he could argue that despite having 'cut myself off from the main current of socialist activity in England', he had found 'sympathy and agreement in unexpected places', and also that there were 'many intellectuals who are fundamentally anarchist in their political outlook, but who do not dare invite ridicule by confessing it'.[92] Read may have had George Orwell in mind here, a figure similarly disillusioned by the failure of war to precipitate radical social changes. Like Read, Orwell had seen a wider significance for European political culture in the defeat of the Spanish Republic. There emerged in his work a representation of Communism as a totalitarian force, an idea that brought a libertarian strand into British left-wing opinion with which anarchism found a degree of sympathy. Read said of Orwell after his death, 'I suppose I have felt nearer to him than to any other English writer of our time.'[93] Orwell expressed sympathy with Read's 'civilizing influence' and championing of 'unfashionable causes', especially his 'guts to speak out against the russo-mania of the last ten years'. But Orwell was confused by Read's correlation of freedom and organization, and mused critically that 'liberty and efficiency must pull in opposite directions'.[94] Nevertheless, it was to Read that Orwell turned in 1939 with the idea of setting up an underground press to counter wartime censorship.

The most important event in Read's wartime experience, and one in which Orwell was also involved, was the defence of four anarchists against charges of subversion launched by the British state. Towards the end of the war the editors of the publication *War Commentary* (titled *Revolt* up to 1939, *War Commentary* during the war and then *Freedom* in 1945), the wartime paper of the anarchist Freedom Press, were tried under emergency regulations on the charge of spreading disaffection in the military. In 1944, the Special Branch of Scotland Yard raided the offices of *War Commentary* and seized membership and subscription lists. Read was the chairman of the Freedom Defence Committee, which he set up in support of the anarchist editors. Members of the Committee included Orwell (as vice-president), T. S. Eliot and E. M. Forster. In 1945 the Director of Public Prosecutions charged the four Freedom Press figures, including Vernon Richards and Marie Louise Berneri, with conspiracy to 'seduce from duty persons in the Forces and to cause disaffection'. The government's case was partly based on a poem distributed in a leaflet, two verses of which read:

Your country, who says you've a country?
You live in another man's flat.
You haven't even a backyard.
So why should you murder for that?

You haven't a hut or a building,
No flowers, no garden, it's true;
The landlords have grabbed all the country;
Let them do the fighting – not you.[95]

The trial and defence of the *War Commentary* editors was an important moment in the emergence of later twentieth-century anarchism in Britain. The trial was seen by the wide sweep of left-wing intellectual opinion as a signal from the government that the same stringent control of speech exercised in the war would continue into the indefinite future. From this it can be seen that the re-emergence of an anarchist sensibility in Britain came firmly from within British radical intellectual circles. The Freedom Defense Committee was formulated to defend the *War Commentary* editors but was more broadly concerned to guard free speech and went on to oppose the continuance of military and industrial conscription after the war.[96] The anarchists found that their profile was raised from magazines of very low circulation to representation in the high distribution daily tabloids in which the case was publicized. The public benches were filled with a wide and varied cross section of bohemian and intellectual British society. Read noted: 'A certain weight of opinion has formed behind [the anarchists] particularly among members of the younger generation.'[97]

Referring to England as the 'Land of Liberty', the terms under which Read expressed his defence of the anarchists indicated his particular sense of the relationship between anarchism and the English sensibility.[98] 'Liberty was always a fine word to make a fury about', he wrote in the introduction to an anthology he compiled called *The English Vision*, 'but only in England do we pursue the idea in calmness of mind'.[99] He framed his oratory in defence of the anarchists on the basis of 'traditional rights which free men in this country have fought for throughout the centuries', and promised the state 'unrelenting strife' on the grounds that it had 'dared to abrogate these traditional rights'. Read claimed that 'It is a small group of anarchists whose freedom is threatened, but, comrades, I do not speak to you now as an anarchist: I speak to you as an Englishman, as one proud to follow in the tradition of Milton and Shelley.'[100] The trial of the anarchists had implications for anyone, he argued, who valued their native rights of free speech, and anyone who sought to resist the growth of 'that foul and un-English institution, the political police'.[101] In his speech after the trial and imprisonment of the *War Commentary* editors, Read continued in this vein 'There is no longer in this land such a thing as the liberty of unlicensed printing for which Milton made his immortal and unanswerable plea: there is no longer any such thing as freedom of expression which ten generations of Englishmen have jealously guarded.'[102] Here Read contrasted an indigenous civil libertarian tradition to the late wartime shape of the British state.

Read interpreted the invocation of war regulations at this late stage in the war as a warning of the authoritarian shape that the post-war state would take. He claimed that the use of Defense Regulation 39A was being prolonged into peacetime in a covert spirit of increasing censorship. As far as Read was concerned, the Freedom Defence Committee was the British wing of the European resistance against the tide of fascism: 'We won the Battle of Britain, but lost the chance of a British Revolution.'[103] The anarchist editors were opposing the rise of 'our home-based fascism openly and directly'.[104] The failure of their defence indicated to Read that 'The front line of the Resistance Movement is now here, in England, and we, *alone* if necessary, will continue the fight against fascism.'[105] Even as the war against fascism was on the verge of being won on the continent of Europe, Read felt it was lost at home while liberties were being curtailed: '[W]e can have no joy in victory, nor ease from strife, until our comrades once more stand beside us as free men.'[106]

It is in relation to Read's patriotic radicalism that we can make sense of his ambiguous relationship to the British establishment, highlighted in 1952 when he accepted a knighthood for services to literature. Read was ostracized from anarchist political circles in Britain for this decision, and uncertainty regarding Read persists in anarchist publications for this reason. It is indeed difficult to make sense of his implicit support for the British peerage in the context of his professed commitment to equality and his hostility to the state. The last of Read's contributions to *Freedom* regarded his knighthood, an anarchist paradox, which, he claimed, 'could only exist in England'.[107] Demonstrating that this was not an act intended to demonstrate the relinquishment of his anarchist philosophy, which it was taken to signify by the anarchist movement, he argued: 'To contract out of society is an idle gesture . . . My convictions have not changed and will not change. I regard war as the curse of humanity and governments as the instruments of war.'[108] His defence of this contradictory position was not strong or convincing enough to sway the hostility of the anarchist community in Britain, including his former friends at the Freedom Press. Read's long association with the Freedom Press was reflected through his friendships with the editors and his many contributions to their publications *Spain and the World*, *War Commentary*, *Revolt!* and *Freedom*, and the individual titles he wrote and edited for Freedom Press, including *The Philosophy of Anarchism* (1940), *Kropotkin: Selections from His Writings* (1942), *The Education of Free Men* (1944), *Freedom: Is it a Crime?* (1945), *Existentialism, Marxism and Anarchism; Chains of Freedom* (1949) and *Art and the Evolution of Man* (1951). This personal and intellectual relationship ended suddenly and dramatically in 1952. Michael Paraskos relates a story told by Read's children that conveys the domestic impact of Read's ostracism from the anarchist community in austerity-era Britain. According to this account, the Read household had enjoyed regular supplies of good coffee beans, a rare commodity in 1950s Britain, sent up to their Yorkshire home from the Italian delicatessen King Bomba in Soho. The shop was owned by Ernidio Recchioni, the father of Freedom Press editor Vernon Richards. Recchioni sent the regular delivery of coffee beans to Read in thanks for his services to anarchism, and, accordingly, the deliveries stopped abruptly in 1952, in observance of Read's exclusion from anarchist circles.[109] Nonetheless, in 1993, Colin Ward, noted the ongoing value of Read's work for the anarchist movement, not least because 'his anarchist propaganda' had been able to reach 'a wider audience than most of us could expect'.[110]

Developing his anarchism in response to his experiences in World War Two, Read persisted in his view that 'War increases in intensity and effect as society develops its central organisation.'[111] He was resolute in his conviction that 'War will exist as long as the state exists' and that 'There is no problem which leads so inevitably to anarchism.'[112] After the war Read argued that the rise of atomic power highlighted the nature of man's relationship with the state in the twentieth century and highlighted the non-violent form that resistance to it must take:

> The power of the State, of our enemy, is now absolute. We cannot struggle against it *on the plane of force*, on the material plane. Our action must be piecemeal, non-violent, insidious and universally pervasive . . . the real revolution is internal . . . the most effective action is molecular . . . only in so far as we change the actual disposition of men do we guarantee the enduring success of the social revolution we all desire.[113]

Read was an advocate of non-resistance, and saw this as the future of the movement, drawing the tradition away from previous, more militant, conceptions of anarchism. It was in this sense that he meant that his conception was 'less political' and more 'humane' although he added that 'I will not admit for a moment that it is less revolutionary.'[114] Read's anarchism rested on the desire to 'secure a revolution in the mental and emotional attitudes of man', discarding the conception of anarchism associated with 'conspiracy, assassination, citizen armies, [and] the barricades' for that kind of agitation had been rendered finally obsolete 'blown into oblivion by the atomic bomb'.[115] The non-violent turn in his anarchism, and the implied rejection of force on internal and political levels, was a break with classic anarchist political thought to which anarchist historian David Goodway assigns 'decisive importance'.[116] Read recognized that the principle of non-violence was not entirely novel in the anarchist tradition, Tolstoy being non-violent anarchism's most prominent advocate. Read asserted that 'Tolstoy's message has not grown out-of-date'.[117] Read saw himself developing the internal implications of Tolstoy's non-violent view by highlighting the psychological form of revolutionary change through education that it implied:

> The only way a biological or organismic change can be induced is by training or education. The word *revolution* should largely disappear from our propaganda, to be replaced by the word *education* . . . a new order of society such as we desire can only be given a firm and enduring foundation within the physique and disposition of the human being, and education in its widest sense is the only means we have of securing such fundamental changes in the whole social group.[118]

In the build-up to World War Two, in applying himself to the problem of war, the 'cancer that threatens to destroy the life of our civilisation', Read had come to a set of anarchist conclusions heavily indebted to psychology.[119] The following statement outlines his case, which is that war and repression are related to psychological pathologies associated with exercise of power:

> There is no problem which leads so inevitably to anarchism. Peace is anarchy. Government is force; force is repression, and repression leads to reaction, to a psychosis of power, which in turn involves the individual in destructive impulses and the nations in war. War, therefore, will exist so long as the State exists.[120]

For this approach, Read drew on the work of Edward Glover, a key figure in the development of psychology in Britain through his involvement in the British Psychoanalytical Society from the 1920s. According to Glover, war was the result of the repression of unsocial feelings that were part of the normal human experience. For Read, without opportunities for the discharge of such feelings 'energy accumulates' and 'there occurs a catastrophic purgation of our overcharged emotional system'.[121] In this manner Read correlated war phenomena with phases of repressed unconscious mental development.[122] Read's distinctive approach to political power and individual neurosis was taken up in the themes of Alex Comfort's 1950 work *Authority and Delinquency in the Modern State*. In recognition of this, in 1951 Read referred to the 'fanatical politicians and journalists' of the Cold War era as 'Dr Comfort's delinquents'.[123] Read added Jungian insights to this perspective. Through these ideas Read asserted the importance of the condition of the mental life of the individual for the quality of society. He mounted an attack on the abstract notion of the state as 'a sort of super-individual', a collective entity endowed with personalized attributes. An abstract unity of this type, he argued, could not exercise the moral quality, creative capacity and self-awareness that were the distinctively human qualities of the individual. The administration of humanity in masses had a 'devastating' effect on the individual both morally and psychologically. The idealization of the state led to a mass psychology of 'big numbers' and 'powerful organisations', the superseding of individuality and human scale, under which 'totalitarian demons are called forth' in the consciousness of men.[124] For Read mass society was destructive of the individuality on which healthy society depended. This idea developed into a devastating moral critique of British war policy in the work of Alex Comfort, who courted widespread public controversy with his anti-militaristic attack on the saturation bombing policies of the allied forces in World War Two.

In light of the growth of the imposition of the state, Read was concerned that British socialism had lost its way. 'Socialism is in retreat', he claimed.[125] In order to counter the ever-accelerating power of the state, its imposition into society, and the growing centralization of political authority, he argued that the socialist movement had to engage in some thorough revitalizing self-evaluation. Left-wing political ideas had adopted the methods of the state, and had corrupted their project by mistaking collectivism for socialism. For Read, the first principles of socialism were those directed towards the 'rational organisation of society to the end that men shall live together in freedom, security and plenty'.[126] He was clear that these first principles did not include the idealization of the state, an idealization that Read traced to Hegel's raising of the state 'to the level of an abstract entity', and reifying it as 'the perfect organisation of all our social activities'. Under such a conception of the state, the importance of freedom was undermined by the belief that 'no activities can be tolerated which interfere with its unity and order'.[127] Read denied that such a view of the state was a core principle of socialism: 'The State is everywhere recognised by the founders of modern socialism – by Marx, Engels and Lenin no less that by Proudhon, Bakunin and Kropotkin – as the product of social distinctions and an instrument of oppression.'[128] According to Read modern anarchism was a reaffirmation or a reminder of the traditional socialist view of the state, rather than being a movement away from its core principles.[129] Resistance to the state, under this understanding, was the true core of socialist principle, and the measure of socialism was the extent to which the state has been dissolved.[130] In 1953 Read wrote the introduction to an edition of *The Rebel* by Albert Camus. Like Read, the Spanish Civil War precipitated Camus's socialist–pacifist turn against the Communist Party and the Marxist–Leninism of the Soviet Union. Read was full of praise for the work: 'With the publication of this book a cloud that has oppressed the European mind for more than a century begins to lift. After an age of anxiety, despair, and nihilism, it seems possible once more to hope – to have confidence again in man and in the future.'[131] With the claim that 'Camus's ideas come close to anarchism', Read identified how closely Camus's ideas and reflections approximated elements of his own socialist perspective.[132] Camus's concerns regarding the state, freedom and tyranny, his stance against all forms of power, his emphasis on the significance of human choice, and the call for moral responsibility in his work were all features of Read's perspective. Read argued that both liberalism and communism tended towards the centralized authority of the state. For this view Read drew on a synthesis of the ideas of Proudhon and Alexis de Tocqueville in a key combination of anarchist and democratic sources. From these he read a warning of the corrupting influence of power which reflected exactly 'the anarchist point of view!'.[133] He also drew from these sources an emphasis on the political significance of small-scale organization, which he traced to ancient Greek philosophy: 'It has always been recognised since the time of the Greek philosophers that the practicability of a free democracy was somehow bound up with the question of size – that democracy was somehow bound up with the question of size – that democracy would only work within some restricted unit such as the city-state.'[134] The only political philosophy that recognized this claim, and was thus most intransigent in its attitude to the state, Read claimed, was anarchism. For Read, anarchism resolutely sought to divide power, and decentralize government to a level of locality and directness within which men could enjoy 'social responsibility' and participate 'immediately' in the social order.[135]

Read drew on his anarchist and psychological influences to postulate a source for socialist renewal. What was necessary for socialism, he argued, was a return to the conflict between Marx and Stirner, exponents of communism and individualism respectively. Read considered Marx to have been the intellectual victor in this conflict, but he argued that the time was ripe for a re-examination of the tensions between the two thinkers. The Second World War brought the problems of individual ethics and public morality to the fore for socialists, highlighting the points of tension between Stirner and Marx and revealing their fresh relevance. Read was animated by the ideas thrown up by this conflict: 'We have to build on the basis of that work; we have to conceive socialist thought as a dialectical development which included Marx, Engels and Lenin no less that Stirner, Proudhon and Kropotkin.'[136] Stirner's plea for a rigorous conception of freedom and individuality, and his warning against preconceived dogmas and abstractions, was based on the assertion that man was only free if he was a unique person, entirely self-determined and unrelentingly self-directed. Marx showed that Stirner's utterly self-contained, self-directed egoist was no less of an abstraction, divorced as it was from the environmental influences that determined the nature of the individual personality. Read argued that, in light of what psychoanalysis had revealed concerning the unconscious egotistic impulses behind our ideals, Marx's criticism of Stirner's subjectivism had lost some ground.[137] Read identified Stirner's conception as a psychological understanding of freedom by linking it to the work of contemporary psychologists. He argued that figures like Jung, Burrow, Reich and Fromm were in accord with Stirner's claim that freedom was essentially a process of self-liberation and integration of the personality. Read claimed that Fromm in particular was essentially expressing the insight of Stirner when he claimed that without a strong approval and awareness of himself the individual is in a state of anxiety concerning his own self and as such lacks inner security.[138] Marxian criticism had been misguided in its overlooking of the importance of this component of Stirner, Read argued, and only philosophers of the self like Martin Buber had been able to give proper consideration to these ideas.[139] In order to achieve a synthesis between Stirner's individualist criticisms of Marx and Marx's communist criticisms of Stirner, Read turned to the 'personalist' philosophy of Nikolai Berdyaev, the 1943 author of *Slavery and Freedom*. Significantly, Berdyaev was regarded with suspicion by both varieties of early twentieth-century Russian government. He embraced Marxism at university, for which he was expelled by the Tsarist regime. Then, just in time for the October Revolution of 1917, he broke with Marxism and reaffirmed the values of Orthodox Christianity, thus renewing his alienation from the Russian system of government. Read drew on this writer as the medium of his appropriation of an adapted Stirnerite vision. Berdyaev developed a notion of *personality* as the distinctively human mode of existence in the world, and the essence of the unrepeatable value of the person. Under this conception of personality, creativity was the transformation of the self and the world, and the manner in which the individual participated in existence. Personality in this sense had a communal component. Read quoted Berdyaev as saying of Stirner's work that it contained a 'modicum of truth' in so far as it emphasized that the personality must not be subordinate to society or the will of the mass. But Berdyaev resisted Stirner's notion of the entirely independent ego because in it 'personality disappears in the infinity of self-affirmation, in unwillingness to know an other'.[140] Read utilized the philosophy of Stirner in this way in order to formulate a philosophy of individualism in which he was at liberty to introduce social elements without infringing his commitment to the individual, his creativity, and his personality. What Berdyaev and Read recognized about Stirner was that an over-emphasis on an atomized competitive uniqueness, without due consideration of the social aspects of individuality, actually drew the individual away from his own selfhood. The significance of this insight cannot be overstated. Read presents an understanding of individual freedom and social cohesion as linked, as mutually reinforcing, rather than conflicting, impulses. The view of individual freedom as important for the development of social cohesion is part of the anarchist current within socialism, in his development of this principle Read drew on long-established debates and new sources of knowledge about the human self and its relationship with other selves.

Read was one of the 'names', of the Committee of 100, which, according to Goodway, was 'the most important anarchist – or near-anarchist – political organisation of modern Britain'.[141] But, while he took part in 1961 demonstration in Trafalgar Square, Read quickly became disillusioned by the provocative and violent tactics developing within CND and he was, in the end, critical of the anti-nuclear movement: 'We have become a public spectacle, a group isolated from the general body of public opinion and feeling, a rowdy show to be televised.'[142] Thus, while the work of Read is clearly implicated in the anarchist revival of the 1960s he did not demonstrate the later anarchist interest in youth movements of figures like Colin Ward and Paul Goodman. His comments suggest a difference in age and experience that isolated him from the new developments. Feeling that a generation who had not experienced war could not have the requisite drive for renewal, he was not able to perceive how far their distance from the Second World War and its austerity was to be a vital element of later movements. Read maintained that 'Only those who have experienced the anguish and sorrow at the base of human existence are brave enough to seek to transfigure its brief span.'[143]

Education for Freedom

A key site of anarchist influence in the modern era has been the overlap between the related movements of pacifism, war resistance and anti-nuclear sentiment. Read was one of the 'names' of the Committee of 100. However, the passion of his drive to apply anarchism to the political problems of the modern age was directed predominantly towards his project of education for freedom through art. *Education through Art* was Read's most important and influential work, and a striking attempt to apply the principles of anarchism as he had interpreted and developed them. In this book Read attempted to formulate an anarchist programme to restore and regenerate Western culture, which had demonstrated its debasement and degradation in the process of World War Two. Crucially, first appearing in 1943, the book emerged in the context of the widening state remit over schooling as developed by the 1944 Butler Act. In fact, the Freedom Press brought out a shorter pamphlet summary of Read's book, entitled 'The Education of Free Men' in 1944, announcing: 'We are glad to publish this pamphlet by Herbert Read because . . . it covers new ground by relating the problem of education to that of liberty. This is particularly important at a time when many people think that the question of education can be solved by state legislation.' Read's educational writing relied on the anarchist celebration of the individual and his relationship to society and Read's own belief in the regenerative potential of art. It demonstrated his direct development of the anarchist focus on mainstream education as a site of unwarranted suppression and coercion by adding an emphasis on education as a potential mode of social change. It was an explicitly non-violent alternative to revolutionary insurrection. Colin Ward has noted the significance in subsequent decades of *Education through Art* and the Freedom Press pamphlet *The Education of Free Men* for 'giving a climate of respectability to teachers . . . fighting . . . for the recognition of the role of the arts in education.' For Ward personally, Read's writings gave his own later efforts to develop the role of art in environmental education 'an important certificate of intellectual respectability.'[144] Read's project for education through art was the culmination of his consistently unified approach to the development of the insights of radical approaches to art and politics. He saw the rehabilitation of culture as lying in art and allied to the recovery of democratic politics through anarchism. Throughout Read's career his writings on these topics were parts of a cohesive aestheticized anarchist project emphasizing human subjectivity and social awareness, natural spontaneous form and social order. He saw the relationship between individual political freedom and individual artistic consciousness as the root of human civilization. The basis of his aesthetic politics was the unique synthesis he performed between the idea of the objectivity of form, which underpinned abstract art, and the subjective emotionality of romantic art. The result was a singular view of the objective social value of the inner vision of the individual artist. Only anarchism could support his politicized view of creative activity, a celebration of the capacity of the individual and his universal awareness to transform reality.

Education through Art was Read's most influential political work. It led to the foundation, as a subsidiary UNESCO organization, of the International Society for Education through Art. Read's prescription for education through art was his attempt at an explicitly anarchist programme. Read noted that as he was writing *Education through Art* in the early 1940s, bombing raids of unprecedented scale were besieging German cities and European armies were in a bloody deadlock in the Ukraine. This evidence of the 'diseases of the human spirit' was a desperate call for a means by which civilization could restore itself to health and humanity. This was the call which the educational programme outlined in Read's book was designed to answer.[145] Essentially, Read's work on education was a reiteration of his views on the regenerative potential of art, the importance of art in human consciousness, and the importance of the individual and his relationship to society. Read's writing on education enjoyed a wide readership, however what has been overlooked in the mainstream popularity that Read's writing on education enjoyed was the fact that *Education through Art* was an anarchist strategy and an alternative to violent insurrection. Through a change in the way we educate children, Read claimed, a change would be precipitated in society. This represented the culmination of Read's non-violent conception of anarchism. Read regarded the idea of changing society through education rather than political means as his most important contribution to anarchist theory. Many of the principal anarchist thinkers demonstrated a practical or theoretical interest in education. William Godwin, for example, set out a method of education in the eighteenth century based on an equal relationship between the teacher and the student, and a pedagogical relationship in which the student's initiative would be the trigger to his learning. Read was following Godwin's precedent in maintaining that the role of the teacher lay in 'identifying himself with the distinct personality of each child' and preserving 'the child's own line of thought'.[146] As in Godwin's philosophy, Read's ideas included a critique of systems of state education and a denial of the value of punishment and systematic assessment. Read's ideas, however, constituted a more comprehensive manifesto of anarchism-through-education and contained a clearer advocacy of the positive principles towards which education was to be directed. He went so far as to suggest that the school might be the principal focus for anarchist social change. The idea has had a major impact on anarchist ideas about education, and *Education through Art* influenced ideas about curriculum design in primary education policy in the years before the educational reforms of the Thatcher era. The successful efforts of the Thatcher and Blair governments to reverse the pedagogical trends of the post-war years, however, demonstrate the essential weakness of a programme of radical social change through educational innovation alone. They show that the educational system will always be a key site of social and political contestation, and one that cannot be isolated from the struggle for social and political power. To implement a transformative and egalitarian system of education for the purposes of engendering social change requires social and political power, and the project of revolution through education cannot be theorized independently from questions of where that power lies and in whose interests it operates. Nonetheless, Woodcock has noted that Read made it impossible for future anarchist thinkers to overlook the revolutionary potential of educational ideas.[147]

One of the starting points of Read's philosophy of education was his integration of the romantic view of man with the classical notion of objective form, a synthesis that had animated his thought since his reading of Hulme. Read drew from Plato in particular a conception of the relationship between physical form and ethical form, the idea that what is beautiful is good and what is ugly is bad in aesthetic and moral terms. Read added to this a conception of children as beings with a natural aesthetic impulse and sense of form that they expressed spontaneously in art and play. For Read, in the words of Wordsworth, the child was 'nature's priest'.[148] Plato's philosophy of idealized forms led Read to an anarchism based on an assertion of the natural harmony of nature and human perception: 'order in itself appeals to the imagination'.[149] In this vein, he claimed that 'The free man is a man of nature, perfected in natural ways of behavior'.[150] For the relationship between the notion of objective artistic form and human freedom, Read drew inspiration from Schiller, to whom he attributed the insight that until man was capable of perceiving beauty, and its secrets of goodness and truth, he will not be capable of liberty.[151] However, as Read perceived it, Plato's approach was classical; the order of nature was interpreted as rigid and systematic. Against such a conception, Read argued: 'we are endowed with a mind that is not satisfied with such a circumscribed activity – a mind that desires to create and adventure beyond the given.'[152] The recognition of the quality of spontaneity in natural growth was missing from Plato's understanding. Abstracting static concepts from natural processes destroyed the spontaneity 'which in the human personality is the quality of spiritual freedom'.[153] This was supported by the psychology of Erich Fromm, who, Read argued, traced the 'secret of our collective ills as a society' to 'the suppression of the spontaneous creative ability in the individual'. This was because, he argued, an instinct was never repressed without seeking unconscious compensation, so when spontaneity was blocked it became a destructive urge.[154] Freedom thus had an expressive and dynamic character. Art was the 'expression of health: it is exuberance, exhilaration, [and] ecstasy', this was central to freedom, as opposed to the passivity or 'passive absorption' of experience which characterized the un-free or constrained individual.[155]

Another starting point of this work was the development of Read's thinking about the relationship between art and human psychology that was triggered by his encounter with children's art. In 1940 the British Council decided to 'project' British art overseas during wartime by sending drawings by British children. As a prominent figure in British art, Read became involved in the task of assembling the collection and as part of this project he visited schools throughout the country. While visiting British schools to gather material he was struck by the recurrence of an ancient symbol, which he recognized as the mandala, a symbol connected with unity and the self in Eastern and Medieval cultures. Its appearance, 'spontaneously in the minds of English children', struck him as highly significant.[156] This led him to the conviction that images and forms recurred in the human imagination across time and cultures, and corresponded to forms in nature. He related this to Jung's notion of the archetypal symbol and saw it as evidence of the truth of Jung's theory of the collective unconscious. Archetypal symbols in dreams and art were for Jung the result of repeated or powerful impressions, which changed the physical constitution of the brain. Experience imprinted itself on the biological machinery of perception as physical 'records of function'. Thus, the mind of the child, he claimed, 'can discover and reproduce concrete patterns within his consciousness'.[157] The physical changes were reproduced in subsequent generations and produced recurrent symbols which inhabited the collective unconscious and were parts of shared experience: 'They are the revised texts, the final editions, of the electrostatic patterns produced in the cortex by normal phenomenal experience.'[158]

The ideas of Jung offered fertile psychoanalytical concepts for Read's theory that the processes of social integration were facilitated by the relationship of the individual to images in art. This challenged his Freudian view of the artist as the valuable but outcast neurotic, which he had applied most notably in his analysis of Shelley. For Read, the artist was no longer an outsider but a central agent of integration with a crucial social function, his subjective imagery was rooted in a shared, objective store of images, myths and symbols. Such was the nature of Read's conversion that he later became both publisher and editor-in-chief of the collected works of Jung in English. What Read drew from the ideas of Jung was the relationship of the individual artistic imagination to its origins in the root-images of the community. Most important for Read's philosophy was the notion of the collective unconscious, which he could utilize as a key mediating force between the individual and his community. The mandala image Read encountered convinced him that Jung had accurately conceptualized the forces, the common heritage of symbols and dreams, integrating humanity. The Jungian notion of a common biological consciousness had evolutionary implications which resonated with the notions of creativity in evolution which Read had drawn from Bergson. Read's system now contained concrete evidence of the reciprocal relationship between the cultivation of individuality and the integration and health of society. As Read stated in *The Origins of Form in Art*: 'Not only is art a process of experience co-equally important with science for the life and progress of mankind, but it has the unique function of uniting men.'[159]

Read argued that Gestalt psychology provided the vital proof that art was part of the individual's perspective on their place in the world. Under the tenets of Gestalt psychology, human beings were viewed as open systems in active interaction with their environment. It was the interaction of the individual perceptive machinery and the external situation that determined experience. The contribution of Gestalt theory to Read's ideas was an emphasis on the importance of individual discrimination in perceiving the order of nature. For Read, 'It is this faculty of assimilating sensuous impressions from material things and then combining them in significant relationships that the human race found its place in the world.'[160] Gestalt psychology was thus especially suited to Read's understanding of the presence of order and structure in the artist's subjective perception: 'the nervous system develops its organized patterns' as part of a process which is analogous to 'the way the artist paints his pictures'.[161] It provided Read with a scientific basis for his emphasis on the biological importance of subjective perception in the intuition of the universal features of the objective world. For Read and for Gestalt psychologists, the object was perceived in the human mind as part of a coherent pattern. For Read, aesthetic laws conformed to the same pattern as biological laws and were tracked in the consciousness of the individual by following the instinct for 'a heightened sense of aesthetic enjoyment'.[162] In this sense Read's defence of freedom rested on the 'biological significance of uniqueness' in mans interaction with the world.[163] Read was here putting forward a conception of individual and social development as biological individuation.

The subjective aspect was crucial to Read's conception of art and freedom and it led him to an understanding of freedom as based on positive characteristics. Subjectivity relied on the cultivation of those individual capacities that enabled men to make independent judgements. Thus, it was not enough merely to free students from constraint; there had to be some positive principle at work if children were to realize their freedom and change society. The lack of imposition was just the start, the means to cultivate freedom, which led to further effort towards the development of expressive, self-sufficient, self-creative, and spontaneous characteristics.[164] This sense of the creation of the self had parallels with Stirner's principle of freedom as 'ownership of the self'. Read claimed, with Stirnerian emphasis, that it was the 'unique sensational system' that was the agent of values.[165] His conception of freedom, he stated, was that 'Freedom should not be conceived in a negative sense, as freedom from certain wants or restrictions. It is a state of being with positive characteristics, characteristics to be developed in all their self-sufficiency'.[166] Read's conceptions of the individual and the harmony of nature, freedom and society, and the implications of art for anarchist theory, distinguished his ideas from the starkly atomized individualism of Stirner. Art was the expression of feeling in communicable form: 'the ability to represent inner feelings in outward forms'. This social form of self-realization was premised on individual subjectivity because, according to Read, we only express ourselves 'significantly' if we experience our perceptions deeply and coordinate them into patterns.[167] In Read's work this process moved alongside the parallel development of the 'social consciousness' or 'social initiation' because 'society can only function harmoniously if the individuals composing it are integrated persons, that is to say they are whole and healthy, and by that very reason competent to render mutual aid'.[168] The individual development of the child was essential for co-operation because cohesion followed individuation: 'What kind of education will promote social union? The answer is, of course, the same kind of education as that which promotes personal integrity.'[169] The unique individual was valuable to society: 'His touch of colour contributes, however imperceptibly, to the beauty of the landscape – his note is a necessary, though unnoticed, element in the universal harmony.'[170]

Art theory, psychology and a utopian revolutionary sensibility were combined in *Education through Art* into an integrated system of anarchist philosophy through the notion that the inner life of the child was the source for renewal of society: 'I have tried to show in detail how a natural order of education could achieve such individual and social harmony.'[171] Read's view that art was a primary biological process was well established in his art theory. His view of self-development and uniqueness, and the mediation he offered between individual freedom and a healthy society, were firmly supported by his anarchist theory. In *Education through Art* Read was effectively combining these emphases. His assertion that art was part of the physiological constitution of man became the basis of an anarchist political programme. The Jungian and Gestalt varieties of the notion that 'form' was inherent in biological processes pointed to the importance of spontaneous artistic expression. Subjective aesthetic imagery was essential to human thought and development. Read pointed to the wider argument that uniqueness and diversity were principles of human evolution and sources of growth and vitality in human society. Fundamentally underlying his view of the liberatory social potential for art education was his focus on freedom as a necessary biological process. As Read stated: 'Aesthetic activity is biological in its nature and functions; and human evolution in particular, and by exception, is differentiated from animal evolution by the possession of this faculty.'[172] This, alongside his firm reconciliation of individuality and sociability, was his most vital contribution to anarchist political philosophy.

Conclusion

Herbert Read was born at the tail end of the nineteenth century and he died in 1968. In his political and aesthetic writing he responded to the wars and revolutions that decisively shaped the character of the twentieth century. In the year of Read's death Stephen Spender wrote an obituary poem linking Read to the Paris uprisings later that same year, entitled

'Imagination Seizes Power'. Read's contribution to anarchist political ideas emerged in a variety of responses and reactions to political and cultural ideas and events that shaped British culture and social experience in the first half of the century. Anarchism was revived in his work as the only appropriate political idea with which he could formulate his unique response to the conditions of modernity in mid-twentieth-century Britain. Read's experiences in World War One in particular caused him to turn away from mainstream politics and seek sources of cultural renewal outside of conventional political thought. His perspectives on art, culture and politics drew on embedded radical traditions of thought in the British context. Read did not see anarchism as alien to British cultural and political traditions. He utilized anarchism in order to draw these national traditions into a vital political programme with which to challenge the pernicious erosion of liberties in an era of war, mass consumerism and state-growth. In so doing he attempted to revive the anarchist tradition by highlighting its pertinence to contemporary radical dilemmas regarding the exercise of individual conscience, war, nationhood, the growth of the state and the commitments of the socialist tradition. Read drew on the anarchist tradition as the source for a combination of individualistic, egalitarian and libertarian perspectives. He contrasted this with the developing collectivism and manipulation of masses, as he perceived it, by the state and mass consumer capitalism. He developed a view of aesthetics which expressed and supported his political concerns with freedom, spontaneity, and cohesive community. In this he saw himself defending essential but forgotten British traditions supporting creativity and individualism, and a native desire for liberty.

As well as reviving the classical anarchist tradition, Read developed some of its core components, creating a distinctive twentieth-century strand within anarchism. Read's shaping of anarchism particularly developed some of its non-violent components. In one sense this served to emphasize anarchism's challenge to modern states, which for Read were associated with war-like political behaviour. In another sense it illustrated Read's particular emphasis on the subjective aspects of social change. This view was associated with his view of art education as a revolutionary strategy. Read developed the more individualist focuses of anarchist thinkers like Godwin and Stirner on private judgement, subjective reason and individual autonomy into a concrete biological conception of self-creative freedom. Creativity became in Read's work an essential human characteristic and a stable and absolute basis for his defence of freedom. He presented a view of freedom as based on the importance of human uniqueness and independence. Read's utilization and development of anarchism provided him with the view of the mind and the person as inviolable, the psychological and social value of subjectivity, the concrete biological uniqueness of human selves, and the importance of their communication with other unique selves. Artistic form, perception and creation were the analogies to human awareness, freedom, and progress. To this he added a view of modern art that rooted the necessity for freedom in the biology of the human individual. Read drew fields of art theory and psychology into an understanding of human freedom as based on the self and his experiences of the world through his unique and creative physiology. This view of artistic cognition strengthened the individual against the mechanical forces of homogenization and atomization. Read drew psychoanalytical concepts into this emphasis on the importance of creative activity. The desire to create in the human individual thus became in Read's system a concrete psychological phenomenon. It also became a fundamental concomitant to human freedom and social progress.

Read attempted to give a scientific basis to the view that inspiration, individuality and the transgression of convention were the source of human regeneration. Abstract modernism in particular fulfilled the promise of art to create representations of universal qualities upon which a new society could be built. Under Read's formulation anarchism became a form of radicalized modernism infused with the renewing impulse for self-creation. The fate of art and the fate of the individual were closely allied, for art was the expression of the will to self-creation. The world of art was for Read the inner world of the creative self where experimental methods in art forms were used to investigate human experience and purposes. For Read, this represented the recovery of human experience in the face of a collectivizing, soulless modern age. His libertarian, romantic and utopian view of modernism in art presented it as a war on capitalism and an aesthetic transformation of the public sphere.

Read linked the artist's symbolic inner world to exterior realities. The relationship between the subjective creation of art and the representation of social experience rested for its political import on Kropotkin's philosophy of spontaneous order. Of the clusters of political ideas available, anarchism offered the potential intellectual basis for a uniquely sociable subjectivity. According to Read, the sensational awareness that generated important art linked the subjectivity of the creating artist to the universalization of his experience through a form that connected it with the experience of other individuals. The balance of subjectivity and objectivity reflected the synthesis of the individual and social aspects of anarchism which Read consistently emphasized. Read also developed a vision of individuality as developed 'personality', a concept that encompassed both individual and social facets. Read intended *Education through Art* to be an explicitly anarchist political programme and a response to World War Two. It was representative of his non-violent view of anarchist revolution and its particular appropriateness to politicizing culture and human sensibility. It was based on the regenerative potentials of art and anarchism. Read's anarchist programme of revolution through education rested on complete congruity between the biological need for uniqueness and freedom and the social need for integration and solidarity.

Notes

1. Huang Yongping 'A History of Chinese Painting' and 'A Concise History of Modern Painting' Washed in a Washing Machine for Two Minutes' (1987 / 1993).

2. Colin Ward, *Talking Anarchy* (Nottingham: Five Leaves Publications, 2003), p. 44.

3. George Woodcock, *Herbert Read: The Stream and the Source* (London: Faber and Faber, 1972), p. 256.

4. Herbert Read, *Anarchy and Order* (London: Souvenir Press (Educational and Academic) Ltd., 1974, first published 1954), p. 41.

5. Read, *Anarchy and Order*, p. 130.

6. Herbert Read, 'Neither Communism nor Liberalism' (1947), BBC talk, printed in *Freedom* (4 January), reprinted in Goodway (ed.), *Herbert Read. A One-Man Manifesto and Other Writings for Freedom Press* (London: Freedom Press, 1994), p. 115.

7. Herbert Read, *The Contrary Experience. Autobiographies* (New York: Horizon Press, 1973, first published 1963), p. 61.

8. Michael Sadler, Vice Chancellor at Leeds University purchased the first Kandinsky paintings to enter England, and Frank Rutter, an advocate of Wyndham Lewis was appointed Curator of Leeds Art Gallery in 1912 and battled for the acquisition of modern works.

9. Read, *The Contrary Experience*, p. 61.

10. Read, *The Contrary Experience*, p. 128.

11. Read, *The Contrary Experience*, p. 65.

12. Read, *The Contrary Experience*, p. 123.

13. Read, *The Contrary Experience*, pp. 123–4.

14. Read, *The Contrary Experience*, p. 203.

15. Woodcock, *Herbert Read: The Stream and the Source*, p. 241.

16. Rodney Barker, *Political Ideas in Modern Britain* (London: Methuen and Co Ltd, 1978), pp. 71–2.

17. Read, *The Contrary Experience*, p. 209.

18. Read, *The Contrary Experience*, p. 217.

19. Read, *The Contrary Experience*, pp. 217–18.

20. Read, *The Contrary Experience*, p. 65.

21. Herbert Read, *Poetry and Anarchism* (London: Faber and Faber, 1938), p. 15.

22. Read, *Poetry and Anarchism*, pp. 16–17, p. 84.

23. Read, *The Contrary Experience*, p. 68.

24. Read, *Poetry and Anarchism*, p. 43.

25. Read, *The Contrary Experience*, p. 87.

26. Read, *The Contrary Experience*, p. 61.

27. Read, *The Contrary Experience*, p. 177.

28. Herbert Read, 'Naked Warriors'(1919) in *Art and Letters*, p. 5, quoted in David Thistlewood 'Herbert Read's Paradigm', in Benedict Read and David Thistlewood (eds) *Herbert Read. A British Vision of World Art* (Leeds: Leeds City Art Galleries) p. 76.

29. Herbert Read, 'The Method of Revolution' (1938), in *Spain and the World* (16 September), reprinted in Goodway (ed.), *Herbert Read. A One-Man Manifesto and Other Writings for Freedom Press*, pp. 36–7.

30. Herbert Read, *Wordsworth* (London: Faber and Faber, 1930), pp. 50, 135.

31. Read, *Wordsworth*, p. 42.

32. Read *Wordsworth*, pp. 41–2.

33. Herbert Read, *The Philosophy of Modern Art* (London: Faber and Faber, 1964, first published New York: Horizon Press, 1953), p. 261.

34. Read, *Wordsworth*, pp. 36–7.

35. Kevin Davey, 'Herbert Read and Englishness', pp. 270–86, in David Goodway (ed.) *Herbert Read Reassessed* (Liverpool: Liverpool University Press, 1988), p. 271.

36. Read, *The Philosophy of Modern Art*, p. 268.

37. Read, *Poetry and Anarchism*, p. 40.

38. Herbert Read, 'Psycho-analysis and Literary Criticism' (1924), in Herbert Read, *Selected Writings. Poetry and Criticism* (London: Faber and Faber, 1963), p. 107.

39. Herbert Read, 'In Defence of Shelley' (1936), in Read, *Selected Writings. Poetry and Criticism*, p. 157.

40. Read, 'In Defence of Shelley', pp. 170, 174.

41. Read, 'In Defence of Shelley', p. 178.

42. Read, 'In Defence of Shelley', p. 157.

43. Read, 'Psycho-analysis and Literary Criticism', pp. 106–7.

44. Read, *Poetry and Anarchism*, p. 58.

45. Herbert Read, *Art and Alienation. The Role of the Artist in Society* (London: Thames and Hudson, 1967), pp. 154–5.

46. Herbert Read, 'Art and the Evolution of Man' (1951), Conway Memorial Lecture, Freedom Press, 10 April 1951, reprinted in Goodway (ed.), *Herbert Read. A One-Man Manifesto and Other Writings for Freedom Press*, p. 171.

47. Herbert Read, 'Culture and Religion' (1949), BBC talk, printed in *Freedom* (23 July and 6 August), reprinted in Goodway (ed.), *Herbert Read. A One-Man Manifesto and Other Writings for Freedom Press*, p. 143.

48. Herbert Read, 'Art and the Evolution of Man', p. 169.

49. Renato Poggioli, *The Theory of the Avant-Garde* (London and Cambridge, MA: Oxford University Press; Harvard University Press, 1968), pp. 48, 46, 48.

50. Herbert Read, *The Meaning of Art* (London: Faber and Faber, 1931), pp. 39, 48.

51. Read, *The Meaning of Art*, pp. 48–9.

52. Read, *The Meaning of Art*, p. 48.

53. Herbert Read, *Henry Moore. A Study of His Life and Work* (London: Thames and Hudson, 1965), p. 257.

54. Read, *Art and Alienation*, p. 152.

55. Read, *Henry Moore*, p. 255.

56. Read, *The Meaning of Art*, p. 257.

57. Herbert Read (ed.), *Surrealism* (London: Faber and Faber, 1936), pp. 19–91.

58. Herbert Read, 'Surrealism and the Romantic Principle' (1936), in Read, *Selected Writings. Poetry and Criticism*, p. 247.

59. King, *The Last Modern. A Life of Herbert Read* (New York: St. Martin's Press, 1990), p. 157.

60. Michel Remy 'Surrealism's vertiginous descent on Britain' (pp. 19–55) in Alexander Robertson, Michel Remy, Mel Gooding, Terry Friedman, *Angels of Anarchy and Machines for Making Clouds: Surrealism in Britain in the Thirties* (Leeds: Leeds City Art Galleries, 1986).

61. In 1950s and 1960s Blunt himself became a highly influential figure in British art criticism, receiving a knighthood in 1956 which was rescinded in 1979 after his exposure as the fourth member of the infamous Cambridge spy ring.

62. Michael Paraskos, 'The Curse of King Bomba: or how Marxism stole Modernism', pp. 44–57, in Michael Paraskos, (ed.), *Re-Reading Read: New Views on Herbert Read* (London: Freedom Press, 2007), p. 47.

63. Herbert Read, 'Picasso's Guernica' (1938), in *London Bulletin* (October), p. 6, cited by Michael Paraskos, 'Introduction' to Herbert Read (ed. Michael Paraskos), *To Hell with Culture* (London and New York: Routledge, 2002, first published 1963), p. xiv.

64. Anthony Blunt, *Spectator*, 25 March 1938, quoted in King, *The Last Modern*, p. 170.

65. Read, *To Hell with Culture*, p. xxvi.

66. Read, *To Hell with Culture*, p. xxvi.

67. Read, *To Hell with Culture*, p. xxvii.

68. Read, *Poetry and Anarchism*, pp. 45–6.

69. Read, *Poetry and Anarchism*, p. 25.

70. Read, *To Hell with Culture*, p. 9.

71. Alan Antliff, *Anarchy and Art: From the Paris Commune to the Fall of the Berlin Wall* (Vancouver: Arsenal Pulp Press, 2007), pp. 11–12.

72. Antliff, *Anarchy and Art*, pp. 12–13, see also Richard Day, *Gramsci is Dead: Anarchist Currents in the Newest Social Movements* (London: Pluto Press, 2005), pp. 15–16.

73. Proudhon, Du Principe de l'Art et sa Destination Social (Paris, 1865), p. 84, quoted in Antliff, *Anarchy and Art*, p. 26.

74. Emile Zola, 'Proudhon and Courbet', in My Hatreds, Paloma Paves-Yashinsky and Jack Yashinsky (Lewiston, NY: Edwin Mellen Press, 1992) p. 11, quoted in Antliff, *Anarchy and Art*, p. 27.

75. Emile Zola, 'Proudhon and Courbet', in My Hatreds, p. 17, quoted in Antliff, *Anarchy and Art*, p. 29.

76. Robyn Sue Roslak, Scientific aesthetics and the Aestheticized Earth: The Parallel Vision of the Neo-Impressionist Landscape and Anarcho-Communist Social Theory (PhD diss., University of California at Los Angeles, 1987), p. 204, quoted in Antliff, *Anarchy and Art*, p. 45.

77. Alan Antliff, 'Ecological Anarchy: Richard Mock', *Alternative Press review* 10 (2), 2006, p. 7, quoted in Antliff, *Anarchy and Art*, p. 191.

78. 'Richard Mock: Interview with Alan Antliff' (25 June 2001), quoted in Antliff, *Anarchy and Art*, p. 192.

79. Paraskos, 'Introduction', in Read, *To Hell with Culture*, p. xi.

80. Zaslove, Jerald, 'Herbert Read and Essential Modernism: Or the Loss of an Image of the World', pp. 287–308, in Goodway (ed.), *Herbert Read Reassessed*, p. 301.

81. Paraskos, 'The Curse of King Bomba', p. 53.

82. Read, *Anarchy and Order*, p. 154.

83. Paraskos 'The Curse of King Bomba', p. 56.

84. Paraskos 'The Curse of King Bomba', p. 57.

85. Paraskos 'The Curse of King Bomba', p. 57.

86. David Goodway, 'Introduction', in Goodway (ed.), *Herbert Read. A One-Man Manifesto and Other Writings for Freedom Press*, p. 2, and Herbert Read 'The Necessity of Anarchism' (1937), *Adelphi*, vols. 13 and 14.

87. Read, *Poetry and Anarchism*, p. 15.

88. Herbert Read, 'Anarchism: Past and Future' (1947), lecture to the London Anarchists, printed in *Freedom*, (17 May), reprinted in Goodway (ed.), *Herbert Read. A One-Man Manifesto and Other Writings for Freedom Press*, p. 117.

89. Read, *Poetry and Anarchism*, p. 17.

90. Read, 'Anarchism: Past and Future', pp. 117, 119.

91. Herbert Read, 'Neither Communism nor Liberalism' (1947), BBC talk, printed in *Freedom* (4 January), reprinted in Goodway (ed.), *Herbert Read. A One-Man Manifesto and Other Writings for Freedom Press*, p. 115.

92. Herbert Read, *Annals of Innocence and Experience* (London: Faber and Faber, 1946, first published 1940), p. 134.

93. Herbert Read, letter to George Woodcock, 3 August 1966, quoted by David Goodway in 'Introduction'. in Goodway (ed.), *Herbert Read. A One-Man Manifesto and Other Writings for Freedom Press*, p. 22.

94. George Orwell, 'Review of Herbert Read, *A Coat of Many Colours*', in George Orwell, *The Collected Essays, Journalism and Letters of George Orwell, Volume 4, In Front of Your Nose, 1945–1950*, edited by Sonia Orwell and Ian Angus (Harmondsworth: Penguin, 1970), p. 70.

95. *News Chronicle*, 24 April 1935, quoted in King, *The Last Modern*, p. 222.

96. Ruth Kinna has noted that in the post-war period British anarchists associated with the Freedom Press paid particular attention to resisting the censorship of the press, especially on the grounds of indecency, defending the publication of D. H. Lawrence's *Lady Chatterley's Lover*. Ruth Kinna, *Anarchism: A Beginners Guide* (Oxford: Oneworld, 2005), p. 37.

97. Herbert Read, 'Before the Trial' (1945), speech before the trial of the editors of *War Commentary*, printed in *War Commentary*, (21 April 1945), and in *Freedom: Is it a Crime?* (London: Freedom Defence Committee, 1945), reprinted in Goodway (ed.), *Herbert Read. A One-Man Manifesto and Other Writings for Freedom Press*, p. 97.

98. Read, 'Before the Trial', p. 96.

99. Herbert Read, *The English Vision. An Anthology* (London: Routledge, 1939), p. vi.

100. Read, 'Before the Trial', p. 98.

101. Read, 'Before the Trial', p. 99.

102. Herbert Read, 'After the Trial' (1945), speech after the trial of the editors of *War Commentary* printed in *Freedom: Is it a Crime?*, reprinted in Goodway (ed.), *Herbert Read. A One-Man Manifesto and Other Writings for Freedom Press*, p. 103.

103. Read, 'Before the Trial', p. 97.

104. Read, 'Before the Trial', p. 97.

105. Read, 'Before the Trial', p. 97.

106. Read, 'After the Trial', p. 103.

107. Herbert Read, 'A Statement' (1953), *Freedom,* (17 January), reprinted in Goodway (ed.), *Herbert Read. A One-Man Manifesto and Other Writings for Freedom Press*, p. 204.

108. Read, 'A Statement', p. 205.

109. Paraskos 'The Curse of King Bomba: or how Marxism stole Modernism', p. 57.

110. Ward, *Talking Anarchy*, p. 45.

111. Read, *Poetry and Anarchism*, p. 118.

112. Read, *Poetry and Anarchism*, pp. 120, 119.

113. Read, 'Anarchism: Past and Future', pp. 124–5

114. Read, 'Anarchism: Past and Future', p. 124.

115. Read, 'Anarchism: Past and Future', p. 124.

116. Goodway, 'Introduction', in Goodway (ed.), *Herbert Read. A One-Man Manifesto and Other Writings for Freedom Press'*, *Freedom Press*, p. 11.

117. Herbert Read 'The End of an Age', 'Freedom', 13 November 1948, reprinted in Goodway (ed.), *Herbert Read. A One-Man Manifesto and Other Writings for Freedom Press*, p. 133.

118. Read, 'Anarchism: Past and Future', p. 122.

119. Herbert Read, 'The Prerequisite of Peace' (1938), *Spain and the World*, (Supplement, May), reprinted in Goodway (ed.), *Herbert Read. A One-Man Manifesto and Other Writings for Freedom Press*, p. 27.

120. Read, 'The Prerequisite of Peace', p. 29.

121. Read, 'The Problem of War and Peace' (1947), BBC talk, printed in *Freedom*, (20 September), reprinted in Goodway (ed.), *Herbert Read. A One-Man Manifesto and Other Writings for Freedom Press*, pp. 128–9.

122. Edward Glover, *War, Sadism and Pacifism* (London: Allen and Unwin, 1946, first published, 1933), quoted by Herbert Read in 'The Problem of War and Peace', p. 126.

123. Herbert Read, 'A One-Man Manifesto' (1951), *Freedom*, (3 March), reprinted in Goodway (ed.), *Herbert Read. A One-Man Manifesto and Other Writings for Freedom Press*, p. 154.

124. C. G. Jung, *Essays on Contemporary Events* (London: Kegan Paul, 1947), quoted in Herbert Read 'Anarchism: Past and Future', p. 120.

125. Herbert Read, 'The Method of Revolution' (1938), *Spain and the World*, (16 September), reprinted in Goodway (ed.) *Herbert Read. A One-Man Manifesto and Other Writings for Freedom Press*, pp. 36–7.

126. Read, 'The Method of Revolution', p. 32.

127. Read, 'The Method of Revolution', pp. 31–2.

128. Read, 'The Method of Revolution', p. 32.

129. Read, 'The Method of Revolution', pp. 33–4.

130. Read, 'The Method of Revolution', p. 34.

131. Herbert Read, 'Foreword' in Albert Camus, *The Rebel* (London: Penguin, 1965), p. 7.

132. Read, 'Foreword' to Camus, *The Rebel*, p. 8.

133. Herbert Read, 'Americanism' (1950), *Freedom*, (1 April), reprinted in Goodway (ed.), *Herbert Read. A One-Man Manifesto and Other Writings for Freedom Press*, p. 146.

134. Read, 'Neither Communism nor Liberalism', pp. 114–15.

135. Read, 'Neither Communism nor Liberalism', p. 115.

136. Read, 'The Method of Revolution: An Answer' (1938), *Spain and the World*, (12 November), reprinted in Goodway (ed.), *Herbert Read. A One-Man Manifesto and Other Writings for Freedom Press*, pp. 38–9.

137. Herbert Read, 'The Centenary of *The Ego and His Own*' (1946), *Freedom*, (27 July), printed in *The Tenth Muse: Essays in Criticism* (London: Routledge & Kegan Paul, 1957), reprinted in Goodway (ed.) *Herbert Read. A One-Man Manifesto and Other Writings for Freedom Press*, p. 109.

138. Read, 'The Centenary of *The Ego and His Own*', p. 110.

139. Read, 'The Centenary of *The Ego and His Own*', p. 110.

140. Nikolai Berdyaev, *Slavery and Freedom* (London: Geoffrey Bles, 1943), p. 34, quoted by Read in 'The Centenary of *The Ego and His Own*', p. 109.

141. Goodway, 'Introduction' in Goodway (ed.), *Herbert Read. A One-Man Manifesto and Other Writings for Freedom Press*, p. 12.

142. Herbert Read, letter to John Berger, 10 December, 1961, quote by King in *Herbert Read: The Last Modern*, p. 301.

143. Read, *The Contrary Experience*, p. 197.

144. Ward, *Talking Anarchy*, p. 45.

145. Herbert Read, *Education through Art* (London: Faber and Faber, 1943), p. 297.

146. Herbert Read, 'Education through Art', in *Selected Writings of Herbert Read* (London: Faber and Faber, 1963), p. 365.

147. Woodcock, *Herbert Read: The Stream and the Source*, p. 269.

148. Read, *Education through Art*, p. 18.

149. Read, *Education through Art*, p. 30.

150. Herbert Read, *The Education of Free Men* (London: Freedom Press, 1944), p. 6.

151. Read, *Education through Art*, p. 16.

152. Read, *Education through Art*, p. 31.

153. Read, *The Education of Free Men*, p. 11.

154. Read, *Education through Art*, pp. 202–3.

155. Herbert Read, 'Education in Things', in *The Redemption of the Robot* (London: Faber and Faber, 1970), pp. 61, 64.

156. Read, *Education through Art*, p. 187.

157. Read, *Education through Art*, p. 189.

158. Read, *Education through Art*, p. 189.

159. Herbert Read, *The Origins of Form in Art* (London: Thames and Hudson, 1965), p. 158.

160. Read, *The Origins of Form in Art*, p. 154.

161. Read, *The Origins of Form in Art*, p. 154.

162. Read, *The Education of Free Men*, p. 15.

163. Read, *Education through Art*, p. 18.

164. Read, *Education through Art*, p. 6.

165. Read, *Education through Art*, p. 17.

166. Read, *Education through Art*, p. 6.

167. Read 'Education through Art', in *Selected Writings of Herbert Read*, p. 368.

168. Read, *Education through Art*, p. 18.

169. Read, 'Education in Things', pp. 79–80.

170. Read, *Education through Art*, p. 5.

171. Read, *Education through Art*, p. 298.

172. Read, *The Philosophy of Modern Art*, p. 13.

3

The Anarchist Political Philosophy of Dr Alex Comfort

Alexander Comfort by Howard Coster, half-plate film negative, 1943© National Portrait Gallery, London NPG x10884

Introduction

In the following passage, anarchist historian George Woodcock recalls observing the young Alex Comfort attending to the evidence presented at the trial of the Freedom Press anarchists in 1944:

> One day I spotted Alex Comfort in the audience. Alex had blown himself up in a chemical experiment as a small boy and one of his hands had no fingers left and only a thumb that seemed to have elongated with use. That day, listening intently to an obscure passage in the evidence, he began to pick his nose meditatively with that long talon of a thumb. I looked across the court and saw Mr. Justice Birkett in his scarlet robes, equally absorbed in the evidence; he glanced in Comfort's direction and then, equally abstractedly began to pick his nose with a long and bony forefinger.[1]

It is an evocative image of a unique and idiosyncratic individual, but one that emphasizes Comfort's passionate and cerebral engagement with the ideas and issues of the wartime dissident left in Britain. The wartime and post-war writing of Alex Comfort focused on two human experiences which he considered to be fundamentally significant to human society: death and sex. Total and brutal mechanical war was the result, he argued, of the failure to embrace both mortality and sexuality. Comfort was a pamphleteer for and lifelong member of the Peace Pledge Union, a sponsor of the Direct Action Committee, a 'name' in the Committee of 100, a member of the Campaign for Nuclear Disarmament, and a writer, scientist, psychologist and doctor. Publishing books and poems from 1938, he combined his literary endeavours with a prolific scientific and medical career. In 1944 he became resident medical officer at the Royal Waterloo hospital in London and in 1945 he was appointed as a lecturer in physiology at the London Hospital Medical College. Doctoral research in biochemistry and prize-winning research into gerontology ran alongside poetry, prose and criticism, and controversial writing on politics and political sociology. In 1973, he moved to the Center for the Study of Democratic Institutions at Santa Barbara in California and he lectured at Stanford between 1974 and 1983, returning to Britain in his retirement. Comfort tends to be presented exclusively in terms of his personal eccentricities, and too rarely in relation to the social and political concerns and controversies of the wartime and post-war eras. In a recent popular account, for example, Pagan Kennedy gives an account of this 'eccentric visionary' 'building a television from spare parts and glue soaked weetabix'.[2] Insufficient opportunity has been taken to re-examine Comfort's anarchist writings in the wartime and post-war contexts in Britain, and the wider significance of these writings both for the British anarchist tradition and our assessment of the Second World War in relation to British national identity. Engaging with his work in this way also provides insights into the themes and concerns behind the notoriety this figure was to achieve with the controversial publication of the *Joy of Sex* in the later twentieth century.

Anarchist assumptions about the personal and social impact of authoritarian power relationships guided Comfort's controversial interventions into British public debate and literary culture. In particular, he adhered closely to the spirit of this passage from the work of Herbert Read: 'When we can cast out the fear of death and renounce the desire to dominate the least of our fellow men, then we can live in peace and happiness.'[3] On this basis Comfort injected a controversial anti-militarism into British pacifist agendas, which blurred the distinction between the politics of warfare and conscription and the dynamics of interpersonal relations. He condemned the national militarization of civilian life and the rapid development of technologies for killing during and after the war as domestic British 'fascism'. In provocative wartime opinion pieces he called for the prosecution as war criminals of the allied leaders who had directed the saturation bombings of Germany, noting that 'It was a bitter humorist who called our bombers liberators.'[4] Recent re-interpretations of the early twentieth-century British governmental infrastructure as an archetypal 'warfare' state provides a key opportunity to re-examine submerged left-wing challenges to the war-making functions of the state in the mid-century period, in particular Comfort's apocalyptically anarchist campaign against the saturation bombing of German cities during World War Two.[5] This re-examination highlights the engagement of wartime anarchist thought both with contemporary anxieties concerning the technologies of warfare, and also established British intellectual traditions of apocalypse and revelation. The picture of anarchist thought in Britain in the mid-twentieth century that emerges is both more critically active and culturally embedded than is usually assumed to be the case. As well as engaging with native sources of anarchist thought, Comfort made a significant contribution to the revival and reshaping of a 'new' anarchism in the twentieth century. Motifs of his work, including the political significance of personally responsible action, the insights of psychoanalysis and sociology, and the marked evidence-based approach to the vindication of anarchist political theory, were key contributions to the revival of anarchism in the 1950s and 1960s in Britain. These aspects of Comfort's work, which drew heavily on the influence of Herbert Read, made a particularly strong impression on Colin Ward. Comfort's focus on responsibility effectively reconciled the prerequisites of individuality and those of cohesive society, concerns which are erroneously taken to pull the anarchist tradition in two different directions. For Comfort, the primary enemy of individual freedom was the abstraction and impersonalization of political relationships, not the call for social responsibility. This led him to emphasize the immediate and tangible character of responsible human behaviour in individual and social terms. Thus, the individual and his proximate social group were aligned in their struggle against the abstract intangible formulations of the general good imposed by the manipulative agencies of centralized political power. For Comfort, responsibility to society in fact strengthened the individual in his refusal to offer his allegiance to the state.

One aspect of Comfort's anarchist agenda in regard to British culture and politics in the later twentieth century is well known. His lasting fame lay in his early call for what came to be known as the 'new morality' or the 'permissive society', published in social science textbooks such as *Sexual Behaviour in Society*, a book which Nicolas Walter remarks 'must have exploded in the minds of many unsuspecting readers'.[6] Comfort's post-war concerns, including his interest in human sexual relationships, were centred on his notion of 'irresponsible society'. This was his expression of concern about the threats to liberty and sociability presented by centralized, bureaucratic government. The modern 'asocial' society, according to Comfort, exhibited the following characteristics: it had no coherent pattern of individual responsibility and important areas of human conduct were delegated to institutions and centralized authority. This resulted in a loss of individual control over personal relationships. The principal anarchist message of Comfort's work on psychology and sociology was that hierarchical power was not the mother of order in human society but the outcome of personality deviation, and destructive of human social cohesion. Comfort's argument was that morally functional group dynamics depended on individual relationships, direct contact, physical impressions and personal interaction. The politics of mass representation, collective abstraction and centralized power isolated individuals from these face-to-face dynamics. This provided dangerous opportunities for power-hungry personalities to seek and attain power. For Comfort, mass collectivized society inhibited responsibility and its courses of action and modes of thought were wildly at variance with individual standards of human responsibility. The solution was the anarchist re-individuation of the understanding of society and the reinvigoration of the notion of the self as inalienably responsible. Comfort's interest in the social significance of sexual behaviour developed through his use of psychological sources and grew from his dual emphasis on individual liberation and social cohesion. In his work, the solution to social breakdown lay in interpersonal relationships, including his emphasis on the importance of human sexual behaviour, for the health of society. Comfort emphasized the socially cohesive significance of sexual behaviour as a 'chief biological force in the evolution of humanness'.[7] His writing on human sexual behaviour was a response to what Comfort referred to as the modern 'asocial' crisis, by which he meant the simultaneous decline of individual self-awareness and the dissipation of human sociality. 'Asocial' societies are created by the institutions of war, and they make future wars more possible.

The following discussion will focus on the strong connection between Comfort's anarchism and embedded British cultural and political themes. It will be shown that in this respect Comfort's work, like that of Herbert Read, requires us to revise conventional interpretations of anarchism, which assume that it is alien to British political thought and removed from British social experience. Comfort's writing demonstrated the significance of the British social and intellectual context for twentieth-century anarchism. Most notably, his exposure to anarchist themes was filtered through two characteristically British libertarian traditions. First, as we have seen, the influential art critic, and fellow British anarchist, Herbert Read had reinterpreted the romantic tradition as a vital and apposite source of cultural renewal and his ideas were taken up by a generation of war artists, including Comfort, concerned with the mechanization and anonymity of war killing. Secondly, Comfort was a vital and dynamic intellectual figure in the mid-century British pacifist movement. This tradition was perhaps the most fertile twentieth-century ground for British libertarian currents, not least because of its inherent affinity with the ideal of muscular autonomy represented by the figure of the stoic and embattled individual conscientious objector. In drawing on these native libertarian roots and in applying them in his response to the war and then to nuclear weapons, Comfort revealed an important set of continuities in British radical currents over the twentieth century and demonstrated the extent to which the concerns of the anarchist tradition were alive in the political controversies of the era.

Anarchism and the Second World War in National Memory

The allied area bombing campaigns of the 1940s and the technology associated with their execution were concerns for many of Comfort's contemporaries. Adam Piette notes that 'One of the toughest, dirtiest lessons that war taught the blitzed . . . was that the British and American bombers were doing it too, but with infinitely greater ferocity.'[8] Piette is among a number of authors writing on the period that have acknowledged the extent of intellectual and public concern about the allied area bombing campaigns. A. C. Grayling also notes the 'sizable dissenting minority' on the issue of the bombing campaigns and the 'repeated questioning' faced by the wartime coalition government on the issue.[9] George Bell, Bishop of Chichester wrote to *The Times* in April 1941, asking 'if Europe is civilized at all, what can excuse the bombing of towns by night and terrorizing of non-combatants?'[10] In 1941 British Quaker pacifist Corder Catchpol established the Committee for the Abolition of Night Bombing, which organized a petition against the raids, gathering 15,000 names including bishops, MPs, pacifists and non-pacifists.[11] In her book *Seeds of Chaos* written in support of these efforts and detailing the nature and effects of the bombing campaigns, Vera Brittain demonstrated her concerns about moral standards in the conduct of the war. She wrote: 'From the story of our bombing during the past eighteen months only a mental or moral lunatic could fail to draw the conclusion that modern war and modern civilization are utterly incompatible, and that one or the other must go.'[12] These protests were closely related to concerns among figures of the period about the mechanization and indirectness of the technology of warfare and the effect of this on the moral integrity of the individual combatants. R. N. Currey, writing in retrospect about the context and concerns which characterized the war poetry of the 1940s, identified 'a deeper appreciation of the moral implications of killing at a distance.'[13] Currey summarized the distinctiveness of World War Two poetry in terms of its underlying awareness of the 'ease' with which the fighting individual can apprehend the machine but not 'its murderous intention', and he identified it as 'one of the horrors of modern war.'[14] Writing on the poetry and literature of the 1940s consistently reiterates the significance of the accelerating industrialization of killing at a distance and the consequent 'deadening assault upon man's sensitivities.'[15] It was the unattached efficiency of the technological warrior, and the lack of emotion or recoil associated with acts of killing, that concerned Comfort and his contemporaries. As Currey argued, 'This is a civilization in which a man, too squeamish to empty a slop pail or skin a rabbit, can press a button that exposes the entrails of cities.'[16]

A neo-romantic movement in literature in Britain, a self-conscious challenge to the poetry of the Auden generation, placed contemporary concerns about the loss of personal engagement and individuality at the centre of its approach in the 1940s. This was part of a 'wave of romanticism' that surged through English culture during the war years and 'affected all the arts'.[17] The 'best-organised group' within this movement in the 1940s was the Apocalyptic Poets.[18] It was the Apocalyptic circle of poets who embraced their context most fully and they self-consciously placed a concern with the inner life of the individual at the heart of their approach to writing poetry in that period. The first edited volume, *The New Apocalypse*, which collected their work together, was published in 1939, edited by J. F. Hendry and Henry Treece. These authors placed a concern with individual awareness and self-creation at the root of their use of apocalyptic imagery and metaphor. At the heart of the Apocalyptic philosophy was a concern with subjectivity and the internal human condition, specifically as affected by the dislocating and traumatic experiences of war. Theirs was a highly subjective response to the social dislocation of war and the bleak circumstances of wartime Britain. The Apocalyptics drew on surrealist techniques, gothic themes and psychoanalytical ideas in their attempts to create poetry that was less constrained by the systems of what they perceived to be a mechanistic universe. They shared their use of apocalyptic imagery and metaphor with a broad sweep of the intellectual culture of the period. Piette locates Apocalyptic poetry, with its 'aesthetic of destruction', within a range of literary material of the time which employed apocalyptic themes, images and symbols.[19] In London in particular, the bombing raids fuelled the atmosphere of cataclysm and transition. For the Apocalyptics, the horror of the war was 'one of the great *external* stimuli of our time'.[20] By all accounts the results were not very successful as poetry, but, nurtured within their midst, burgeoning writer Comfort went on to mould this apocalyptic turn into an anarchist critique of allied policy in the 1940s, and anti-nuclear campaigns in the 1950s. In his anarchist writing, Comfort was speaking directly to this shared cultural anxiety around what was perceived as a failure of individual ethical engagement. This is clearly reflected in a line from one of his poems, 'Bait' written in 1940: 'Did I do that? I do not understand'. In 'Recruits' written about the same time, Comfort reflects gloomily on the conscripts, seeing the 'quiet skull' in the yet living faces. Comfort again reflects these fears about the pernicious impersonalization of wartime society in his 1944 novel *The Power House*, in which he creates a subjective narrative account of 'the droves of dutiful citizens who are making the world a desert'. He constructs the following account of the failure of individual ethical engagement, perceived in the course of daily social perceptions:

> There is a fellow that you know, with whom you've drunk or argued, whom you think you understand as you do your hat – possessing certain fairly definite qualities that go to make up sanity: humane (he has a normal detestation of violence for its own sake), upright (with exceptions), stupid, because stupidity is a virtue: you meet him one day, unchanged save that now he has abrogated a small part of himself, joined a body of others like himself, agreed to take orders from them, and *without changing any of those attributes* which you recognise comes to you and drinks with you again and tells you what he's been doing – bombing a city, murdering Jews, concocting the most malicious lies about other people like himself, blockading a continent, raising hell and high water in a fashion that the foul Fiend himself couldn't equal, and still he is humane, upright, and stupid.[21]

Comfort's engagement with contemporary anxieties surrounding the mechanization and distance of wartime roles in Britain has wider and more profound ongoing political and cultural implications. Piette argues that British wartime culture limited the public expression of these anxieties and this 'hollowed and emptied out the private mind' and 'anaesthetized feelings'. He argues that the private experiences of manipulation, drudgery, social conflict and trauma were submerged in public transcripts about the stoicism and heroism of British social life, to the detriment of cultural confidence and expression.[22] This point is closely related to recent political and economic re-examinations of the British wartime state, which highlight the militarization of civilian society and culture in the period. Recent revisions of established historiographies of the twentieth-century British State focus on its readiness for international war, including the development, acceleration and entrenchment of military industries, technologies and infrastructure, as a defining characteristic. David Edgerton highlights the 'military-industrial-scientific' complex underpinning the development of the British state in the twentieth century and depicts it as the 'pioneer' of modern, 'technologically focused' warfare and arms exporting, with a state machine operated by militarily oriented bureaucrats and technicians.[23]

Accounts such as this contribute to a better understanding of the impact of the military ordering of British life on the society, culture and dissident politics of the era. The 'hopeless role-playing forced upon minds during the war', argues Piette, alongside the 'fabricated communal feelings', 'military regimentation' and above all the 'gigantic energies and complexities of the war-machine' have had longer-term negative implications for British culture.[24] This point gives weight and context to key concerns iterated by anarchists about the impact of highly centralized and bureaucratized systems of organization on individual development and social relationships, especially those expressed by Comfort in relation to World War Two and its impact on post-war society in Britain.

Exploring Comfort's anarchist writing and campaigning of the period also helps us to re-examine what Angus Calder has referred to as the 'myths' about the heroism and virtue of British policy during the Second World War, public transcripts which cannot accommodate the British bombing strategy of deliberately targeting civilians, and do not acknowledge the lack of popular consensus over this policy.[25] In reflecting on the post-war failures of British policy to assist in the prosecution of war criminals, David Cesarani has demonstrated the ongoing negative impact of these myths and highlighted the need for a popular reinterpretation of the era. National myths about the spotless honour and justice of the allied military operations hamper national debate and informed popular engagement in public matters related to the war. Cesarani points to the furore in March 1994 over the question of German military participation in VE-day celebrations, which led to Britain's highest circulating tabloid newspaper being able to boast that 'The Sun Bans the Hun'. He also highlights the British public indignation and incomprehension in 1993 surrounding German protests about the erection of a statue in London honouring Sir Arthur Harris, the figure most closely associated with the policy of carpet bombing in German civilian areas. Cesarani shows that national myths about the war not only limit public debate around incidents like these within a constricting cultural milieu of unquestioning celebration of British actions, but have also hampered the identification, investigation and prosecution of Nazi collaborators in Britain. To acknowledge the presence of unpunished Nazi war criminals in Britain after 1945 would have involved a dramatic challenge to national memories of 'the Good War' and exposed the ambiguities of British war aims.[26] This point, that national dishonesty about the morally questionable nature of British war actions has limited the appropriate treatment of Nazi war criminals in Britain, was made by Cesarani at the turn of the twenty-first century.

Alex Comfort made these connections in 1944, linking the dishonesty over British war policies to wider deficiencies in the handling of war criminals, most directly in a letter published in October of that year in *Tribune* entitled 'War Criminals':

> I doubt if there is any prospect which intelligent people in all coun-
> tries will regard with greater enthusiasm than that of the punishment
> of war criminals. If it takes place we shall be seeing it for the first time
> in human history. I think that the readers of *Tribune* and other men
> of good will should get busy at once in the compilation of lists . . .
> and I feel that there is considerable urgency in undertaking the work
> before all the possible candidates for trial have been co-opted on to
> the Bench of Judges.[27]

As Cesarani argues, echoing points made by Piette, 'British national memory needs to be recalibrated to reflect our greater knowledge about the history of the war and its aftermath.'[28] Examining the culturally and politically embedded challenges of Comfort's work contributes to the important task of re-examining the British popular interpretation of the era by focusing on challenges and resistance to war policies that were raised *at the time*. Crucially, Comfort's response to the British experience of war highlights alternative idioms of British national identity at work in the period.

Romanticism, Apocalypse and Direct Action

One reviewer wrote of Comfort's novel *The Powerhouse* in 1944, 'The horror seems to have given him a touch of second sight' yet 'the picture is grim, mad, desolate and evil'.[29] Comfort's anarchist input into public debates on war policy addressed the wider concerns among writers of the period about area bombing and the mechanized nature of total war, and drew on the apocalyptic tone of contemporary literature. This is immediately evidenced by his membership of the Apocalyptic group of wartime poets, but in fact his model of suffering and renewal in the face of chaos and death demonstrates a more profound engagement with the apocalyptic tradition in British literature than was the case with this group of neo-romantic poets. The Apocalyptic group took their name from D. H Lawrence's *Apocalypse* in which he cast the first horseman of the apocalypse as a symbol for man's inner self.[30] In this posthumously published title, Lawrence engaged with the recurrent romantic attraction to the apocalyptic passages of the Bible in order to express his distaste for what he saw as the debased era in which he lived. Identifying themselves with Lawrence's symbol, the Apocalyptic Poets highlighted the importance both of heightened subjectivity and the related romantic notion of suffering and destruction in the struggle for individuality. By using Lawrence as their reference for their interpretation of apocalypse, the Apocalyptic group was signalling its uptake of a subjectivist and critical interpretation of the apocalyptic strain in the English romantic tradition. Lawrence writes of the 'living death' and the 'dead and dreary' state of modern man, who is 'dead-alive', stripped of 'emotional and imaginative reaction', 'feeling nothing' except 'boredom and deadness'.[31] According to Lawrence, humanity had been reduced to 'half-dead little modern worms stuffing our damp carcasses with thought-forms that have no sensual reality'.[32] He saw the destruction and disaster of the First World War, and the subsequent era of decadence, as a signal to a fresh start or a moment of transition. His prose anticipates the fears of detachment and disinterestedness which emerged in the poetry and writing of World War Two.

Despite the conservative impulse of Lawrence's interpretation of apocalypse, the influence of anarchist ideas on the Apocalyptic group was also evident from the outset. In particular, the anarchist cultural commentator Herbert Read was *the* major intellectual influence on the poetry and prose of these writers. Romanticism was for Read, and even more so for Comfort, who followed Read as the main theoretician of the neo-romantic sensibility, ideally suited to the dilemmas of British wartime culture. The Apocalyptic Poets both reflected his aesthetic philosophy and also consciously followed his assertion of the libertarian political implications of romanticism. The following statement by Read reflects what was most influential about his work for the emerging neo-romantic sensibility: 'Art, we conclude, is more than a description or "reportage"; it is a dialectical activity, an act of renewal. It renews vision, it renews language; but more essentially, it renews life itself by enlarging the sensibility, by making man more conscious of the terror and beauty, the *wonder* of the possible forms of being'.[33] Read acted as spokesman of the Apocalyptics in articles such as 'The New Romantic School' in *The Listener* in 1942 where he championed the rise of a modern sweeping romanticism.[34] From 1942 to 1947 Read developed a series of publications to include the poets Comfort, J. F. Hendry, Julian Symons, George Woodcock, and others, publishing the anthologies *The White Horseman* in 1941 and *Eight Oxford Poets* in 1942.

In deploying the romantic imagery of apocalypse in his critique of the allied saturation bombing policies of the Second World War, Comfort was drawing on anarchist concerns about agency and responsibility. A wider and more radical tradition of apocalypse in English writing also conditioned Comfort's use of themes and ideas introduced by the Apocalyptic group. Vera Brittain, for example, chose her title for the important anti-area bombing text *Seeds of Chaos* from Alexander Pope's *Dunciad* Book IV: 'Then rose the seed of Chaos, and of Night / To blot out order and extinguish light', and her epigraph from the Book of Jeremiah 6.15: 'Were they ashamed when they had committed abomination?'[35] Paley notes in relation to the role of apocalypse in the work of Coleridge, Blake and Wordsworth, and the 'apocapolitical' work of Shelley in particular, 'the tendency of such discourse . . . to urge radical action'.[36] Christopher Rowland similarly observes that in the English tradition 'apocalyptic has expressed a critical response to the injustices of the world, frequently on behalf of the powerless, and opened eyes closed to realities which have become accepted as the norm'.[37] Following this strain of apocalyptic radicalism, Comfort's romantic apocalypticism was based on the following agency-focused understanding of the tradition: 'The romantic believes that the particular qualities which make up humanness – mind, purpose, consciousness, will, personality –. . . exist only so long as Man himself exists and fights for them . . . an insecurity which begins at the personal level of mortality'.[38] Comfort used anarchist and apocalyptic themes to attack the abstract formulations of the greater good and the 'Just War' which underpinned the defence of allied war bombing policies. His apocalyptic prose likened the policies of the war to 'walking on corpses', and he described the principle effects of the war as 'repression, destruction and famine'.[39] Amid the triumphant atmosphere surrounding the closing months of the war, Comfort remarked bitterly that 'Europe stinks of blood and groans with separation'.[40] His identification of 1940s Britain as apocalyptic drew anarchist-utopian themes into his critique of wartime and post-war policy, moulding a darkly optimistic agenda for action premised on an 'awareness of death'. It was the catalyst for his highly politicized advocacy of a muscular autonomy which he referred to as 'responsibility'. He used it in response to shared popular and intellectual concerns about the mechanization of total war and the effect as he saw it on the moral and political culture of Britain.

In a poem published in *Tribune* in June 1943, under the pen name Obadiah Hornbrooke, Comfort wrote of 'that smell so strong of murder', of 'German corpses laid in endless rows', calling for a 'purge' or a 'vast satanic comet' to 'blast this wretched tinder, branch and root'. He writes of the 'howl' that 'dying systems utter, mad with fear, In darkness, with a stinking of the bowls.'[41] Examining Comfort's prose of the 1940s, it is well to bear in mind Rowland's observation that 'To read apocalypses is to be overwhelmed – and perhaps alienated – by what seems unsavory and at times profoundly unhealthy.'[42] Indeed, Stephen Spender noted in his 1943 review of Comfort's novel *Cities of the Plain*, in *New Statesman*, 2 October 1943: 'Alex Comfort's horrified obsession with uncomfortable events . . . produces the same kind of effect as photographs of atrocities.' George Orwell was moved to respond critically to the self-important 'poet tutting from the sandbagged portal' in the issue of *Tribune* that followed the publication of the 'Hornbrooke' poem.[43] Comfort's use of dark visceral images reflects his use of the apocalyptic concept of renewal or revelation as the product of destruction, decline and chaos, and the romantic concept of suffering as a source of revelatory insight and heightened perception. During the crisis of wartime, in the atmosphere of destruction and chaos, 'When', in Comfort's terms, 'human beings eat each other', he warned that a man must be 'on his guard' to be sure 'that the bread he eats wasn't kneaded inside someone's skull and greased with his brains'.[44] The importance of mortality and self-awareness in Comfort's intellectual make-up significantly shaped his understanding of the moral limitations of hierarchical collective entities. As he wrote in April 1943, '[W]e seem to be in the hands of a Government which wishes to cover itself in detail with every infamy it has denounced in the enemy. The containment of what they have done will extend to all of us, individually, and no repudiation or expostulation will serve to restore us.'[45]

Comfort's wartime writing engages with core characteristics of the apocalyptic tradition as it has been identified by writers on the subject. Apocalyptic writing in general concerns the meaning of crisis; specifically it identifies crisis as a harbinger of imminent change. It is possible to discern three main defining elements of an apocalyptic model of writing, or a theory of apocalypse, according to the consistent and overlapping themes across the essays in Malcolm Bull's edited collection *Apocalypse Theory and the Ends of the World*. These are, first, apocalyptic theory claims to reveal an underlying reality; secondly, it contains a dynamic of transition and anticipation; and thirdly it delivers judgement on contemporary conditions. The key point emphasized by the authors collected in Bull's volume and elsewhere is the integral relationship between the experience of crisis and ending, and the awareness of renewal. Authors on the subject, such as Burdon, agree that the key feature of apocalypse as it has been used in various contexts is that it is succeeded by millennium, or that it 'opens up other worlds' or 'new perspectives on the familiar world'.[46] Similarly,

Rowland argues that the purpose of Revelation itself was 'to reveal some-thing hidden' which would 'enable the readers to view their present situation from a completely different perspective'.[47] Thus, the apocalyptic myth balances terror and hope, or endings and beginnings, in a dynamic tension. A significant characteristic of this genre of writing that focuses on crisis and renewal is an unsurprising emphasis on the anticipated imminence of the transition precipitated by the crisis, and a slightly more surpris-ing focus on human action or 'goal-directed behaviour' as necessary to precipitate the imminent change.[48] The dynamic of transition and antici-pation highlights agency and immediacy rather than suspension or delay. As Rowland notes of apocalyptic theory, 'The present has become a time of fulfillment'.[49] McGinn also argues that 'This form of imminence tends to condense past actions and future hopes into attitudes and decisions to be realized in the present moment'.[50] In line with this model, Comfort's view of the 1940s highlighted the pervasive proximity of threat and death and emphasized the potential for the regeneration of a direct and personal sense of responsibility and individual engagement. In short, the crisis of war would renew social relationships.

In Comfort's work the apocalyptic aspect of the romantic tradition, specifically the emphasis on an intensified and transforming awareness achieved by means of fear and suffering in cataclysmic circumstances, became specifically focused on the significance for individual human development of an awareness of human mortality. Comfort's writing on romanticism focused on the significance for individual human devel-opment of an individual awareness of death. He argued that the sheer mechanized scale of human death in the Second World War and the sub-jection of the individual to military conscription brought this awareness home to the individual in the modern age. According to Comfort's inter-pretation, romanticism was a philosophy that emerged from a tragic and heroic awareness of death. It was an ideology of intellectual and emotional honesty and responsibility with humanistic and individualistic impli-cations. Like Camus's argument in *The Rebel*, Comfort argued that men attempt to escape from the reality of solitary mortality by submerging and enslaving themselves in the immortality of the human species. According to Comfort, man found his own death difficult to contemplate because of his unique awareness of himself. Awareness of death and self-awareness were the roots of the capacity for personal responsibility 'which differenti-ates human relationships from superficially similar animal societies'.[51] The attempt to deny death entailed the denial of individual personality and responsibility, for to admit individuality meant admitting the truth that individuals have a finite existence. The man who sought to identify himself with supra-individual entities, abstractions, and timeless causes lacked the courage to recognize his mortality, 'He will pay any price to rid himself of the selfhood which, subconsciously, he knows must die.'[52]

According to Comfort, the tendency to avoid an awareness of death by identifying with some great timeless cause and the notion of society as a single immortal entity were both attempts to deny the fact of mortality rather than attack it. The allegiance called on by collective identities was the refuge from the self for those without the courage to recognize their own individual mortality and as such it entailed the corrosive abrogation of moral responsibility.[53] This was the cause of 'the obedience of so many populations to rogues and brutes who pull the strings and make Leviathan walk.'[54] The lack of individuality and the flight from personal responsibility was the source of the brutality and barbarism of the modern warring age. This was because 'The courses of action which the group mode of thought imposes upon the individual members are so grotesque and so wildly at variance with reason and with normal constructive activity that by reference to individual standards of human responsibility they are clinically insane.'[55] A society, such as the one he observed in Britain, in which individuals have 'lost their nerve' and fail to exercise individual judgement 'is a society of onlookers, congested but lonely, technically advanced but utterly insecure, subject to a complicated mechanism of order but individually irresponsible.'[56] In such a homogenized, atomized society the individual 'can alternately serve as firing squad and target, bomber and bombed, with little change in his personal attitude, because barbarism has already pulled up the social roots of his humanity.'[57] Romanticism, like anarchism, was 'against power' and postulated the countering force of 'alliance of all human beings against the hostility of the universe'. Most importantly, like anarchism, it resisted 'the attempt to push off the burden of personal responsibility on to other shoulders'.[58] While Comfort's emphasis on selfhood was consistent with his relationship with the Apocalyptic group, his political engagement, his focus on action and his view of science as a romantic endeavour were not in line with their rejection of all objectivity. As he stated: 'The ethic of romanticism is an ethic derived entirely from man, and for the artist and the scientist, concerned with humanity and nothing else, it is true and coherent.'[59] Under Comfort's romantic approach art and science were allies because they were both on the side of man against death and against power. Comfort's outlook also had a more explicitly political orientation; he focused throughout his work on the unending conflict between the

subjectivity of the responsible individual and the mechanized collectivity of irresponsible society. Comfort's neo-romanticism was formulated
in support of a politically activist anarchist agenda. He deployed the
apocalyptic turn in British literature of the period to face the truths about
the saturation bombing. Most notably, early in 1944, Comfort drafted a
declaration against the allied bombings and organized the signing of the
petition by writers, artists and musicians. A key element of Comfort's
relationship to the anarchist tradition was his focus on immediate human
goals over distant, abstracted ones. This was reflected in the ethic of direct
action, the importance of congruity between means and ends, and the
rejection of 'lesser evils' in the struggle for human progress. Twentieth-
century anarchism developed a collection of related concerns focused on
the importance of the present. In Comfort's case this included a specific
and characteristic understanding of the nature and boundaries of the
human sense of responsibility, which was both limited to immediate and
direct interpersonal contact and subverted by the indirectness of abstract
political goals and representative political practices.

'Responsible' Anarchism: Against Power and Collectivity

Comfort's urgent libertarian theorizing was triggered by his experiences
of war. He perceived an accelerating collectivizing and homogenizing
dynamic in wartime and post-war Britain. In Comfort's case, as a non-
combatant unlike his immediate anarchist predecessor Herbert Read, it
was the irresponsibility of individuals and intellectuals and the barbarity
of war policy that drew him into controversial public debate as a vocal
and eloquent anarcho-pacifist, a position which equated violence and
war with hierarchical power and centralization. During the war, Comfort
was blacklisted by the BBC for his vociferous heading of protests against
indiscriminate allied bombing. In a controversial wartime opinion piece
he called for the prosecution as war criminals of the allied leaders who
had directed the saturation bombings of Germany. The following statement is indicative both of his literary style and his understanding of the
relationship between anti-war and anti-authoritarian sentiments: 'Our own
government, if it wants to make butchers or bomber pilots of our children,
is as much our enemy as the Germans ever were.'[60] Faced with the unap-
pealing choice between 'a butcher's life and a sheep's death', argued Comfort,
we must instead recreate ourselves as 'human beings and masterless men'.[61]
Anarchism was the ideology of masterless, responsible men which underpinned Comfort's career of libertarian critique. Driven by his revulsion

for the brutality and corrosion of liberty associated with the prosecution of the Second World War, Comfort's anarchism was also his response to 'collapsing culture', the decline of civilization which for him was 'very obvious in England and America' at the close of the war.[62] Amid the triumphant atmosphere surrounding the closing months of the war, Comfort remarked bitterly that 'Europe stinks of blood and groans with separation.'[63] In 1946 he noted as evidence of the decay of civilization in the allied countries the fact that:

> Few people can remember what it was like to be sane, to live in a world where one could not earn a decoration for butchering a few thousand civilians, where a good many national heroes would have qualified for the gallows and the mental hospital, and where a single news bulletin of the present time would not have produced nation-wide nausea and vomiting.[64]

Those with any vestiges of responsible human feeling, he remarked, must, like himself, 'dread the restitution of our sense of shame'.[65] Comfort saw the war as a watershed, a catastrophe that called for an urgent reassessment of Western civilization by a generation willing to call it to account. 'It was upon our generation that the decision was forced', he stated, and this was due to the fact that they came to maturity under the certainty that they 'would be killed in action on behalf of an unreality against insanity'.[66] For Comfort, the familiar progressive radical frameworks were inadequate for the reassessment of values which the mid-century era called on committed radical intellectuals to make:

> As we look at Europe today, we cannot see it as writers of the 'thirties saw it. We do not see a clear-cut issue between progress and reaction. We see defrauded and deluded peoples engaged in utterly purposeless destruction, because the objects for which they fight are unreal hopes dangled in front of their noses by the respective governments of their countries.[67]

Anarchism equipped Comfort with a political focus on individuality, freedom and subjectivity, which he ranged against the modern British state in the era of total war. He utilized the anarchist tradition primarily in the formulation of the core component of his critique, the interpretation of individual freedom as the capacity to exercise personal responsibility. The ideas which Comfort developed and his political commitments throughout his career demonstrated the role which anarchism played in key twentieth-century debates in Britain. In a general sense, these included war, collectivism and the state. Comfort's anarchism also played a role in debates surrounding nuclear weapons and most notoriously (but equal in controversy to the majority of Comfort's contributions to public debate) sexual behaviour. Throughout his work, 'Anarchism is that political philosophy which advocates the maximisation of individual responsibility and the reduction of concentrated power.'[68] His individualist focus was the source of a social awareness, advocating individual resistance alongside mutual aid practices. His anarchism drew on models of political behaviour far removed from traditional images of political participation but directly inspired by modes of individual activity and organization generated by the war. These were 'the deserter' and 'the Maquis':

> The positive expression of such ideas is not in the ballot box but in the individual restoration of responsible citizenship, the practice of recalcitrant mutual aid, not in political organisation but in the fostering of individual disobedience, individual thought, small responsible mutual-aid bodies which can survive the collapse and concentrate their efforts upon the practice of civilisation. It is the philosophy of direct action, of the deserter and the Maquis, the two most significant and human figures of every barbarian age.[69]

Comfort came to anarchism as a political ideology through his pacifism. In fact, it would be most accurate to describe his anarchism as anarcho-pacifist; such were the concrete connections between the two traditions in his thought. This connection emerged in the anarchism of Herbert Read and marked the whole later twentieth-century tradition of anarchism. It was in Comfort's philosophy, however, that the nature of the connection between anti-militarism, individualism and conscience was most developed, drawing anarchist and pacifist traditions indissolubly together. This link was an important aspect of anarchism's later twentieth-century significance and influence. The key point for Comfort was that the violence and killing of war was the result of the characteristics of states as centralized sources of power. The dangers of fascist-type behaviour like war and mass killing, according to Comfort, underlay all representative government. This is the core of his anarchist anti-militarism. Fascism, at home and abroad, 'teaches that the individual is unreal, and therefore death, the termination of the individual, is unreal also'.[70] To counter this ideology of power and statehood, the anarchist worked to reassert the reality and moral significance of the individual as the primary unit of human society. The urgency with which Comfort pressed his readers to reassess conventional views of their political and social relationships was a marked feature of his project, for, he argued, 'unless we achieve some very rapid changes in the pattern of political society, more of you may die by war than by physical disease.'[71] In short, war was the clearest symptom of a political and social culture debased by centralization and power. Anarchism, as the philosophy of the socially responsible individual, was the apposite response. Both communism and liberal democracy, making 'closely similar assumptions about human behaviour', failed to provide the necessary focus on individual social responsibility because they 'assume that institutions are the main means of altering conduct, and both regard power as a necessary element in maintaining society'.[72]

Western civilization, according to Comfort, was in collapse due to the failure of the individual to assert his resistance to irresponsibility. The emerging situation as he described it was one of barbarism and irresponsibility caused by obedience. Barbarism, with all its implications of roughness, cruelty and coarseness, was in Comfort's writing the polar opposite of civilization, defined as a group ethic in which the individual retained his individuality and sense of responsibility. This combination of individuality and personal responsibility was combined with the notion that 'we have boundless responsibility to every person we meet' and was met for Comfort in the practise of mutual aid.[73] Underlying Comfort's resistance to war was his suspicion of the social habit of obedience: 'Atrocities are not only the work of sadists – your friends and relatives who butchered the whole of Hamburg were not sadists – they are the result of obedience, an obedience which forgets its humanity.'[74]

Comfort reconciled the importance of individually responsible disobedience with the anarchist belief in natural order through his insistence on the humanist potential of the individual moral choice and the potential for agency at that level to discern the morally significant forms of disobedience: 'We do not refuse to drive on the left hand side of the road, or to subscribe to national health insurance. The sphere of our disobedience is limited to the sphere in which society exceeds its powers and its usefulness.'[75] Law and coercion were only necessary to regulate behaviour in centrally organized societies. This was because the anonymity of centralization isolated the individual from primary group controls. In small groups social dynamics were direct and immediate, the individual moral sense could function unhindered and participate in the shaping of the mores that regulated group activity. It is through this kind of understanding that

Comfort referred to centralized society as 'asocial'. Centralization was for Comfort a cause of psychological disorder and violence because it served to disable the human moral and social senses. In contrast to the Hobbesian notion of a natural state of brutal war against all, Comfort advocated the sociological conclusion that man was a social animal, regulated by custom and the social group with an innate predisposition towards sociability. For Comfort, under a centralized political conception of society, 'Leviathan becomes Frankenstein'.[76] This presentation of two contrasting images of the socially made man, the tyrannical personification of the collectivity and the socially constructed monster, neatly encapsulated his anti-collective view.

Anarchist themes formed the basis of Comfort's conceptualization of responsibility as based on an interpersonal morality of immediate and direct human communication. This image of social order effectively reconciles the anarchist commitment to both individuality and social cohesion. Anarchism was also the source for Comfort's closely related and distinctive rejection of abstract, intangible, distant and supra-personal human goals. This perspective was drawn from the same conceptual family of anarchist concerns as the ethic of continuity between means and ends, a cluster of focuses on directness and immediacy in social activity towards change. This group of ethical commitments values temporally proximate goods over the deferred realization of ideals and favours a prefigurative view of social change. This view stipulates that means must be consistent with ends in order to be effectively realized. For Comfort the rejection of the abstract and impersonal was at the same time the embracing of the immediate, tangible, overridingly human-centred endeavour. He urged that we focus on immediate and proximate threats to liberty and solidarity rather than abstract, intangible formulations of the social or political good. He saw the former as the 'responsible' approach. As Comfort stated: 'By responsibility I mean the refusal to abandon the basic conception of humanness for any extraneous object whatsoever – victory, democracy, the nation, the party, the civil list.'[77] This ethic of immediacy and tangibility was opposed to the state and centralized power because these institutions fostered the kind of allegiance which interfered with the individual's responsibility to other people.

For the modern atomized man living in an asocial mass society who failed to enjoy adequate contact with real human beings, extraneous allegiances to institutions, abstractions, personified collectivities, and political symbols were 'substitutes for human beings'. They 'capture our spare social impulses' and 'live on our frustrations'.[78] No moral sense or humanist inclination could survive the abstractions of society conceived as a single entity or the abstract formulation of grand hypothetical goals. Comfort strongly resisted the abstract personification of human collectivity, and the adjacent conception of society as a unity with a singular will or identity. Such social collectivization was 'the enemy of man'.[79] However, according to Comfort, 'civilisation goes on, and personally responsible action goes on within and in opposition to the structure of organised societies'.[80] Comfort's ideas in this respect relied on a distinct picture of the nature of the human personality and its moral capacity. Our moral sense, he argued, could only function reliably under the direct and immediate types of relationship which existed between individuals. Human morality required conditions of direct personal engagement between individuals in order that they could recognize each other in human terms. This was an ethic of direct immediate contact against one of representation. Representation and abstraction undermined the immediate, personalized nature of the human moral capacity. The resistance to abstract goals was strongly linked to the ethic which stated that means and ends must be congruent. The central thesis was that good ends could never emerge through the use of evil means. He applied it in particular to prove war's incompatibility under any circumstances with the ends of a humane and democratic society. Comfort similarly urged his readers to resist the use of hypothetical evils to justify acts of inhumanity. He called on individuals to reject the goals of war if the necessary path involved 'walking on corpses'.[81] For Comfort, a man was a morally unique entity, but his distinctive human moral capacity functioned at the level of personal human relationships. The moral sense of man was utterly subverted by the indirectness and intangibility of representative political notions like 'the general good'. This perspective on the unique but limited moral capacities of man was, in effect, a critique of hierarchical power.

Tracing the philosophy of individual responsibility through Comfort's work on pacifism, romanticism and anarchism and on to his ideas on psychology, sociology and sexuality reveals these as important sources of a revitalized, freshly popular perspective on anarchism in the post-war era. The emphasis on social change through personal redemption rather than institutional revolution emerged in the work of Comfort in a manner characteristic of his relationship with neo-romantic currents in mid-twentieth-century British thought. His attitude towards revolution as a personal and unending process was a facet of his anticipation of and influence on anarchism in the late 1950s. In his work on the characteristics of the 'new' anarchism of this period, David Apter identifies a number of developments in the tradition that directly indicate the significance of Comfort's influence on the twentieth-century growth of anarchist ideas. According to Apter one of the core characteristics of the new anarchism was the balancing of emotionality and rationality in a manner that retained the importance of spontaneousness. This directly reflected Comfort's combination of Godwinian rationalism, Kropotkonian rational scientism, a Proudhonian awareness of the dark forces in man, and the romantic belief in the importance of the subjective emotion and creativity of the individual. Also, Apter mentions 'personal vision', 'regeneration of the self as a continued approach to social betterment' and the 'tyranny of the collectivity' as key modern anarchist concerns.[82] These features of anarchism observed by Apter in the twentieth century closely reflected the influence of Comfort's interpretation of the tradition. New anarchists, Apter also highlights, relied for part of their analysis of society on the insights of Freud, and he noted the related emphasis on sexuality as an emphasis on 'physicalism which produces an erogenous solidarity'.[83] This observation was in part a description of Comfort's anarchism and in part evidence of his influence on the concerns of the tradition. All the features of the new anarchism that Apter identifies relate directly to the various facets of Comfort's ideas and this illustrates how deeply significant Comfort was as an intellectual source of anarchist revival.

Comfort's own scientific background led him to draw on the fields of sociology and psychology as empirical grounds for his anarchism. His ideas heralded an evidence-based, pragmatic defence of anarchism. This came to be most strongly represented in the journal *Anarchy*, established in 1961 by Colin Ward, as a monthly journal for the discussion of anarchist theory in the light of modern sociological, psychological, anthropological and educational theory. The following statement by Comfort was a typical evidence-based argument against the need for coercion in human society: 'The power of prohibition to make men good is something sociology consistently fails to detect.'[84] The roots of this approach were discernible in the anthropological work of Kropotkin in *Mutual Aid* in which he demonstrated that ethnological observations had applicability to the struggle against the coercive society. Comfort's approach in this respect stemmed from his commitment to scientific modes of enquiry and his adherence to a rationalist model of scientific humanism. In *The Pattern of the Future* Comfort demonstrated the libertarian significance of the entry of scientific values into a moral culture premised on Christian tradition. Notions of life after death, the possibility of entering into a personal relationship with the deity, sin, revelation, and creation, he argued, 'no longer stand up to the tests of truth.'[85] As such, the time was ripe to reassess the Christian 'pattern of belief about man's place in physical reality' and its 'pattern of ethics governing his relationships with other men.'[86] The moral conclusions reached by honest reflection on these subjects, he argued, led us to recognize not the moral order of God but the 'orderliness of the human mind', for 'we can see no signs of moral purpose or of standards anywhere save in man.'[87] 'The more fully we study the human mind', continued Comfort, and 'the more we learn about the pattern of its desires and fears', the more honestly are we compelled to recognize that it is not the 'righteousness of God' underlying 'natural order', 'ethical value' and 'conceptions of beauty and truth', but 'his own voice' and 'his own purpose and will'. In sum, 'The God of his tradition is a mirror in which he sees himself.'[88] For Comfort the standards of 'justice, uprightness, love, mercy, truth' came from 'a common human tradition' rather than religious revelation.[89] They were among the characteristics which identified humans from lower orders of species. What this meant for humanity was that 'Their future is in their own hands.'[90] The direct political statement of this sentiment was that 'This revolution is something no party or government is going to do for you. You have to do it yourself, beginning tomorrow.'[91] Comfort's 'do-it-yourself' model of social change developed in the work of Colin Ward into a direct action philosophy with widespread implications for later twentieth-century and early twenty-first-century social movements. Comfort's action-focused, secular humanism also fed into his revision of conventional codes of sexual morality in the early 1970s.

'Man's survival depends on the outcome of his struggle with a morally neutral universe', Comfort argued, but also it depended on 'the maintenance of responsibility between men'.[92] As the moral scaffolding of the Christian tradition fell away, Comfort argued, the imperative for human responsibility and solidarity became stronger not weaker. This was especially the case under the conditions of widespread irresponsibility during war: 'human beings must at all costs stick together if they hope to survive for this generation, let alone in the future.'[93] The concept of responsibility here worked as the agent of human sociability. Responsibility was depicted as responsibility towards other humans. Elsewhere in Comfort's work the notion of responsibility took more of an individual focus. At these times in Comfort's work responsibility was an inner condition of developed selfhood, a condition of rigorous individuality and developed autonomy.

In these cases responsibility denoted the personal capacity for facing truths, accepting consequences, and taking responsibility for the outcomes of activity or inactivity. The important point about the two senses of the notion of responsibility in Comfort's work, responsibility for others and responsibility for self, social and individual imperatives respectively, was the connection between them. The notion of responsibility was the mode both of human individuality and human sociality. This illustrated the modern anarchist case, developed in the work of a number of twentieth-century anarchist writers, which is that only the developed individual self can enter into truly social interpersonal relationships and participate as part of a healthy functioning social unit.

British Pacifism and the Nuclear Disarmament Movement

Comfort's pacifist commitments highlighted anarchism's relationship to British ideological traditions and social movements. There is a strong link between the traditions of British pacifism and anarchism. Too much has been made of the question of how far the two doctrines can overlap until anarchism accepts a rejection of interpersonal violence on a doctrinal level, and pacifism embraces a comprehensive critique of the state. In fact, the point at which the two doctrines converge is the rejection of war. As Jenny Teichman notes, 'the very word *pacifism* was coined to mean *anti-war-ism*', its core commitment is the principled rejection of the violence of war between nations.[94] Historically, however, the anarchist response to war had been more ambiguous. Proudhon wrote a defence of war, Bakunin postulated the need for total destruction before total reconstruction could be made possible, and during the First World War Kropotkin announced his support for the allied cause. However, for both anarchists and pacifists the emergence of total war in the twentieth century came to be seen as closely related to the power-seeking behaviour of nation–states. The impact of war and the growth of the state were equally important for non-violent and anti-state radical ideologies, which saw their agendas merge significantly in response to conscription. This reflects the shared commitments of pacifist and anarchist traditions in so far as they both reject the militarization of civilian life, although they may not agree over the extent to which the state is inherently a militaristic or war-seeking institution. Overlooking this, Martin Ceadel argues that the pacifist faces the problem of having adopted a contradictory attitude because he challenges the state over war but does not challenge it over other social and political evils. Ceadel refers to this as an incoherent 'selective anarchism', which demonstrates a fundamental misunderstanding of the relationship between anarchism and pacifism in Britain.[95] Both traditions challenge the right of the state to engage in, and conscript its citizens for war. Both anarchism and pacifism reject the militarization of society inherent in the prestige attached to soldiering, the maintenance of a powerful army, the insistence on conscription and the repeated emphasis on threats to national survival. Fundamentally, both anarchism and pacifism agree on the anti-militarist principle that war entails unacceptable social control. Ceadel further misrepresents the political nature of British pacifism by ignoring those non-selective, consistent anarchist pacifist figures exemplified by Comfort. For figures like Comfort the anti-war sentiment *was* part of a more general challenge to the state. The flaw in Ceadel's argument gives us the opportunity to consider two things. First, we realize the extent to which anarchist involvement in pacifist movements in Britain has been overlooked by commentaries on the subject. Secondly, in addressing this oversight we recognize the coherent and fluid connection between pacifist and anarchist perspectives in philosophical and historical terms. In general, the literature on pacifism in Britain contains a good measure of unwitting testimony to the anarchist current within this movement. However, it lacks explicit discussion of anarchism. Focusing on Comfort in this context highlights the significance of the relationship between anarchism and pacifism in the twentieth century. It also demonstrates the continuity of the tradition of politically engaged British pacifism through the wartime period, an era generally treated as barren of pacifist political engagement. This helps to link the strong and popular pacifism of the 1930s with the strength of pacifist sentiments in the anti-nuclear movements of the 1950s and 1960s. This focus also emphasizes the strong links between anarchism and anti-nuclear politics, one of the main sites of anarchist influence in the twentieth century.

In Britain, pacifism hovered on the fringes of anarchism even before the First World War, most significantly in the Brotherhood movement which was based on the ideals of Tolstoy. It was, however, the First World War and its aftermath which made the issue of violence crucial, and linked it with the issue of conscription. The pacifist movement in Britain can be traced to the spring of 1916, when the passing of Military Service Act, providing the legal grounds for civilian conscription, was greeted with protest. Radicals saw this act as an affront to individual responsibility and a transgression of the terms of the relationship between citizen and state. Pacifism is one of the key ways in which the individual conscience has conflicted with the demands of political society. Conscription, as described by Comfort, was 'the final impudence of the demand that men should put their bodies and consciences in hands that they may not question'.[96] From the dock, in the early twentieth-century wave of British anti-conscription sentiment, Bertrand Russell expressed the terms clearly: 'It is not only I that am in the dock; it is the whole tradition of British liberty . . . for that liberty of the individual I stand.'[97] Comfort too was well aware of the pacifist tradition in which he stood, remarking that the internationalist, liberal socialist traditions from which peace politics grew 'seems to me the most positive resource in Britain's political culture'.[98] Conscription was important evidence of the expansion of the role of the state and its collectivizing momentum in Britain. It was a key issue in British pacifist traditions. It linked non-violent and anti-authoritarian political thinking together in a manner that is crucial for understanding twentieth-century anarchism and its relationship to contemporary protest movements. Confrontation with the state in these individual terms provided a conducive breeding ground for a domestic brand of anarchism. As Comfort stated: 'For me, pacifism rests solely upon the historical theory of anarchism.'[99]

The Peace Pledge Union, formed in 1934, was a kind of libertarian analogue to the proto-Communist Left Book Club. It advocated a much more strongly individualist kind of philosophical outlook. This was related to the strand of British radical thought which advocated the ideal of human brotherhood, rather than class allegiance, as its radical principal. The fraternal ideal, and the requisite change in individual moral values, was seen as enduringly at odds with the pugilistic struggle for power. This notion of individual moral imperative and individual conscience represented the kind of ideas with which anarchists found natural allegiance. A prominent pacifist-anarchist of the 1930s, Ethel Mannin, wrote that 'Graduating through Marxism to anarchism, pacifism is only one step further on.'[100] Pacifism as a social faith was also recognized as akin to anarchism by a number of the younger pacifist figures in the 1930s and 1940s including figures like Frank Lea and Maurice Cranston. The newer type of pacifist that emerged in the 1930s was moving away from the older political traditions of non-conformist individualism towards a position that was related to anarchist or atheistic pacifism. Ceadel has referred to this as 'the libertarian activist' model of pacifist commitment, typically secular and bohemian, with a commitment to individual liberation.[101] Comfort reflected this newer style of membership. Ceadel remarks of this group that 'Taken as a whole the younger generation of thirties pacifists represented within the British tradition of dissent a transitional stage between the Nonconformist conscience and the beatniks.'[102] This was a crucial link. The style of the younger 1930s pacifists, represented by the figure of Comfort, provided a continuity in British social movements between the radicalism of the 1930s and the movements of the 1950s and 1960s.

During the later 1930s, war became a real fear and the morally and politically progressive radical activist core of the pacifist movement found that they were outside the mainstream of progressive values, which had become increasingly anti-fascist and hostile to pacifism. In the late 1930s radical opinion began to divide between those who advocated the complete rejection of all war and those who accepted military conflict in the service of a cause deeded to be just. The relationship between mainstream socialism and pacifism in the British movement thus became a tense one. There was a divide between pacifism and Marxist forms of socialism that reflected the traditional antagonism between anarchism and Marxism. The reaction of mainstream Marxist-influenced socialists to the Second World War on the one hand, and that of the pacifists and anarchists on the other, signalled an important break in British radical thought. This rupture drew pacifist, anti-militarist, anti-collectivist, individualistic and anti-authoritarian sentiments together, and Comfort's anarchism developed within these alliances. Events in the 1930s contributed to finally separating pacifism from its temporary allies among the socialists, League of Nations internationalists and left-wing militants. Most came to accept that a war against Germany was also a democratic cause. The real threat of war drew many intellectual figures and other Marxists away from pacifism. The Bloomsbury set, A. A. Milne, and even the most unambiguous pacifists of previous years like Fenner Brockway and Bertrand Russell rescinded their pacifism. George Orwell attacked the remaining pacifists, claiming that they constituted a 'fascist gang'. By 1941 he was complaining of the moral collapse of British pacifism, claiming that it was now impossible to tell the difference between PPU pacifists and Blackshirts. It became difficult in Britain to be politically anti-fascist and anti-war.

Comfort's deep involvement in the radical political debates concerning the war demonstrated the relevance of the developing twentieth-century current of anarchism to the central concerns of political intellectuals in the 1940s. In 1943, writing for *Partisan Review*, Comfort complained that the 'youngest poets' were under pressure to become 'the literary propagandists of the war, devote themselves to the study of Brooks, and write choric odes to the air force'.[103] Refusing to be a propagandist, Comfort publicly denounced the war and headed the agitation against indiscriminate bombing.

As part of this project Comfort drafted declarations against the allied bombings and organized the signing of the petition by writers, artists and musicians, including Herbert Read, Benjamin Britten, Julian Symons and George Woodcock. One such invective ran thus:

> The bombardment of Europe is not the work of soldiers nor of responsible statesmen. It is the work of bloodthirsty fools. I doubt if the devotion of a citizen Air Force could be more bitterly insulted than by the tasks which our present leadership expects it to perform . . . It seems to me that a particular responsibility belongs to the English writers and artists. There are times when denunciation is both a moral and an aesthetic duty. The present seems to be one such, and I invite other writers who share my feeling to say so publicly and as soon as possible.[104]

For public letters such as this, Comfort was officially blacklisted by the BBC. In the ages of *Partisan Review* Comfort wrangled with George Orwell over the sincerity of pacifist commitments to resisting fascism. The energy and commitment of both parties in the disagreement between Comfort and Orwell illustrated just how immediate and important the issues were for both men. These included resistance to totalitarianism, the freedom of the individual, the nature of political goals, the imperative for action, and the political significance of the war. Comfort's commitments to pacifism during World War Two extended directly into his total objection to the proliferation of nuclear weapons in the post-war era. His relationship to the post-war anti-nuclear and direct action movements, including CND and the Committee of 100, highlighted the significance of anarchism in the ideological formation of these movements. More generally it also highlighted the relevance of the anarchist tradition to the concerns of dissonant political movements in the later twentieth century.

As figures like Orwell attacked the pacifism of Comfort in the name of anti-fascism, so Comfort attacked those intellectuals like Orwell who came to depict the war as a responsible course of action. The conflict between the two figures, carried out in the pages of contemporary cultural journals, was indicative of their shared concern with the moral rigour of literary commentary. The concerns that they shared were their common fears of powerful government. The tension between the ideas of the two men was subtle and crucial, both aimed at resistance to totalitarianism, only for Orwell this necessitated fighting the fascists abroad, and for Comfort the fascists within the ranks presented an equal if not greater threat. Orwell's position was that Hitler had to be fought even if the British leadership was flawed. Comfort argued that no government could be trusted to fight a war of principle, and that men cannot trust their individual human consciences to government. For the former: 'Objectively, whoever is not on the side of the policeman is on the side of the criminal, and vice versa. In so far as it hampers the British war effort, British pacifism is on the side of the Nazis.'[105] For him the case was straightforward: 'In practice, "he that is not with me is against me."'[106] For Comfort, such simple dichotomies were misleading. The responsible individual, in his fight against coercion and manipulation, must be able to recognize 'filth from food, whatever the wrapper'.[107] Fascism was not a characteristic of a particular nation–state, he argued. Rather, like brutality and incarceration, it was 'the occupational disease of the twentieth century'.[108] He argued that 'Hitler's greatest and irretrievable victory over here was when he persuaded the English people that the only way to lick Fascism was to imitate it', this included 'sitting on the Press "because this is Total War"' and 'making our soldiers jab blood bladders while loudspeakers howl propaganda at them'. Only the pacifists, he argued, were sincere in their resistance to fascism by their refusal to accept its tenets: 'The men who, like Orwell, could have helped, are calling us Fascists and presumably dancing round the ruins of Münster Cathedral.'[109] Intellectuals like Orwell, mourned Comfort, 'have utterly failed to learn the lesson of war'.[110] The lesson was that when governments waged war, the people always lost. Comfort, consistent with his anarchism and pacifism, held that 'War will liberate nobody from anything.'[111] Against Orwell, he argued that intellectuals 'who charge romantic individualism with losing its nerve' are, in their failure to recognize realities with honest responsibility, 'imitating the man who smashes the barometer because it points to rain'.[112]

There is a key difference in the way in which Orwell and Comfort were using the term 'fascism' in this debate, which reflects the wider anti-militarist commitments underpinning Comfort's pacifism. Orwell used the term to designate the particular ideological commitments of the German state, while Comfort used the term in a wider sense to condemn the unjust and dominating social hierarchies which underpin war, and militarize civilian populations in the interests of the state. Comfort uses the term 'fascism', as the domestic ideological counterpart to militarism, to attack the government imposition of reasons of state on civilian culture and society. This is what he means when he describes the British leadership and governing institutions as 'fascist', and it follows the anarchist perception of the state as an inherently militaristic institution. One of the classic anarchist arguments regarding the state, and reiterated in relation to World

War Two, is that 'Governments need wars to survive and without them they would collapse.'[113] The two anarchistic aphorisms 'War is the trade of governments' and 'War is the health of the state' present this case.[114] For the anarchist, the war-making tendencies of states are closely related to their socially disintegrative characteristics, war is seen as one of the ways in which the institutions of the state corrode and inhibit spontaneous social cohesion. Herbert Read included in his indictment of the state its propensity to undermine human freedom and solidarity via the waging of wars: 'I regard war as the curse of humanity and governments as the instruments of war.'[115] He was resolute in his conviction that 'War will exist as long as the state exists' and that 'There is no problem which leads so inevitably to anarchism.'[116] Further, anarchists, with their ontological commitment to the distinction between state and society, particularly to the idea of a spontaneous social cohesion that emerges outside of the impositions of state-imposed ordering, are particularly sensitive to the infiltration of military concerns in civilian spheres. Thus, the overlap between pacifism and anarchism is not only evident when pacifists turn their critiques of war onto the state agents that propagate them, but in the very challenge posed to militarism from within both bodies of political thought. The affinity between pacifism and anarchism is not limited to instances of shared commitments to non-violence or hostility to the state per se, if and when these emerge, but lies in a shared resistance to militaristic assumptions about the inherent justice of war and the benefits achieved by a military ordering of civilian life. The affinity between anarchism and pacifism does not rely then on anarchists professing non-violent philosophies, or pacifists espousing anti-state commitments.

Another core point of contention between Orwell and Comfort was the extent of the latter's commitment to the purism of anarchism's ethic of means and ends. His unshakable conviction was that there are no lesser evils because means and ends are indistinguishable: 'You can abolish firing-squads only by refusing to serve in them, by jamming the rifle down the throat of the man who offers it to you if you wish – not by forming a firing-squad to execute all other firing-squads . . . we cannot defend the bad against the worse.'[117] More importantly, the abstract good never outweighs the immediate good, especially not if it calls for the sacrifice of humanity or freedom in the present. In Comfort's novel *On This Side Nothing*, the character of Szmul emphasizes Comfort's total rejection of the notion of acceptable inhumanities or 'lesser evils': 'When human beings eat each other, nobody who isn't a political vegetarian has a right to open his mouth, and even he has no right to let a word out of it unless he is on his guard to see that the bread he eats wasn't kneaded inside someone's skull and greased with his brains.'[118] In the case of World War Two: 'Acquiescence in the murder of the population of Lidice is as evil as acquiescence in the murder of the population of Hamburg.'[119] Still arguing against the notion of war as the lesser evil, Comfort extended his case to nuclear weapons: 'The atomic bomb has brought home to increasing numbers of the public at large that tyranny is not a greater evil than war, because war itself is an instrument of tyranny on the largest scale.'[120]

Anarchist figures like Comfort maintained throughout the later twentieth century an obstinate and continual source of doubt about the notion of 'good' or 'progressive' war. Comfort injected his anarchism into the post-war period with an immediate attack on the achievements of the war, which he described as 'The historical vindication of the pacifist case'.[121] He stated that 'They have replaced famine, destruction and repression with repression, destruction and famine.'[122] Comfort predicted that pacifism would re-emerge, from its unpopularity during the war, after the atomic attack on Japan. At the same time he demonstrated the fluid shift of his own pacifism from resisting war to resisting nuclear weaponry: 'It was not more that two years ago . . . that we were hearing it confidently reiterated that pacifism could have no conceivable future for the intelligent or the politically relevant individual. I have the feeling that since the events of August last we shall hear that remark with decreasing frequency.'[123] It was the development of nuclear weapons that confirmed for Comfort the parallel responsibility for civilization which scientists shared with artists. Comfort argued that scientists must recognize, especially in the face of new technology, their duty to react against the misuse of science, for: 'Now he finds himself, often to his great alarm, being asked to put unlimited powers of genocide, coercion and destruction into the hands of limited groups of individuals, many of whom show themselves by all their public gestures quite unfit to control a sporting gun, let alone a vast military machine.'[124] Comfort's reaction to the dropping of atomic bombs on Japan was marked by a ferocious outrage at the barbaric nature of the attack, the debasing of civilization and humanity, and the degeneration of personal responsibility that it reflected, 'It is high time we tried our own war criminals' he declared (again).[125]

Comfort engaged in an anarchist anti-militarist attack on the British actions in the Second World War in terms of the militarization of civilians and the untenable social control exercised by the state, but he also condemned the international policies of the wartime leaders of Britain using the more conventionally accepted tenets of Just War theory. For a war to be a Just War it must be initiated by a proper authority, fought for a just cause with right intentions and it must employ just and proportionate means. Following the twentieth-century mechanical revolution in warfare, the use of aerial bombardment in particular demonstrated to concerned parties that technologies of warfare were not going to be used to human- ize war, but rather to intensify its deadly and indiscriminate features. Teichman identifies a distinct conditional strain of pacifism which does in principle admit the possibility of a Just War. This position argues that war is no longer an admissible mode of conduct, no longer 'just' in the appropriate sense, when the technology and weapons used will kill large numbers of civilians or when the combatants are pressed or conscripted into conflict. This position in practice rules out the possibility that modern warfare could fulfill the precepts laid out in Just War theory 'which were supposed to make the activity all right'.[126] Ceadel refers to this position as 'Modern War' pacifism: 'just wars were once possible but are no longer so in view of the indiscriminate destructiveness of modern technology.'[127] While the anarchist position constitutes an unconditional rejection of war, this conditional argument played an important part in Comfort's rejection of war and the technologies of modern warfare. Comfort deployed this 'Modern War' strain of pacifism alongside his principled, anti-militarist anarchism:

> I know that it is all war, and not this particular manifestation of bombing, which I believe to be unjustified, but there are times when a single act of folly and brutality seem so signal that one dare not remain silent. I am not interested in Sinclair or General Quade's remarks about 'legitimate operations of war.' Even if I believe that no operation of war is legitimate, some are less so than others . . . I want to able to go about in Europe without having to wear a poster saying: 'I am English, but I didn't do it . . . there are some things that not even a soldier who accepts war should stomach.[128]

In 1945 Alex Comfort observed that 'The atomic bomb is not dif- ferent in kind or in result from the other weapons and methods of war which characterize contemporary society.'[129] His campaign against nuclear weaponry was a continuation of his attacks on the allied use of aerial bombing technologies and this reflects his emphasis on the social and political significance of the technologies of warfare. 'Sir', he wrote to the *New Statesman and Nation* in August 1945, 'The announcement of the "atomic bomb," and the tone in which that announcement was made, made me feel that we are entitled to ask whether the Allies are committed from now on to the indiscriminate extermination of the whole Japanese civil population, and, if so, whether the British labour party endorses that policy.' He continued, with characteristic emphasis, 'It seems to me that a party or a people which is prepared to condone or applaud the annihilation at a single blow of a city of 300,000 inhabitants has reached a level of irresponsibility without historical parallel.' He concluded that 'the failure of English liberal thought to dissociate itself immediately from such actions, and to demand their immediate end, is likely to cover us with well-merited disgrace in the eyes of history and of every sane contemporary.'[130]

One of the persistent themes of Comfort's anti-militarism was the moral implication of modern technologies of war. His habit of depicting the visceral effects of military technologies was a clear political attempt to make them tangible to his audiences and bring them within their subjective and empathetic grasp. He brought distant technologies of war into a humanly discernible sphere of terminology by offering accounts of the individual damage they caused. In 1952 he gave such an account of the use of napalm: 'Napalm is not merely a minor advance in the use of fire as an agent of war; it represents an enormous increase in the ability to start fires, and almost instantaneously to sear and char organic material whether that be vegetable, animal, or human.'[131] Following this, in a public letter to *The Times* written in July of the same year, Comfort wrote, 'The burns inflicted by napalm are among the most painful wounds which any weapon can produce.' He commented on the 'barbarity of the weapon' and highlighted that it was 'indiscriminately used against inhabited places', signalling the 'deterioration of our values'. He argued that the 'time has come for humane men to make an organised protest'. This letter was signed by a number of public figures, including H. N. Brailsford, Benjamin Britten, Tom Brown, Barbara Castle, G. D. H. Cole, R. H. S. Crossman, Clifford Curzon, Christopher Fry and Compton Mackenzie.[132] Implicitly, the argument here is that barbaric means significantly colour the moral probity of the ends they serve, and this applies whether or not you raise wider political concerns about the aims underpinning the conflicts during which they are used. Just War theory makes an explicit distinction between 'just cause' in waging war and 'just means' in warfare, examining the premises for each independently. In short, this means that a war can be interpreted as 'just' according to the relevant criteria, but the means used in its prosecution can still be deemed 'unjust', specifically if they are disproportionate to the means sought, or involve the deliberate target-ing of civilians. Other recent British anarcho-pacifist challenges have also demonstrated a marked focus on military technology in their critique of British war policies. The political output of anarcho-punk band Crass has highlighted this anti-militarist character of British anarchism, emphasiz-ing personal responsibility and the visceral effects of military technologies. They released the single 'Nagasaki Nightmare' in 1980, the insert for which depicts the leaders of the nuclear powers grouped together amid the ruins of Nagasaki and the victims of the blast, including the charred corpse of a child. The song relates the politician's shared willingness to 'do it again'. The approach of the band to the Falklands conflict also demonstrated key anarchist themes of responsibility and the physical effects of warfare. The lyrics of Crass's 1983 album 'Yes Sir I Will' calls on the observers of state violence in warfare to withdraw their support. The original essay, which was adapted into lyrics for the album, was followed by an addendum that aimed to demonstrate the horrors of acquiescence to authority, especially in relation to war: 'A squaddy, horrifically burnt [and permanently disfig-ured] in the Falklands War, was approached by Prince Charles during a presentation. 'Get well soon' said the Prince, to which the squaddy replied, 'Yes Sir, I will.'[133]

Writing for the journal *Anarchy* in 1962, Nicolas Walter claimed that Comfort was 'the true voice of nuclear disarmament'.[134] The war-time pacifism of Comfort was extended seamlessly, first to Suez and then to the movement resisting the proliferation of nuclear weapons. He also played a notable part in the PPU's 1950 campaign against cold war government propaganda for civil defence. A leaflet signed by Comfort and entitled 'Civil Defence – What YOU should do now!' caught the attention of the press, and was discussed in parliament. In 1951 Comfort was a signatory of the Authors' World Peace Appeal, but resigned from its committee when it began to be taken over by Soviet sympathisers. Later in the decade he actively supported the Direct Action Committee (DAC) against nuclear war, the Committee of 100 and CND. When the Committee of 100 was formed, he went to prison for a month, alongside Bertrand Russell, for refusing to be bound over not to take part in the Trafalgar Square mass sit-down in September 1961. Focusing on Comfort as a political intellectual serves to emphasize an important point about the British anti-nuclear movement. This is its direct relationship to the pacifist tradition. From the outset there was an inherent relationship between the anti-nuclear movement and the current of British anarchism that was a persistent feature of the pacifist tradition. Comfort as a public intellectual figure highlights the continuity between the Peace Pledge Union, representing the early twentieth-century pacifist movement, the DAC, which grew from the younger generation of PPU members, and the Committee of 100, a movement with a key relationship to the British New Left of the early 1960s. The development of direct action philosophies within the anti-nuclear movement over the post-war period was built at least partly on the firm pacifist links with anarchist traditions. Richard Taylor has rightly asserted that the fusion of the two traditions of anarchism and pacifism lies at the heart of the Western tradition of non-violent direct action.[135] Of crucial importance in the DAC was the emphasis on means rather than ends. The ethic of direct action is related to this idea and to the affiliated cluster of anarchist focuses on immediacy, direct experience and interaction, and prefigurative forms of social change. The focus on means and ends in particular was a key link with pacifist figures like Aldous Huxley and with the rising popularity of Gandhian ideals.

In January 1952 the DAC organized a sit-down outside the War Office. This demonstration marked the beginning of the direct action movement in Britain. They planned the next demonstration for April and this became the first Aldermaston March. Taylor remarks that '[T]he DAC can be seen as a staging post along the road of radical pacifism within the anti-nuclear movement which begins, in the post-war context, with the PPU and ends with the mass civil disobedience and quasi-anarchistic orientation of the later Committee of 100.' Taylor notes the testimony of figures like Michael Randle that the DAC was in the 'socialist/anarchist' tradition and far removed from the ideologies of orthodox social democracy and Communism.[136] The anarchist paper *Freedom* claimed that direct actionists were 'pioneers in a struggle which, by its very nature, brings to the fore at once the contemporary relevance of anarchist ideas: the struggle between people and governments'.[137] The radical wing of the nuclear disarmament movement was dominated by direct action politics from the outset. From 1957–1961 the DAC was the main organizational and ideological focus for direct action politics. However, it was not until the Committee of 100 that the direct actionists began to move towards a more generalized libertarian socialist critique of the 'warfare state', and argued for the need for confrontation with the power of the state in order to instigate a wholesale social change. David Stafford notes that from 1962 the Committee of 100 'both under the influence of anarchists within its ranks and through a process of self-generating anarchism' developed the idea that 'Ban the Bomb means ban the State', which included a campaign of direct action regarding military projects.[138]

The formation of the Committee of 100 was a response to growing sense of urgency in the nuclear disarmament movement. As David Widgery notes, this 'committee of arty bigwigs camouflaged some very determined politicos'.[139] Bertrand Russell and Ralph Schoenman gathered together a prestigious collection of prominent supporting figures, including Comfort, with the aim of arousing unmanageable public protest, in the form of civil disobedience, over the nuclear issue. Some years before even the creation of the DAC Comfort had stated the necessity for seeing resistance in these terms: 'The only barrier between this country and war is public opinion, public resistance, the certainty in the minds of those who wish to make war that they cannot make it with us.'[140] In his speech to the founding meeting of CND at the Central Hall, Westminster on 17 February 1955, Comfort reiterated his direct action approach: 'This is the function of the campaign which we are launching here tonight: to make every individual reassume the moral responsibility for opposing public insanity. The issue is one for direct action by every one of us.'[141] In a policy statement of 1964 the Committee of 100 clearly related its campaign against the bomb to a wider struggle against the distribution of power within society, a move Stafford describes as the 'anarchization' of the Committee of 100.[142] It is a move in which we can also discern the anti-militarization of the anti-nuclear agenda, which accompanied the anarcho-pacifist rejection of war as developed in the work of Comfort. The affinity between anti-nuclear and anarchist ideas became more prominent after the expression they were given in the new monthly journal *Anarchy*, edited by Colin Ward. In many ways Comfort anticipated Ward's applied, pragmatic anarchism as he expressed it in the editorship of the journal and his own writing, and Ward acknowledged the significance of Comfort's influence in this respect.[143] Heavily influenced in particular by Comfort's anti-militaristic anarchism, Ward himself was to ask:

What if we are forced to conclude that the same coercive power which controls national law and order is responsible for the threat to world peace and survival? What if we are driven to see war and the threat of war as implicit in the nature of government and the state, to conclude in fact that war is the *trade* of government, the *health* of the state? If we are impotent about the bomb it is because we are impotent about everything else, and we have surrendered our power over our own desires, and if we are ever to get it back we need to start thinking about a different kind of politics rather than see the issue in constitutional or electoral terms.[144]

In a number of articles for *Anarchy*, Nicolas Walter provided a contemporary analysis of the links between the anarchist tradition and the Committee of 100. He emphasized the essentially anarchist commitment to the congruity of means and ends and the distinction between this ideal of libertarian insurrection and the Marxist socialist idea of revolution. Particular elements that indicated anarchist synergies within the Committee of 100 were the notion of personal responsibility, the importance of individual action and the significance of direct action against the authority of the state. Comfort's advocacy of individual responsibility against the power of the state played an important role in the approach of the Committee of 100. Walter drew on the ideas of Comfort for at least one of his discussions on the subject, using his terms to assert that the struggle was between life, freedom and resistance versus obedience, war and death. On this basis, Walter stated that for the anarchists in the peace movement, pacifism and anarchism were essentially the logical correlates of each other.[145]

Delinquency, Mass Society and the Socializing Role of Sexual Behaviour

Comfort's other great concern in the post-war era, apart from nuclear weaponry, was the rise of mass 'asocial' society and the irresponsible 'delinquent' individual. For Comfort, writing in 1950, the primary concern of the anarchist was the modern pattern of administered, collectivized, power-centered human social order: 'congested but lonely, technically advanced but personally insecure, subject to a complicated mechanism of institutional order, but individually irresponsible and confused for lack of communal sanction.'[146] This is a clear development of his anti-militarist agenda, which condemned the imposition of military purposes on civilian life during war and saw it as an authoritarian sociological phenomenon associated with centralized government even in peacetime. Comfort accused the British state of militarism on both counts. He understood the experiences of military social organization during the war, conventionally justified according to the demands that the state may legitimately make on citizens during war, as providing a reliable model for anticipating the likely pattern of state impositions on civilian life after the war. This perspective reflected Comfort's characteristic anarchist link between militarism as a feature of warfare in particular and militarism (or 'fascism') as the more general hierarchical political principle of state-directed social order. The link was reiterated in his concerns in 1945 about the state regulation of doctors after the war under the auspices of the British Medical Association as part of the arrangements underpinning the NHS. He argued that 'the subjection of medicine to a Minister would be comparable to the transfer of the Red Cross from international to national sponsorship.' The doctor, he argued, has exclusive responsibilities to the health of the patient, responsibilities which would be compromised by accountability to the state. He illustrated the dangers of this tension by drawing analogies with the position of medical and psychiatric practitioners during the Second World War: 'A certain psychiatrist who advised a man to refuse orders was very nearly court-martialled.' 'The state today is not a reliable quantity', he argued, adding that 'there is no evidence that the danger of a totalitarian degeneration in this country is over'. Thus, he concluded, 'every responsible body which can be put in a constitutionally unassailable position should be put there.'[147] As his discussion in this respect demonstrates, Comfort does not make a distinction between the demands on civilians by the state under conditions of war and those of a state in peacetime. As he argued, doctors must be immune from the partiality of state demands, and their underlying political goals, in both cases. If we look forward to the work of Colin Ward in this respect, we can see that this argument does not entail a rejection of social welfare arrangements per se, merely their dependence on state institutions. In a talk Comfort delivered in Oxford in 1947 he correlated the experiences of the British population during wartime with the increased incidence of marriage breakdown after the war. There he argued that 'Military conscription was an important contribution to the breaking up of the marriage institution.' His argument was that centralized state ordering during the war had destroyed social relationships, for 'Real marriage in a militarised society was impossible.' He further argued that the barbarism of state-administered urban life accounted for the breakdown of families in the post-war era.[148] Thus, it was a clear and logical expression of his anti-militarist agenda to mount two parallel campaigns in the late 1940s, one against the continuation of conscription, and the other to foster greater intimacy between individuals. The biological human need for intimacy offered humanity the opportunity to counter the fragmenting dynamics of the state's regimentation of society. He argued in *Tribune* in November 1946 that 'If we do not smash conscription it will smash us' and the following summer he wrote, albeit for medical audiences, that 'ignorance of erotic technique among married people is a bad and deplorable thing', adding 'I wonder how our health would fare if the entity which is optimistically described as "public morality" took the same view of cookery as it does of sexual technique.'[149]

After the war, Comfort was deeply affected by Albert Camus's first novel, *The Outsider*, which, according to Comfort, was a documented study of a new yet typical figure of modern urban societies – the affect-less delinquent. The terrifyingly indifferent central figure of the novel, Comfort argued, was 'not tough so much as stunted, not vicious so much as utterly emptied of sociality. He is a terrifying clinical picture of one of the main psychiatric problems of a century.'[150] As World War Two drew to a close Comfort prophesied that 'The giant enemy of the next ten years will not be a class but irresponsible society.'[151] This signalled the direction of Comfort's ideas after the war. These were oriented around concerns about mass, administered, bureaucratic society precipitated by large-scale social administration. The most explicitly anarchist book of his career, Comfort's *Authority and Delinquency in the Modern State*, published in 1950, focused on the phenomenon of the atomized, irresponsible individual, incapable of individuality or responsibility, and the parallel rise of asocial human order. His sociological analysis in this respect was linked with a growing component of psychological analysis in his work. The irresponsible individual, the delinquent personality of the modern 'society of onlookers', and the 'congested but lonely' society they inhabited, both exhibited the signs of insanity.[152] Comfort's view of freedom as mental health was apparent even in his early pacifist writing. He posed his criticisms of the Second World War and specific bombing campaigns in terms of sanity and madness, terms that he used in tandem with civilization and barbarism. Throughout the war, Comfort attacked the heavy bombing of German cities, and later, the atomic bombing of Japan, describing them as evidence of 'criminal lunacy', and 'the ethical product of the mental hospital'.[153] Similarly, Comfort described the Nazi regime as a 'psychopathic manifestation'.[154]

The figure of the power-seeking ruler, illustrated by 'The Churchills and Hitlers of this world', were, Comfort argued, illustrations of the irresponsibility bred by centralized political power. They were 'the essential products of the State in the total divorce between their pretension and their practice, and their own utter inability to comprehend the nature, quality and results of their action'.[155] Wars originated as the result of mentally deranged individuals who secured office, and the compliant behaviour of irresponsible collectivities. Publics tolerated wars because they replaced the individual responsibility and the social purpose and unity lost to them through centralization. Under what he referred to as the 'criminology of power', Comfort argued that centralized society rested on unadjusted individuals and their delinquent behaviour.[156] The principal anarchist message of Comfort's work on psychology and sociology was this: 'There is a growing body of evidence to show that the desire to govern by coercion, to control or rely upon the state machinery, which Western political thought has traditionally regarded as the basis of social order, is in itself an abnormal impulse, an outcome of personality deviation.'[157] His view was that 'Anti-social conduct and delinquency, in the sense of action and attitude prejudicial to the welfare of others, are psychiatric entities.'[158]

In these areas of his thought Comfort developed his anarchist focus on the crucial qualitative difference between direct and immediate human interaction and the indirect representation of political relationships through systems of centralized, administered authority. This posited the individual capacity for personal responsibility against the pernicious abstract formulation of political goods. In the post-war era his reliance on psychology for the formulation of this argument became more marked. Cruelty, he claimed, was commonplace in psychiatry as abstract fantasy. It was harmless on that individual level, he argued, as long no individual possessed the opportunity to enact fantasy undisguised on a larger scale. Thus, he argued, 'Buchenwald undoubtedly exists, potentially, in the unconscious of a great many individuals who would pass muster as normal. Given certain social conditions, it can re-emerge as cold fact, whether as the open sexual violence of the SS, or as the censored equivalent which produced the atomic bomb and unlimited warfare.'[159]

While Comfort recognized that human sociability was fragile, he maintained that human beings always behaved socially and humanely at the personal level, the level at which they recognized each other as individual human beings. Further, the individual nature of human psychology meant that individuals could not retain a sense of the human subjectivity of others in the absence of direct and personal relationships with them. In the absence of these relationships, moral judgements were impaired because the human 'social sense is bearing a weight which it was never designed to carry'.[160] Political leaders in centralized political systems 'are like men who are detailed to carry the packs of an entire battalion'.[161] Not only was their moral sense incapacitated but the system of centralized authority exaggerated the effects of their unbalanced asociality: 'A pin dropped in Downing Street can demolish a city. A headache in the Kremlin can deport a nation to Siberia. A hangover or an attack of indigestion in Washington can touch off a hysterical train of propaganda ending in an atom bomb. A neurosis in the State Department or the Foreign Office can kill the lot of us.'[162] These concerns lay behind Comfort's involvement in the Center for the Study of

Democratic Institutions at Santa Barbara in California, where he moved in 1973. The centre was a radical think tank which attempted to draw some of the most prominent and respected intellectuals of the era into collaborative work concerning democratic practice in America. This aim was served through discussion and criticism, publications and public meetings. Political leaders, academics, scientists, social scientists, legal scholars, journalists, theologians, labour leaders and community leaders brought their expertise to interdisciplinary discussions on questions of critical concern to democratic society. Topics included, among others, modern technology, war and nuclear weapons, ecological imperatives, the responsibilities and control of the mass media, minority and constitutional rights, and world peace. The centre soon folded, but Comfort remained on the West Coast, in a series of medical and academic posts until 1985 when he retired to England.

For Comfort, 'The greater the concentration of authority, the greater the strain on those who accept it, the greater the likelihood that psychopaths will come to the top, and that those who do come to the top will be psychopathic.'[163] This was what made the politics of representation, collective abstractions and centralized power so dangerous in human society. Comfort's argument was that morally functional group dynamics depended on individual relationships, direct contact, physical impressions and personal interaction. The functional level of group psychology was 'face-to-face' contact. In the absence of these relationships, human activities were increasingly limited to techniques, and patterns of individual responsibility disappeared. This lack of personal relationships in modern systems of power was a fundamental feature of centralized government. Mass collectivized society inhibited responsibility and thus its courses of action and modes of thought were wildly at variance with individual standards of human responsibility. The solution was the anarchist re-individuation of the understanding of society and the reinvigoration of the notion of the self as inalienably responsible. In Comfort's imagination, responsibility, civilization, individuality, disobedience and sanity were pitted against barbarism, society, obedience and insanity: 'It looks as thought the sole remaining factor standing between the possibility of living a sane life and its destruction by lunatics is the disobedience of the individual.'[164]

Despite Comfort's recurrent emphasis on disobedience for the restoration of responsible individual selfhood, he focused on the interpersonal sources of the development of the mature and liberated human personality.

This emphasis was manifest in Comfort's interest in the social significance of human sexual behaviour. Comfort's interest in the importance of sexual behaviour developed through his interest in psychological fields of enquiry. Freud's schema of child mental growth and its profound effect on the personality of the adult fed into Comfort's developmental sense of the maturity of the free personality. Especially influential was the Freudian belief in the negative effect on subsequent behaviour of the obstruction of any phase of development. For, in the Freudian system, once the self-exploratory stages of development were carried through, the child transferred its interest to the world outside its own person and sought normal relationships with others. These childhood developmental phases were those referred to by Freud as 'autoerotic' and were related to the child's experimental attempts to find physical satisfaction. The progression through these phases was taken to significantly affect future behaviour in both sexual and non-sexual fields and it was this close relationship between sexual and non-sexual behaviour which was the greater part of Freud's influence on Comfort. As Comfort argued, 'Any attempt to isolate sexual behavior from the other factors in a social pattern is bound to hinder our comprehension of it and lead to false emphases.'[165] Responding in the pages of *Freedom* to the publication in America of Kinsey's infamous *Sexual Behavior of the Human Male*, published in 1948, Comfort introduced his interest in the survey by noting that: '[A]s anarchism is coming to rely more and more for its support upon social psychology and anthropology, those who accept it as a hypothesis cannot afford to neglect any new evidence.'[166]

Comfort's emphasis on the anarchist significance of empirical observations about human sexual behaviour reflected his desire to move beyond the ethical traditions of the Christian tradition and reinforced his scientific humanism. Comfort's view was that 'no form of sexual behaviour can be regarded as inacceptable, sinful, or deserving of censure unless it has demonstrable ill effects on the individual who practices it, or on others.'[167] He aimed to challenge the persisting religious morality underlying modern beliefs, supported by the medical profession, that sexual desire is unhealthy, abnormal or mentally harmful. The assertion of the importance of evidence was very much a statement of the new anarchism of the 1950s and 1960s, but Comfort utilized the field of research related to human sexuality as something more than evidence. His work on sex and freedom seemed to stand as a core component of his ideas concerning the anarchist case for the existence of a natural order that supported human liberty. Comfort's argument about the political importance of uninhibited sexual contact was a direct reinforcement of his rejection of ideologies that emphasized the institutional moulding and control of human behaviour through law, coercion or punishment. His emphasis on the socializing function of natural human sexual desire was part of his focus on spontaneous patterns of human order that operated through the mores and natural social patterns of individual interaction and small group dynamics. He argued that this conception challenged two erroneous assumptions: 'that individual conduct can be determined institutionally, and that punishment is effective in preventing anti-social behaviour in adults.'[168]

The overriding message Comfort drew from the data in Kinsey's survey was the statistical undermining of the conception of normality. Comfort was deliberately moving past the moral weighting of concepts of deviance such as sadism, masochism and fetishism. In doing so he also rejected the Freudian notion of the socializing function of sublimation, especially the sublimation of sexual desire. Put simply, for Comfort, the frustration of positive emotions such as sexual desire led to their expression as destructive ones. Sublimation, according to Comfort, caused the diversion of the repressed desire into a compensatory desire to have power over others and regulate their conduct. Comfort asserted that this exercise of power, in Freudian terms the continuance of an externalized super-ego into adulthood, prevented the individual from developing personal responsibility and accounted for many of the social features of fascism. Comfort's stringent notion of personal responsibility was thus combined with a permissive notion of liberation. More important for Comfort's anarchism than this libertarian understanding of the relationship between desire, freedom and personal autonomy was his emphasis on the socially cohesive significance of sexual behaviour.

Comfort came to the opinion that sexuality was a 'chief biological force in the evolution of humanness'.[169] In this he was echoing the work of Kropotkin, who had demonstrated in *Mutual Aid* that ethnological observations had applicability to the struggle against coercive society. Comfort was also following the work of Kropotkin, who saw play as a form of social training and communication, in his assertion of the importance of sexual play. Play behaviour was for Comfort a cohesive force and, he argued, offered the possibility for the discharge of certain forms of aggression. The repression of sexual play and the increase in 'sexual maladjustment' in modern industrial civilizations was part of Comfort's understanding of the 'asociality' of modern society that elsewhere in his work he related to the centralization of power. In the following statement, Comfort bolstered these psychological assertions of the socializing function of human sexuality with primatological claims, and linked these ideas to his romantic philosophy:

> [W]hat, if any, are the social and mental forces which can make humans fully social, give them the power of joy without limiting their capacity for necessary sorrow, and enable them to be free of anxiety without blinking the facts of the human situation? . . . the psychiatric evidence seems now, in many people's view, to point to the same force which socialized primates, made us able to live in families, and motivated our personal and social behaviour, namely sexual love – extended, through the peculiar role it has come to play in human economy, far outside its original context of the desire to copulate, and made more similar to the poet Schiller's idea of 'joy' . . . spilling over into all types of relationship.[170]

Comfort developed a view of sexual interaction as inherently liberating and socially cohesive. For Comfort, conventional and repressive sexual morality was the logical concomitant of authoritarian society. This position was developed according to his precisely elaborated, scientifically humanist, romantic, anti-militarist ideological framework, underpinned by the utilization and development of the anarchist tradition of political thought. By the early 1960s, he established himself as one of Britain's most prominent advocates for 'free love'. In his 1963 publication *Sex in Society* and his public discussions of the work, he courted controversy with his radical agenda, identifying chastity as a health problem, arguing for legalized prostitution and celebrating the sexual identities of children. At the Sandstone free love community in Topanga Canyon, Comfort met many of the other writers behind the sexual revolution, including Betty Dodson, a feminist writer who championed masturbation, and a pioneer in women's sexual liberation, who published her first book *Self Liberation* in the early 1970s. Comfort sought to bring these ideas to wider audiences. In *Sex in Society* he argued that 'There is a strong case for a literature of sexual enjoyment which treats the elaboration of sexuality as Indian and Arabic work have treated it – at the level of ballroom dancing.'[171] Given that, as he observed in 1963, 'There are virtually no European works of this kind', it was clear that his authorship of *The Joy of Sex* was directed towards providing, in his terms, an urgently needed reference for the development of human sociality in an age of asocial, delinquent crisis.[172] In 1972, *The Joy of Sex* went to the top of the bestseller lists and stayed there for most of the decade. By writing about sex as if it were fashionable French cooking, Comfort's book eventually brought his anarchist agenda of 'sexual liberation' within the remit of acceptable mainstream expectations. Contrary to his calculations in this regard, however, the challenges he raised to traditional mores regarding human sexuality does not seem to have limited the incidence of warfare in the years since his guide was published.

Conclusion

Comfort put his utilization of anarchist themes and concepts to work in a lifetime of controversial twentieth-century public debate and critique of war, state violence, centralized and collectivized social administration, and stultifying convention. He is most well known for his challenge to conventional views of sexual morality, but this aspect of his work was just one feature of his attempt to challenge mainstream culture using the thorough and exacting standards of liberty which he drew from the anarchist tradition. Recognized by Arthur Salmon as 'the most important contemporary artist representing anarchist ideas and policies', he is remembered solely for the controversial publication of a sex manual in the 1970s.[173] Insufficient attention is paid to his singularly critical position on the Second World War and the twentieth-century dangers of collectivism, or to the vision of liberty and society that made sense of his later emphasis on human sexual relationships. Comfort's challenge to conventional views of politics and individual behaviour draw on thoroughly embedded intellectual and political currents, and his ideas developed the anarchist tradition of political thought in a way that made it particularly applicable to the dynamics of war and barbarism, which for Comfort marked the modern era.

Anarchism underpinned Comfort's approach in a number of ways. The key feature of Comfort's thought, to which he remained committed in all his work, was his morally individualist perspective. This shaped and directed all his ideas about the nature of human freedom and the limits of political power. Comfort's perspective on social cohesion, the key dilemma for anarchist theorists, followed his strict individualism. Anti-social behaviour, being the result of the loss of individuality engendered by the centralization of society, could be checked and managed, he argued, without law or coercion, in decentralized social groups where group dynamics and organization took place at the level of direct individual interactions.

The notion of personal responsibility was the main theme of his focus on the individual. The concept of responsibility had a flexible character in Comfort's work. He used it both as an inward looking conceptualization of developed selfhood and an outward looking imperative for social awareness. This reflected his reconciliation of traditional anarchist concerns with individual freedom and natural social order. Another key element of Comfort's relationship to the anarchist tradition was his focus on immediate human goals over distant, abstracted ones. This was reflected in the ethic of direct action, the importance of congruity between means and ends, and the rejection of 'lesser evils' in the struggle for human progress. Twentieth-century anarchism developed a collection of related concerns on the importance of the present. In Comfort's case this included a specific and characteristic understanding of the nature and boundaries of the human sense of responsibility, which was both limited to immediate and direct interpersonal contact and subverted by the indirectness of abstract political goals, representative political practices, centralized administration and power. Comfort's interest in the spontaneous and creative sources of human liberation, including the significance of desire, was combined with a marked emphasis on the liberating rationalism of scientific models of enquiry and verification. Both these emphases have played marked roles in the anarchist tradition.

Comfort's ideas and public campaigns were one of the main ways that anarchism was made available to later twentieth-century social and political thought. His ideas reflected the emergence of the fields of psychology and sociology in anarchist ideas. For anarchists, Comfort's work was a key source of a scientifically aspirant, evidence-based form of anarchist ideology which constituted the revival of anarchism in the 1950s and 1960s, often referred to as 'new' anarchism. The importance of Comfort in the pacifist movement also put anarchism firmly in the milieu of British dissonant currents in the twentieth century. The relationship between anarchism and British social movements was particularly highlighted by the ideological composition of anti-nuclear movements in the late 1950s and 1960s, movements in which Comfort was a key figure. The ideas which Comfort developed and his political commitments throughout his career demonstrates the role which anarchism has played in key twentieth-century debates in Britain, including those concerning war, collectivism and the state, the individual and society, nuclear weapons, and sexual behaviour. The theme of selfhood, with both individual and social components, developed in his work as a response to accelerating mass social administration, and was triggered by the pivotal moment that World War Two proved to be for the revival of the anarchist tradition. Focusing on Comfort as a figure not only enhances our understanding of the twentieth-century history of ideas, including the trajectories of pacifism, romanticism and anti-nuclear movements, but it also dramatically challenges the popular understanding of anarchism. Instead of a moribund, incoherent, archaic cluster of ideas, anarchism can be found in the ideas of figures like Comfort to be operating as a vital and applied response to the challenges of twentieth-century political and social developments.

Notes

1. George Woodcock, *Letter to the Past: An Autobiography* (Canada: Fitzhenry and Whiteside Ltd, 1982), pp. 267–8.

2. Pagan Kennedy, *The Dangerous Joy of Dr. Sex and Other True Stories* (Santa Fe: Santa Fe Writers project, 2008), pp. 8, 9.

3. Herbert Read, *Poetry and Anarchism* (London: Faber and Faber, 1938), p. 79.

4. Alex Comfort, *Tribune*, 9, 16 April 1943.

5. David Edgerton, *Warfare State: Britain, 1920–1970* (Cambridge: Cambridge University Press, 2006).

6. Nicolas Walter, 'Anarchism in Print Yesterday and Today', in David E. Apter and James Joll (eds), *Anarchism Today* (London and Basingstoke: Macmillan, 1971), p. 132.

7. Alex Comfort, *Sex in Society* (London: Gerald Duckworth, 1963), p. 12.

8. Adam Piette, *Imagination at War: British Fiction and Poetry 1939–1945* (London and Basingstoke: Papermac/Macmillan, 1995), p. 76.

9. A. C. Grayling, *Among the Dead Cities* (London: Bloomsbury Publishing, 2006), pp. 194, 195.

10. Letter to *Times*, 17 April 1941, quoted in Grayling, *Among the Dead Cities*, p. 179.

11. Grayling, *Among the Dead Cities*, p. 179.

12. Vera Brittain, *Seed of Chaos* (London, 1944). Published for the Bombing Restriction Committee by New Vision Press, quoted by Grayling, *Among the Dead Cities*, p. 200.

13. R. N. Currey, *Poets of the 1939–1945 War* (London: Longmans, Green & Co Ltd., 1967), p. 8.

14. Currey, *Poets of the 1939–1945 War*, pp. 46–7.

15. Warren French (ed.), *The Forties: Fiction, Poetry, Drama* (Deland, FL, Everett/Edwards, 1969), p. 27.

16. Currey, *Poets of the 1939–1945 War*, pp. 46–7.

17. Linda M. Shires, *British Poetry of the Second World War* (London and Basingstoke: Macmillan, 1985), p. 26.

18. Shires, *British Poetry of the Second World War*, p. 24.

19. Piette, *Imagination at War*, p. 44.

20. J. F. Hendry and H. Treece (eds), *The Crown and the Sickle* (London: P. S. King and Staples Limited, 1945), p. 10.

21. Alex comfort, *The Power House* (London: Routledge, 1944).

22. Piette, *Imagination at War*, pp. 2, 4.

23. Edgerton, *Warfare State: Britain, 1920–1970*, pp. 292, 1, 13, 287, 13.

24. Piette, *Imagination at War*, pp. 2, 4.

25. Angus Calder, *The Myth of the Blitz* (London: Jonathan Cape, 1991) p. 43.

26. David Cesarani, 'Lacking in Conviction: British War Crimes Policy and National Memory of the Second World War', pp. 27–44, in Martin Evans and Ken Lunn (eds) *War and Memory in the Twentieth Century* (Oxford: Berg, 1997,) pp. 27, 28, 36.

27. Alex Comfort, 'War Criminals', Correspondence, *Tribune*, 6 Oct 1944.

28. Cesarani, 'Lacking in Conviction', pp. 27, 28, 36.

29. Richard Church, re. *Powerhouse, John O'London's Weekly*, 6 Oct 1944.

30. Shires notes this in *British Poetry of the Second World War*, p. 31.

31. D. H. Lawrence, 'Apocalypse' (1930), pp. 59–149 in D. H. Lawrence (ed. Mara Kalnins) *Apocalypse and the Writing on Revelation* (Cambridge: Cambridge University Press, 1980), p. 92.

32. Frederick Carter, 'Introduction' to D. H. Lawrence *The Dragon of the Apocalypse* (1930), in D. H. Lawrence, *Apocalypse and the Writing on Revelation*, p. 54.

33. Herbert Read, 'Surrealism and the Romantic Principle' (1936), reprinted in *Selected Writings* (London: Faber and Faber, 1963), p. 282.

34. Herbert Read, 'The New Romantic School' (1942), *The Listener* (23 April), p. 533, quoted in Shires *British Poetry of the Second World War*, p. 29.

35. Vera Brittain, *Seed of Chaos*, quoted in Grayling *Among the Dead Cities*, p. 182.

36. Morton D. Paley *Apocalypse and Millennium in English Romantic Poetry* (Oxford: Oxford University Press, 1999), pp. 22, 112, 242.

37. Christopher Rowland, 'Upon Whom the Ends of the Ages have Come': Apocalyptic and the Interpretation of the New Testament', pp. 38–57, in Malcolm Bull (ed.), *Apocalypse Theory and the Ends of the World* (Oxford: Wiley-Blackwell, 1995) p. 56.

38. Comfort, 'Art and Social Responsibility: Lectures on the Ideology of Romanticism', (1946), reproduced in David Goodway (ed.), *Writings against Power and Death. The Anarchist Articles and Pamphlets of Alex Comfort* (London: Freedom Press, 1994), p. 57.

39. Comfort, 'Peace and Disobedience', *Peace News* Pamphlet, p. 80.

40. Comfort, 'Peace and Disobedience', p. 31.

41. Obidiah Hornbrooke, Letter to an American Visitor, *Tribune*, 4 June 1943.

42. Rowland, 'Upon Whom the Ends of the Ages have Come', p. 56.

43. George Orwell, 'As One Combatant to another (a letter to "Obadiah Hornbooke"), *Tribune*, 18 June 1943.

44. Alex Comfort, *On This Side Nothing* (London: Routledge and Kegan Paul Ltd., 1949), p. 145.

45. Alex Comfort, 'Bombing Policy', *Tribune*, 2 April 1943.

46. Christopher Burdon *The Apocalypse in England Revelation Unravelling, 1700–1834* (Basingstoke: Macmillan, 1997), p. 2.

47. Rowland, 'Upon Whom the Ends of the Ages have Come', p. 46.

48. Malcolm Bull, 'On Making Ends Meet', pp. 1–17 in Malcolm Bull (ed.), *Apocalypse Theory and the Ends of the World*, p. 6.

49. Rowland, 'Upon Whom the Ends of the Ages have Come', p. 46.

50. Bernard McGinn, *The End of the World and the Beginning of Christendom*, pp. 58–89 in Malcolm Bull (ed.), *Apocalypse Theory and the Ends of the World*, p. 60.

51. Comfort, *Art and Social Responsibility* (London: Falcon Press, 1946), p. 20.

52. Comfort, *Art and Social Responsibility*, p. 21.

53. Comfort, *Art and Social Responsibility*, p. 20.

54. Comfort, *Art and Social Responsibility*, p. 21.

55. Comfort, *Art and Social Responsibility*, p. 20.

56. Alex Comfort, *The Novel and Our Time* (London: Phoenix House Limited, 1948), pp. 8, 12.

57. Comfort, *The Novel and Our Time*, p. 19.

58. Alex Comfort, 'Art and Social Responsibility: Lectures on the Ideology of Romanticism' (1946), reproduced in Goodway (ed.), *Writings against Power and Death*, p. 65.

59. Alex Comfort, *Art and Social Responsibility*, p. 25.

60. Comfort, *Art and Social Responsibility*, p. 83.

61. Comfort, *Art and Social Responsibility*, pp. 32, 28.

62. Comfort, *Art and Social Responsibility*, p. 35.

63. Comfort, *Art and Social Responsibility*, p. 31.

64. Comfort, *Art and Social Responsibility*, p. 79.

65. Comfort, *Art and Social Responsibility*, p. 80.

66. Comfort, *Art and Social Responsibility*, pp. 27, 24.

67. Comfort, *Art and Social Responsibility*, p. 31.

68. Alex Comfort, preface to Harold Barclay, *People without Government* (London: Kahn and Averill, 1996), p. 7.

69. Comfort, *Art and Social Responsibility*, p. 23.

70. Comfort, *Art and Social Responsibility*, p. 17.

71. Alex Comfort, *The Pattern of the Future* (London: Routledge and Kegan Paul, 1949), p. 33.

72. Comfort, *The Pattern of The Future*, p. 34.

73. Alex Comfort, 'Art and Social Responsibility: Lectures on the Ideology of Romanticism' (1946), reproduced in Goodway (ed.), *Writings against Power and Death*, p. 61.

74. Alex Comfort, 'Peace and Disobedience' (1946), *Peace News* Pamphlet, reproduced in Goodway (ed.), *Writings against Power and Death*, p. 83.

75. Alex Comfort, 'October, 1944' (1944), *NOW*, reproduced in Goodway (ed.), *Writings against Power and Death*, p. 41.

76. Comfort, 'Art and Social Responsibility: Lectures on the Ideology of Romanticism', in Goodway (ed.), *Writings against Power and Death*, p. 69.

77. Alex Comfort, *The Novel and Our Time* (London: Phoenix House Limited, 1948), p. 19.

78. Comfort, *The Pattern of the Future*, p. 28.

79. Alex Comfort, 'October, 1944' (1944), *NOW*, reprinted in Goodway (ed.), *Writings against Power and Death*, p. 37.

80. Alex Comfort, 'Imagination or Reportage?' (1946), in *Readers News*, January, reproduced in Goodway (ed.), *Writings against power and Death*, pp. 91–2.

81. Alex Comfort, 'Peace and Disobedience', p. 80.

82. David Apter, 'The Old Anarchism and the New – Some Comments', in David E. Apter and James Joll (eds), *Anarchism Today*, p. 6.

83. Apter, 'The Old Anarchism and the New – Some Comments', p. 12.

84. Alex Comfort, *Sexual Behaviour in Society* (London: Gerald Duckworth and Co. Ltd., 1950, reprinted as *Sex in Society*, 1963), p. 114.

85. Comfort, *The Pattern of the Future*, p. 10.

86. Comfort, *The Pattern of the Future*, p. 9.

87. Comfort, *The Pattern of the Future*, p. 13.

88. Comfort, *The Pattern of the Future*, pp. 14–15.

89. Comfort, *The Pattern of the Future*, p. 22.

90. Comfort, *The Pattern of the Future*, p. 15.

91. Comfort, *The Pattern of the Future*, p. 52.

92. Comfort, *The Pattern of the Future*, p. 26.

93. Comfort, *The Pattern of the Future*, p. 23.

94. Jenny Teichman, *Pacifism and the Just War* (Oxford: Basil Blackwell, 1986), p. 4.

95. Martin Ceadel, *Pacifism in Britain 1914-1945* (Oxford: Clarendon Press, 1980), pp. 16–17.

96. Comfort, 'Peace and Disobedience', pp. 83–4.

97. Bertrand Russell, quoted in Caroline Moorehead, *Troublesome People. Enemies of War 1916–1986* (London: Hamish Hamilton, 1987), p. 11.

98. James Hinton, *Protests and Visions. Peace Politics in 20th Century Britain* (London: Hutchinson Radius,1989), p. viii.

99. Comfort, 'Peace and Disobedience', p. 80.

100. Ethen Mannin, *Privileged Spectator*, p. 304, quoted in Ceadel, *Pacifism in Britain 1914–1945*, p. 291.

101. Ceadel, *Pacifism in Britain 1914–1945*, p. 229.

102. Ceadel, *Pacifism in Britain 1914–1945*, p. 232.

103. Alex Comfort, 'English Poetry and the War', *Partisan Review*, March–April 1943.

104. Alex Comfort, *Tribune*, 2 April 1943.

105. George Orwell, review of Alex Comfort's *No Such Liberty*, *Adelphi*, 1941, included in Sonia Orwell and Ian Angus (eds) *The Collected Essays, Journalism and Letters of George Orwell, Volume 3* (New York: Secker & Warburg, 1968), pp. 166–7.

106. George Orwell, in D. S. Savage, George Woodcock, Alex Comfort, George Orwell 'Pacifism and the War. A Controversy' *Partisan Review* (1942), September–October, p. 419.

107. Comfort, *The Novel and Our Time*, pp. 25–6.

108. Comfort, *On This Side Nothing*, p. 135.

109. Alex Comfort, in D. S. Savage et al., 'Pacifism and the War. A Controversy', p. 417.

110. Comfort, *Art and Social Responsibility*, p. 82.

111. Alex Comfort, 'What Can We Do To Stop Them? (1951)' Speech at Public meeting organised by the London Anarchist Group, 28 March 1951, printed in *Freedom* (14 April), reproduced in Goodway (ed.), *Writings against Power and Death*, p. 137.

112. Comfort, *Art and Social Responsibility*, p. 35.

113. Derrick A. Pike, 'Conscientious Objectors in World War Two', in *The Raven: Anarchist Quarterly*, 29, vol. 8, no. 1, Spring 1995, pp. 48–9.

114. Colin Ward, quoting Randolph Bourne, 'The State' (1919), in 'The Awkward Question', *Freedom*, 17 August 1957.

115. Herbert Read, 'A statement', *Freedom*, 17 January 1953, reprinted in David Goodway (ed.), *Herbert Read. A One-Man Manifesto and Other Writings for Freedom Press* (London: Freedom Press, 1994) p. 205.

116. Herbert Read, *Poetry and Anarchism* (London: Faber and Faber, 1938), pp. 120, 119.

117. Comfort, *Art and Social Responsibility*, p. 85.

118. Comfort, *On This Side Nothing*, p. 145.

119. Comfort, *Art and Social Responsibility*, p. 30.

120. Comfort, 'Peace and Disobedience', p. 84.

121. Alex Comfort, 'An Anarchist View: The Political Relevance of Pacifism' (1945), *Peace News* (7 December), reproduced in Goodway (ed.), *Writings against power and Death*, pp. 50–1.

122. Comfort, 'Peace and Disobedience', p. 80.

123. Comfort, 'An Anarchist View: The Political Relevance of Pacifism', p. 49.

124. Alex Comfort, 'Social Responsibility in Science and Art' (1951), BBC talk, published as a *Peace News* Pamphlet (1952), and in *Freedom* (1 and 8 December, 1951), reproduced in Goodway (ed.), *Writings against Power and Death*, p. 141.

125. Alex Comfort, 'Criminal Lunacy Exposed' (1945), *War Commentary*, (25 August), reproduced in Goodway (ed.), *Writings against Power and Death*, p. 49.

126. Teichman, *Pacifism and the Just War*, p. 5.

127. Ceadel *Thinking about Peace and War*, p. 143.

128. Alex Comfort, *Tribune*, 9, 16 April, 1943.

129. Alex Comfort, 'An Anarchist View: The Political Relevance of Pacifism', p. 49.

130. Alex Comfort, 'Indiscriminate'. Correspondence, *The New Statesman and Nation*, 11 August 1945.

131. Alex Comfort, 'Napalm', Published by Science for Peace (London, 1952), p. 7.

132. Alex Comfort, letter to the *Times*, 8 July 1952, re. Napalm Bombs.

133. Alan Antliff, *Anarchy and Art: From the Paris Commune to the Fall of the Berlin Wall* (Vancouver: Arsenal Pulp Press, 2007), pp. 183–6.

134. Nicholas Walter, quoted in Goodway (ed.), *Writings against Power and Death*, p. 15.

135. Richard Taylor, *Against the Bomb. The British Movement 1958–1965* (Oxford: Clarendon Press, 1988), p. 248.

136. Taylor, *Against the Bomb. The British Movement 1958–1965*, p. 137.

137. *Freedom*, 9 Jan. 1960, quoted in Taylor, *Against the Bomb. The British Movement 1958–1965*, p. 142.

138. David Stafford, 'Anarchists in Britain Today', in David E. Apter and James Joll (eds), *Anarchism Today*, p. 87.

139. David Widgery *The Left in Britain 1956–1968* (Harmondsworth: Penguin, 1976), p. 110.

140. Comfort, 'What Can we Do to Stop Them?', reproduced in Goodway (ed.), *Writings against Power and Death*, p. 138.

141. Alex Comfort, 'The Duty to Rebel', in David Widgery, *The Left in Britain 1956–1968*, pp. 115–16.

142. Stafford 'Anarchists in Britain Today', in Apter and Joll (eds) *Anarchism Today*, p. 99.

143. David Goodway *Anarchist Seeds beneath the Snow* (Liverpool: Liverpool University Press, 2006), p. 251.

144. Colin Ward, 'The Future of the Committee of 100: An Anarchist View', *Peace News*, 26 January 1962.

145. Nicholas Walter, 'Direct Action and the New Pacifism', *Anarchy*, 13 March, 1962, and 'Disobedience and the New Pacifism', *Anarchy*, 14, April, 1962, and 'The Committee of 100 and Anarchism', *Anarchy*, 52, June, 1965, referenced in Taylor, *Against the Bomb. The British Movement 1958–1965*, pp. 247–8.

146. Comfort, *Sexual Behaviour in Society*, p. 43.

147. A Physician (Alex Comfort), 'Must we Deal with the BMA?', *Tribune*, 27 April 1945.

148. Alex Comfort, Oxford Talk on Sexual Ethics, Reported in *The Oxford Mail*, 31 May 1947, under the heading 'Urban Life "Barbaric"'.

149. Alex Comfort 'Conscription', *Tribune*, 15 November 1946, Alex Comfort, 'Medical aspects of Marriage Guidance' (Medical Publication, c. June 1947).

150. Alex Comfort, 'Keep Endless Watch' (c. 1949), *Readers News*, reproduced in Goodway (ed.), *Writings against Power and Death*, p. 117.

151. Comfort, *Art and Social Responsibility*, p. 83.

152. Comfort, *The Novel and Our Time*, p. 12.

153. Comfort, 'Criminal Lunacy Exposed', p. 49, and Comfort, 'An Anarchist View: The Political Relevance of Pacifism', reproduced in Goodway (ed.), *Writings against Power and Death*, p. 50.

154. Alex Comfort, 'Psychopaths in Power' (1950), *Freedom* (14 October), reproduced in Goodway (ed.), *Writings against Power and Death*, p. 123.

155. Comfort, *Art and Social Responsibility*, p. 83.

156. Alex Comfort, *Authority and Delinquency in the Modern State* (London: Routledge and Kegan Paul, 1950), p. 46.

157. Alex Comfort, 'The Individual and World Peace' (1954), *Resistance* (New York, June), reproduced in Goodway (ed.), *Writings against Power and Death*, pp. 151–2.

158. Comfort, *Authority and Delinquency*, p. ix.

159. Comfort, 'Psychopaths in Power', p. 124.

160. Alex Comfort, 'The Right Thing to do'(1948), BBC talk, December 1948, published as a *Peace News* Pamphlet and in *Freedom* (24 December 1948), reproduced in Goodway (ed.), *Writings against power and Death*, p. 112.

161. Comfort, *The Pattern of the Future*, pp. 39–40.

162. Comfort, *The Pattern of the Future*, pp. 39–40.

163. Alex Comfort, 'The Right Thing to do', p. 112.

164. Alex Comfort, 'An Exposition of Irresponsibility' (1943), *Partisan Review* (October), reprinted in Goodway (ed.), *Writings against Power and Death*, p. 35.

165. Alex Comfort, *Sex in Society*, p. 48.

166. Alex Comfort, 'The Kinsey Report' (1948), *Freedom*, (1 May), reproduced in Goodway (ed.), *Writings against Power and Death*, p. 100.

167. Comfort, *Sex in Society*, p. 15.

168. Comfort, *Sex in Society*, p. 128.

169. Comfort, *Sex in Society*, p. 12.

170. Alex Comfort, *Nature and Human Nature* (London: Weidenfeld and Nicolson, 1966), p. 182.

171. Comfort, *Sex in Society*, p. 155.

172. Comfort, *Sex in Society*, p. 155.

173. Arthur E. Salmon, *Alex Comfort* (Boston: Twayne Publishers, 1978), pp. 17–18.

4

Colin Ward and the Future
of British Anarchism

Colin Ward © East Anglian Daily Times, Evening Star & Associated Papers, Ipswich

Introduction

At the end of December 1944, Special Branch officers led by Detective Inspector Whitehead searched the belongings of soldiers in various parts of the country, hunting for evidence of anarchist subversion in the military. A reluctant young conscript, Colin Ward, was subjected to such a search at Stromness in Orkney. He wrote of the experience to Lilian Wolfe, an important figure in the Freedom Press circle:

> Whitehead drew my attention to the article 'All Power to the Soviets' in the November *War Commentary*, and to the duplicated Freedom Press forces Letter of about the same date, and asked if I had read them. I said 'Yes' . . . He asked what conclusions I drew from these two articles in conjunction, and whether I considered them an incitement to mutiny. I gave a non-committal reply.[1]

Ward was subsequently called as a witness for the prosecution during the trial of the Freedom Press anarchists in 1945, to establish that the offending material had been received by him, and to ascertain the degree to which he had been influenced by its content. He insisted in their defence that he had not been radicalized by the material. The truth, of course, was that he most certainly had been. 'My own marginal part in the proceedings', he wrote, many years later, 'brought me a rich reward. The defendants became my closest and dearest friends.'[2] Through his involvement with the Freedom Press, and subsequent independent publishing career, Colin Ward became one of the most calmly forceful British voices in the anarchist canon. He is also an important source of inspiration for pluralist and mutualist social movements. Mutualism in political and social ideas aims to promote mutual organizations to meet social needs, including mutual insurance systems and mutual funds. In economic terms mutualism grows out of anarchist schools of thought, originating in the writings of Pierre-Joseph Proudhon, who propounded a labour theory of value whereby the exchange of goods was strictly based on the direct equivalence of the labour time invested in their production. Mutualism also makes a virtue of the pluralism of human life, something Ward celebrates. Political and social pluralism of the kind celebrated by Ward, which he referenced using the work of André Gorz, recognizes the co-existence of various ways of working, producing and living, according to the lived experience and aspirations of real people. This perspective is something that classical Marxist doctrine has traditionally dismissed as petit-bourgeois individualism. Conversely, Ward celebrates the diversity of private human lives and 'all those freedoms which people actually value'.[3] Through his enthusiasm for various historical and contemporary examples of mutualist practice, such as food co-operatives, credit unions, tenant self-management, and Local Exchange Trading Systems (LETS), Ward highlighted the direct link between anarchist political thought and the plurality of mutualist traditions in the British context.

With disarmingly effective gentleness, he showed his readers the extent of the damage done to the flourishing of ordinary human life by the wars and social policies of the British state. More importantly, Ward aligned anarchism with the informal habits and traditions by means of which marginalized groups traditionally protest and survive in hierarchical societies. These traditions were for Ward a model of what a mutually produced social order could look like. In line with this, he took as his definition of anarchism the opening lines of the article on anarchism that Kropotkin wrote for the *Encyclopedia Britannica* in 1905, in which he identified anarchism as:

> . . . the name given to a principle or theory of life and conduct under which society is conceived without government – harmony in such society being obtained, not by submission to law, or by obedience to any authority, but by free agreements concluded between the various groups, territorial and professional, freely constituted for the sake of production and consumption, as also for the satisfaction of the infinite variety of needs and aspirations of a civilised being.

As Alex Comfort put this idea, in his own terms, 'civilisation goes on, and personally responsible action goes on within and in opposition to the structure of organised societies'.[4] Ward was heavily influenced by Comfort's call, in *Authority and Delinquency in the Modern State*, published in 1950, for anarchism to become a kind of libertarian sociology, drawing on the evidence offered by sociological research regarding self-regulating patterns of social order in order to vindicate anarchist conclusions. As we have seen, Comfort's own scientific background led him to draw on the fields of sociology and psychology as empirical grounds for his anarchism. His call for an evidence-based, pragmatic defence of anarchism came to be most strongly answered in Ward's editorship of the journal *Anarchy*, established in 1961.

Ward argued that the already existing practices of voluntary association and mutual aid showed the utopian anarchist the means and tools available, not for direct warfare with the state, but for a kind of insidious guerrilla confrontation with its effects. This was in the spirit of one of Ward's favourite quotations, from the work of Gustav Landauer, 'The state is not something which can be destroyed by a revolution, but is a condition, a certain relationship between human beings, a mode of human behaviour; we destroy it by contracting other relationships, by behaving differently.'[5] Thus, from the apocalypse wrought by the 'warfare state' as it was ferociously depicted by Alex Comfort, emerged the 'here and now' populist utopia of spontaneous civilian face-to-face community-building as warmly portrayed by Colin Ward. The overriding concern of his career was the aim to forge a close correspondence between anarchist political ideas and contemporary debates and problems. '[T]he historians wrote that anarchism finally died when Franco's troops entered Barcelona in 1939', noted Ward. He countered the historians' claim with one of his own, arguing that 'Anarchism, instead of being a romantic historical by-way, . . . [is] an attitude to human organisation which is more relevant today that it ever seemed in the past.'[6] In line with his aims in this respect, his work in promoting mutualist and Do-it-Yourself (DiY) approaches to social and political change has had an impact well beyond strictly anarchist social movements.

Ward's anarchism was a response to wartime and post-war social administration. During the Second World War, prior to his conscription, Ward worked in the Ilford Borough Engineer's office where he developed his strong and abiding dislike for the governmental mentality behind council housing. Consequently, years later, in an interview with David Goodway he was to claim that 'as anarchists, we deplore the statist, bureaucratic version of socialism that the Fabian Old Gang bequeathed to Britain.'[7] During the war he came into contact with the Freedom Press anarchists and became a regular contributor to the anarchist publication *Freedom*. From 1947, Ward was on the editorial board of *Freedom* and in 1961 he established and edited the monthly journal *Anarchy* for the Freedom Press. After his training as an architect he worked for Sidney Caulfield, who had been articled to John Loughborough Pearson and taught by Edward Johnson, Eric Gill and W. R. Lethaby and was thus a direct link to the Arts and Crafts Movement. Ward also followed a career as a teacher from 1964–71. He combined these interests when in 1971 he became education officer for the Town and Country Planning Association (TCPA), founded by Ebenezer Howard as the Garden City Association, and edited their journal, *The Bulletin of Environmental Education*. Throughout the 1960s and 1970s Ward allied himself with movements in schooling, housing, industry and a whole variety of community organizations. Always this was in the spirit of highlighting the already existing anarchist tendencies within society and emphasizing the constructive, pragmatic approach to change that he attributed to anarchism.

While still working within the *Freedom* circle, Ward developed as a more prominent figure in the 1970s and 1980s. As part of the more mainstream appeal that Ward's journal *Anarchy* brought to the Freedom Press, and the interest in his ideas outside anarchist circles, he began to contribute regularly to other publications, most notably *New Society*. In 1978 he was invited to become a regular contributor to the full-page 'Stand' column. This, alongside the first few titles in what would become a consistent stream of books on a wide range of subjects, established Ward as an important figure in British social and political commentary. In the 1980s and 1990s Ward's ideas helped shape a new approach in protest politics. The edited volumes *DiY Culture* (1998) and *Richer Futures* (1999) pay tribute to his influence on direct action and DiY approaches to social change. Ward drew on the anarchist tradition as the theoretical framework for his ideas, utilizing its traditional emphases on individuality, mutual aid and federation. He also utilized and enriched some of the distinctive twentieth-century developments of the anarchist tradition, including the characteristic overlap between individualist and communitarian concerns, and between anarchist and utopian thinking. His ideas contributed to the importance of self-development within the anarchist tradition. Ward's editorship of *Anarchy* gave him the intellectual space to update British anarchism with contemporary sources, and to highlight its relevance using modern applications. At the same time, for Ward, anarchism in the modern era was the expression of older British libertarian socialist traditions. This view challenges the perception of anarchism as unrelated to embedded ideological tradition. This is especially relevant in the British context where anarchism has been treated as a predominantly continental phenomenon. With its characteristic preoccupations with land, the relationship between town and country, its non-conformist sources and its romantic roots, Ward's anarchism demonstrated a strong British character. Ward approached anarchism from a background of architecture, town planning, the Garden City movement and the Arts and Crafts tradition. These influences fed into his brand of idealistic and constructive radicalism.

Ward developed thematic and conceptual affinities between utopian styles of political imagining and anarchist philosophical approaches. These affinities fed into a unique and invigorating approach to political change which emphasized pragmatic and piecemeal programmes of change as well as maintaining the commitment to idealized conceptualizations of freedom and equality. Ward's utilization of utopian currents of thought fed into a significant area of his contemporary influence, the direct action and DiY approach to radical activity. Both utopian and anarchist traditions have been represented as archaic and dormant. The relationship between them has been characterized as a shared extreme and unwieldy idealism concerning the future. Emphasizing the relationship in Ward's ideas between anarchist and utopian traditions of thought highlights a unique view of social change and a different perspective on the nature of political utopianism. Ward's anarchist utopianism rests on an alternative set of understandings of the relationship between action and ideals, and the relationship between the present and the future. His perspective presents a proactive approach to the here-and-now and also emphasizes the efficacy of such a focus for the attainment of future-oriented social goals. Ward drew an idealistic but specifically non-revolutionary picture of anarchist social change. This was fuelled by some of the influences on which he drew, which included architectural and planning traditions of thought, and working-class mutualist practices. Implicit in Ward's perspective was the assertion that mutual aid and self-help were a much more fundamental part of the actual functioning of human societies than mainstream political thought has been prepared to acknowledge. As such, Ward was deeply interested in oral histories, informal traditions and marginal movements, the hidden transcripts of human social life. His central commitment, however, was to installing anarchism on the mainstream ideological agenda.

In the contexts in which his work has been recognized, Ward is regarded as an important and dynamic intellectual source. In the wider arena of political ideology his impact on twentieth-century approaches to political activity has been less well acknowledged. This has served to reinforce the erroneous under-emphasis on the role of anarchist political theory in the twentieth century, especially in the British context. Ward's writing challenges conventional interpretations of anarchism as a violent, impractical and isolated ideological tradition. It also challenges the traditional division of anarchism into either exclusively individualistic or communitarian strands. The individualist notion of self-help and the more communitarian emphasis on mutual aid combined comfortably in the writing of Ward to form the underpinning for his notion of freedom as socially responsible autonomy. Ward highlighted the anarchist tradition as relevant to contemporary concerns and an appropriate approach to modern politics. Through his books, his contributions to *Freedom* and his editorship of *Anarchy* Ward developed a pragmatic, policy-oriented perspective on anarchism

and presented it as the reasonable alternative to bureaucratic state administration in the twentieth century.

The Anarchism of Colin Ward

Ward's ideas were orientated around an anarchist ideology that he pro-
claimed was 'a social philosophy based on the absence of authority'.[8]
Anarchism was for Ward the only political philosophy that supported a
configuration of anti-authoritarianism, libertarianism and socialism.
For Ward, this combination of values was necessary for the development
and survival of vibrant, self-governing communities and independent,
autonomous individuals. On this issue Ward noted: 'Herbert Read used
to say that the only *real* politics are local politics, and you can push the argument further to claim that the only real local politics are personal politics.'[9]
Ward's book *Anarchy in Action* drew on a wealth of sociological material as
evidence for the social efficacy of freedom and spontaneous organization.
In this vein, Ward argued that 'There is an order imposed by terror, there
is an order enforced by bureaucracy (with the policeman in the corridor)
and there is an order which evolves spontaneously from the fact that we
are gregarious animals capable of shaping our own destiny.'[10] The primary
goal of the book was to 'look at a variety of aspects of daily life in the light of
traditional anarchist contentions'.[11] Martin Buber's distinctions between the
'political principle' and the 'social principle' were also highly significant to
Ward's thought. Ward noted that 'One is embodied in institutions, the other
in associations.'[12] He said of these distinctions that 'The political principle
is seen in power, authority and domination, the social principle in families,
groups, unions, co-operative bodies and communities.'[13] In Ward's interpretation the social principle was represented in voluntary organization and
grassroots association. Anarchism as an ideology embodied this principle
because it advocated 'an extended network of individuals and groups,
making their own decisions, [and] controlling their own destiny'.[14]

Ward was to a significant extent working within a framework of ideas
established by Kropotkin in *Mutual Aid*. Ward humbly remarked that
his book *Anarchy in Action* was 'simply an extended, updating footnote
to Kropotkin's *Mutual Aid*'.[15] He also considered Proudhon to be a pertinent figure, stating that his famous invective against political rule would
be 'perfectly comprehensible to any citizen who steps out of line in any of
the totalitarian regimes of the Right or Left that today govern the greater
part of the world'.[16] In *Anarchy in Action*, Ward's most important work of
anarchist political theory, he wrote that 'These famous names of anarchism

recur in this book, simply because what they wrote speaks, as the Quakers say, to our condition.'[17] Central to Kropotkin's *Mutual Aid* was the idea that evolution was the result of the development of mutual aid within a species rather than hierarchy and competition. The argument of both Kropotkin and Ward was that anarchism was in keeping with existing tendencies within nature and society. As Ward argued in one of his most characteristic anarchist statements, 'once you begin to look at human society from an anarchist point of view you discover that the alternatives are already there, in the interstices of the dominant power structure.'[18] This led the way for Ward's advocacy of the hidden traditions of self-help within British working-class movements. In *Anarchy in Action* Ward argued that individuals were naturally co-operative and that current societies and institutions, however authoritarian, capitalist and individualist, survived only because of the real subterranean forces of mutual aid and voluntary association. Thus, for Ward, 'Anarchists are people who make a social and political philosophy out of the natural and spontaneous tendency of humans to associate together for their mutual benefit.'[19] Like Kropotkin, Ward did not focus on revolutionary organization but emphasized the ongoing state of struggle between authoritarian and libertarian tendencies. His emphasis in this respect was such that he effectively wrote out any notion of climactic revolution from his perspective in favour of an emphasis on the piecemeal activity of cooperative groups. Ward differed from his Freedom Press colleagues on this. His difference in emphasis was, in part, to be explained by his background in architecture, town planning, the Garden City movement and utopian traditions. These influences were all threads in the pragmatic idealism that was characteristic of Ward, expressed in the statement that 'If you want to build a free society, the parts are all at hand.'[20]

Conscription brought Ward into contact with anarchism in the latter years of the Second World War. When Ward was 18 he was sent to Glasgow, at that time a city with a significant indigenous anarchist movement, and he attended the anarchist meetings held above a local pub. From there Ward submitted his first article for the radical paper *War Commentary* (the wartime name for *Freedom*, the anarchist newspaper set up by Peter Kropotkin and Charlotte Wilson in 1886). In a 1968 interview for BBC Radio 3 entitled 'Conversations about Anarchism', a handful of contemporary anarchists, including Ward, discussed the significance of World War Two in their conversions to anarchism. One of these interviewees, Donald Rooum, traced his anarchism to a period of imprisonment as a conscientious objector and the influence of a copy of *War Commentary* he read while on a Government potato-picking scheme in 1944. Another,

Bill Christopher, identified his disillusionment with the Labour Party and the ILP over German rearmament and the hydrogen bomb as the root of his anarchist politics. Ward himself had this to add: 'I became an anarchist when I was a soldier in the army. I think that's enough to make anyone an anarchist.'[21] He later wrote, supporting the anarchist affinity with pacifism: 'In the nineteenth century T. H. Green remarked that war is the expression of the "imperfect" State, but he was quite wrong. War is the expression of the State in its most perfect form: it is its finest hour.'[22] There was, however, more to Ward's wartime contact with anarchism. In 1945 as the war was drawing to a close, the four editors of *War Commentary*, Vernon Richards, Marie Louise Berneri, John Hewetson and Philip Sansom, were prosecuted for conspiring to cause disaffection in the armed forces. The Director of Public Prosecutions charged the editors of *War Commentary* under Defence Regulations for attempting to 'undermine the affections of members of His Majesty's Forces'. Ward was among four servicemen subscribers called to give evidence for the prosecution and along with the other three he testified in support of the editors. Three of the four accused were imprisoned for nine months. Ward's experience of governmental authority and the growth of the British state during and after the Second World War was a significant catalyst in his development of anarchism beyond its eighteenth- and nineteenth-century sources. The war era established Ward as a regular contributor to *Freedom*. In the following year, serving in the South of England, Ward reported on the post-war squatters movements that had emerged in response to housing shortages in nine articles for *Freedom* and upon discharge in 1947 Ward joined the editorial group. Ward regarded the squatters movement, which saw ordinary working-class families take over and adapt disused military bases, as an example of the human tendency for direct and cooperative self-help, and thus a key model of 'anarchy in action'. His perspective on the squatters' movements was key to what was distinctive about his approach to anarchism, and for a time his colleagues at the Freedom Press were not sympathetic to the extensions and revisions he was making to the tradition.

In the 1940s, *Freedom* enjoyed relative success, drawing regular contributions from well-known figures and increasing its publication from fortnightly to weekly. Dwight Macdonald headed a parallel wartime anarchist turn in American left-wing journalism in the journal *politics,* which Ward admired and which brought the ideas of American anarchist Paul Goodman to his attention.[23] In the late 1950s and 1960s, anarchism achieved a measure of renewed popularity and Ward began to gain status as a radical public commentator. In 1961 Ward was given editorship of a new monthly journal,

Anarchy, in which to exercise his view of anarchism as a reasonable and rational ideological position, and to give anarchist propagandists 'the chance to stop and think'.[24] This was important for the formulation of his pragmatic, non-revolutionary conception of social change. Other members of the Freedom Press Group maintained a more traditional anarchist perspective, looking back to the workers' and Soldiers' councils of the Russian Revolution and the collectives of the Spanish Civil War. They initially considered Ward a diluted, revisionist kind of anarchist. It was not until Ward had already published a book on the subject of housing with the Architectural Press in 1974 that the Freedom Press considered publishing his work in book form. He in turn would state in defence of his perspective that 'One of the weaknesses of the anarchism movement throughout the world, it seems to me, is a preoccupation with its own past.'[25] Interviewed for BBC Radio in 1968, Ward stated: 'In *Anarchy* what I try to do is to find ways of relating a way-out ideology like anarchism to contemporary life and to find those positive applications which people are looking for . . . What I would like anarchism to have is intellectual respectability.'[26] The emergence of *Anarchy* coincided with the rise of the New Left and the nuclear disarmament movement and it published a wide range of articles concerned with these developments. Ward was concerned to frame anarchism as a relevant, constructive approach to contemporary problems. The effect of this immediate and imminent approach to an ideology so at odds with established social and political assumptions is far from quiescent or unchallenging.

The direction Ward took in *Anarchy* with themes like housing and squatting, progressive education and sociological topics, provided him with a much wider audience in the 1960s. In 1969 he wrote: '*Anarchy* has tried . . . to take it for granted that anarchism is in the mainstream of modern social ideas, and to address itself to the outside world rather than the in-group. This has involved going outside the usual circle of contributors to the anarchist press.'[27] He intended *Anarchy* to be an intellectual examination of anarchist theory and ideas. As he put it, he was concerned to '. . . put anarchism back into the intellectual bloodstream, into the field of ideas which are taken seriously.'[28] Anarchism for Ward was not a 'way-out' idea and this gave his work its underlying energetic optimism. He wanted to point out the anarchist values inherent in the existing practices of 'normal', 'practical' people: '. . . if you have a revolutionary ideology in a non-revolutionary situation, what exactly do you do? If you've got a point of view which everybody considers to be way out, do you act up to it, or do you lean over backwards to show how normal and practical your ideas are? What I would like anarchism to have is intellectual respectability.'[29]

Kropotkin's *Mutual Aid* charted the destruction of the social institutions that embodied the human tendency for mutual aid by the growth of the nation–state. Ward updated this critique of statehood with his attack on the principles of state welfare. State welfare in Britain, he argued, swept away the working-class self-help and mutual aid welfare organizations that preceded it. Throughout his work Ward saw anarchism as part of a British libertarian tradition of socialism. His anarchism was in part a response to the post-war rise in Britain of a municipal, state-directed form of socialism. Ward reflected that when this form of socialism had achieved power in Britain it created 'Monopoly capitalism with a veneer of social welfare as a substitute for social justice'.[30] The state welfare tradition as he saw it was a powerful agent of social authority, locking individuals into dependent relationships with centralized government agencies. Conversely, the imminent, self-help, self-governed tradition of mutual aid grew from and developed human autonomy and social responsibility. Ward attacked the Marxist critique of the self-help tradition, specifically in relation to housing. He summarized this critique as follows: self-help housing increases the amount of unpaid labour in society, devalorizes labour power and lowers pressure for wage increases by excluding housing costs from wages. It also reduces the need for public subsidies to housing since the reproduction of labour is done by the efforts and costs of labour itself. Further, self-owned housing is economically expansionary for consumption demands, incorporates people into the mentality of the petty bourgeoisie, isolates people from each other and their discontent, and inhibits collective actions and solidarity. Ward responded to this critique with vehemence: 'Alas these comments illustrate what a grotesque distorting mirror Marxist economic analysis applies to reality.'[31] He takes up these themes again when he writes about the self-help activities embedded in domestic and unofficial relationships, which he termed the 'informal economy'. The Marxist critique of self-help activity, as it was identified by Ward, ignores the mutual and reciprocal relationships in the private and domestic spheres that actually make human life possible, even in the formal economic sphere. For example, a pertinent point recently made by Alvin Tofler in a question put to Fortune 500 executives, *Fortune* magazine's annual list of the top 500 U.S. companies, highlights the importance of the 'informal economy'. Tofler provocatively asked this group of business leaders 'How productive would your work force be if they were not toilet trained?'[32] Recent attempts to quantify the value of productive labour in the U.S. 'informal economy' calculate that they exceed at least 40 per cent of the GDP. Similarly, a calculation made in 2002 of the economic value of the unpaid labor in the United States that keeps elderly individuals out of residential care exceeded $250 billion dollars.[33] The point is that reciprocal family and neighbourhood relationships of mutual aid and self-help *are* economic activity, in the broadest sense. Ward also wondered rhetorically how self-help activity could reduce the non-existent wages of the very poor, especially in the shanty-town fringes of modern third-world cities, or similarly how this kind of activity could affect their position in a labour market in which they have no significance. As well as his libertarian objection to council housing, Ward also argued that state welfare as a whole enlarged social inequality. The middle classes benefited more from the public education system and other public benefits and the working classes paid more into social services than they drew out. Thus: 'The great council house myth was one of those illusions of the early post-war years – along with the folklore of the welfare state.'[34] Ward considered the post-war socialist support for state-administered welfare a grave mistake of the British left. In this he was reopening the terms of the debate that heralded the very emergence of 'social policy' as a distinct field of state activity and academic enquiry in Britain with the publication of the 'majority' and 'minority' reports of the Royal Commission on the Poor Law in 1909. The 'minority report' set the pattern for welfare in Britain realized after 1945. At this point, according to Ward, 'The great tradition of working-class self-help and mutual aid was written off, not just as irrelevant, but as an actual impediment, by the political and professional architects of the welfare state.'[35]

Ward was aware of a firm connection between radical intellectualism and anarchism in the British context. In particular he maintained an enduring interest in the works of George Orwell, setting out the 'paradoxical links between Orwell and anarchism' in a series of articles for *Freedom* in 1955. In the first instance, the radical literary sympathy for anarchism was clearly illustrated by intellectual responses to the Freedom Press raids. The 1945 establishment attack on and prosecution of the *Freedom* anarchists had been presaged towards the end of 1944 when the Special Branch of Scotland Yard raided the offices of *War Commentary* and impounded membership and subscription lists. This raid evoked many protests among British intellectuals. Orwell wrote about it in *Tribune* and, along with others, including T. S. Eliot and E. M. Forster, signed a letter circulated by Herbert Read that was hostile to the police actions. Orwell regarded the prosecution of the anarchists as an ill-portent for the fate of peacetime freedom of speech. His concerns about this and other attacks on the anarchist left and his dissatisfaction with the Communist-dominated National Council for Civil Liberties led him accept the role of vice chairman of the Freedom Defence Committee of which Herbert Read was chairman and George Woodcock was secretary. During the war Orwell had bitterly opposed the anarchists for their pacifism and their opposition to the war effort but he nonetheless had many friends and acquaintances among the British anarchists, a sympathy fed by his experiences with anarchist and communist factions in the Spanish Civil War and by his suspicion of state strength and centralization. Ward did not claim that Orwell's instinctive anti-authoritarianism made him an anarchist, but he did point out the critical position on the British left that Orwell shared with the anarchists. He noted that on many issues, including amnesty for wartime deserters and resistance to the internment of Spanish refugees: 'Orwell and the anarchists raised their voices, and the political left as a whole remained silent.'[36] Ward quoted, as further evidence of Orwell's affinity with anarchist political concerns, his bleak warning to Western civilization: 'The autonomous individual is going to be stamped out of existence.'[37]

A collection of essays published in 1984 commemorating Orwell's novel included a contribution by Ward entitled 'Big Brother Drives a Bulldozer'. In his attack on corporate approaches to planning and social housing, Ward highlighted Orwell's themes of nostalgia, environmental decay, the betrayal of ordinary human aspirations by the educated classes and the superiority of the values by which poor people survive. Ward used Orwell's novel to present his own reflections on town planning; the butchery of inner cities by post-war redevelopment, the resultant undermining of urban communities and the death of the extrovert social life that supported the self-help and mutual aid of local poor residents. The Orwellian 'men of power' were responsible, through 'the sinister alliance between the planning industry and property developers', for what Ward termed 'the shift from a fine-grained to a coarse-grained environment'.[38] Ward interpreted the ambiguously optimistic phrase of Winston's, 'if there is hope it lies with the proles', to mean that revolutionary potential lies in the social individualism which survives in informal, marginal, unofficial activities in which people engage outside of the state in a world of friends, relatives and neighbours. Ward thus saw his anarchism as thoroughly connected to British traditions of left-wing critique.

Ward's anarchism leads us to revise a number of conventional interpretations of the anarchist tradition. Ward was concerned both with the freedom of the individual and the cohesion of social groups. He posited anarchism as an ideology which rejected states, hierarchies and centralization and

supported individuals and communities in their efforts to govern themselves. Ward also aligned libertarianism with socialism. In doing so he
eroded the dichotomy that is usually posited between individualist and
communitarian traditions of anarchism. Ward also drew a specifically
non-revolutionary picture of anarchist social change. His anarchism was
inspired at least in part by the wartime administration of Britain. Following
from this, his anarchism was also a reaction to post-war social administration, specifically welfare institutions. In this he demonstrated his view
of the modern applicability of anarchism. Not only did Ward criticize the
post-war welfare measures of the British State in the name of individual
and community independence, he also challenged the ideological tradition on which it was premised in the name of socialism. He highlighted
libertarian traditions of socialism and linked them to anarchism in the
British context. This both undermines the image of anarchism as exterior
to ideological tradition and the understanding of it as unrelated to British
political traditions.

Autonomy, Community and Freedom

Ward's socialist value system was orientated around autonomy and self-
government on individual and social levels. There is a continuity between
Ward's anarchism and traditionally British sources of libertarian socialism as identified in the classic study by W. H. Greenleaf. In the words
of Greenleaf, we can say that in the post-war era Ward attacked the
'development of the collectivist tendency' as part of 'the rearguard action
of libertarianism'.[39] It is in this sense that Ward claimed that he sought
to 'rescue socialism from itself'.[40] As part of his rejection of state-strong,
bureaucratic welfare provision in favour of self-help, mutual aid welfare
associations, Ward expounded what he called the 'social psychology of
Direct Action'.[41] In describing the post-war squatting movements that were
the response of homeless families to housing shortages in the late 1940s he
noted that those who had seized housing opportunities for themselves, for
example by moving into unused army bases, engaged in extensive activity
to make their environments habitable. Those who were later placed in
similar accommodation by local councils were inert, dependent and apathetic. Ward made the morally weighted distinction between: '[T]he state
of mind that is induced by free and independent action, and that which is
induced by dependence and inertia: the difference between people who
initiate things and act for themselves and people for whom things just
happen.'[42] This was an example of Ward's commitment to a rigorous notion

of freedom as independence, activity and personal autonomy. Ward was strongly committed to the sentiment expressed in the following quote from the work of American anarchist Paul Goodman: 'For me, the chief principle of anarchism is not freedom but autonomy, the ability to initiate a task and do it one's own way.'[43]

Ward's use of the notion of autonomy in his conception of freedom challenges one influential line of thinking about freedom. In this sense anarchism has important contributions to make to thinking about the concepts and problems of political theory. Steven Lukes identifies the concept of autonomy as one of the component features of the notion of individualism and elucidates the concept thus: '[A]n individual is autonomous to the degree to which he subjects the pressures and norms with which he is confronted to conscious and critical evaluation, and forms intentions and reaches practical decisions as the result of independent and rational reflection.'[44] This is closely related to the understanding of freedom which Isaiah Berlin identified as 'positive' liberty and which holds the following to be of central importance: 'I wish my life and decisions to depend on myself . . . I wish to be the instrument of my own, not other men's, acts of will. I wish to be a subject, not an object; to be moved by reasons, by conscious purposes, which are my own.'[45] Berlin regarded this positive understanding of liberty as ultimately totalitarian because he interpreted it as an overly proscribed view of the type of human behaviour which should be considered as expressive of freedom. Once liberty can be proscribed, and the individual can be 'forced to be free', in the famous dictum of Rousseau, then the concept has been stretched beyond what can reasonably be considered 'freedom'. Berlin argued that a 'negative' view of freedom was a more authentic view of liberty, linked as it was to the defence of an entirely unproscribed sphere of human behaviour in the private sphere. What is clear in the anarchism of Ward, however, is that the notion of autonomy remains a highly libertarian value. The development of freedom as autonomy in the individual personality depended centrally on the free and un-coerced development of the individual capacity for will and judgement, entirely undirected or manipulated by forces outside of the individual. As Lukes comments on Berlin's fears about the authoritarian consequences of a 'positive' conception of liberty: '[T]his ominous progression is neither logically compelling not in itself relevant to the consideration of the idea of the autonomy of the individual. All ideas can be put to evil uses.'[46] The anarchist view of freedom as the developed capacities of the individual self and the un-coerced experience of the individual challenges the dichotomy between positive and negative conceptions of freedom.

Ward saw individual autonomy as the necessary premise for social interaction and coordination. He perceived a firm connection between individual independence and community self-government. His understanding of freedom ran along individualist lines and he related liberty to healthy sociability. This challenges the conventional theoretical dichotomy between individualism and communitarianism. Among socialists, as Lukes points out, individualism has typically been contrasted with cooperative social order. Ward's anarchism challenged this view of individualism by linking the development of vigorous individuality with the functioning of vital, self-governing communities. Lukes's analysis of the concept of individualism is useful for understanding Ward's integration of individualist and socialist impulses. Lukes examines and defines two contrary traditions of thinking about individuality. One, he concedes, identifies it as a distinctly a-social position. Under what Lukes refers to as the French kind of understanding, of Tocqueville for example, individualism involves the apathetic withdrawal of individuals from public life into a private sphere and their isolation from one another, and a consequent weakening of social bonds. This is the notion of 'individualisme' that Durkheim identified by the twin concepts of 'anomie' and 'egoism' and the breakdown of social solidarity. It is an understanding of individuality as social and moral isolation and dissociation from social purposes. A second tradition of thinking about individuality, however, ties it to human self-development and distinctness. This is identified by Lukes as the characteristically German tradition, rooted in the romantic notions of individual uniqueness, originality and self-realization, and opposed to the uniformity and isolation generated by industrial society.[47]

This second understanding of individuality is orientated around the creative, independent freedom of the individual personality. In one direction this view of individual freedom is tied closely to a view of the healthy social life of communities. It is related to the more complex understanding of individualism that emerged within socialism, an understanding related to self-assertion and independence from authority. Charles Fourier, Lukes tells us, denied any basic opposition between individualism and socialism, while Jean Jaures argued that socialism was the logical development of individualism. In this tradition socialism was a means of furthering individualism.[48] Lukes concludes that the notion of self-development is not logically committed to an anti-social or extra-social position. Significantly, Lukes cites Kropotkin as an example of a thinker who ties individual self-development to genuine community. Ward's own view of individual freedom belongs in this tradition. Like Kropotkin, Ward identified mutual aid as a significant enabling factor in the full development of individual faculties.[49] As Lukes notes of this view of individualism, 'certain forms of self-development – such as that resulting from political participation – depend essentially on our interaction with others.'[50] Ward saw self-help and mutual aid as building strong supportive communities but also preserving autonomy, responsibility and the capacity for initiative. This is a notion of individuality and society as mutually supportive. Ward had this personal observation to add: 'I scarcely need to tell you that the most individualistic people I have known have been people who rejected ideologies of individualism, and firmly believed in communist anarchism. I don't say this as a joke but as an everyday observation.'[51] According to this view, the freedom and vitality of both individuals and social groups are threatened by the political behaviour of corporate and governmental bodies.

Urban and Rural Utopias

Historically and in terms of shared figures and themes anarchism overlaps with utopian traditions. This relationship was particularly relevant to the composition and pertinence of Ward's ideas, and to particular developments of the anarchist tradition. The overlap between anarchist and utopian approaches in his political thought has fed an ongoing utopian element in twentieth-century anarchist political thought. In Ward's work there were a number of facets to the link between anarchist concepts and traditions and utopian modes of political thought. One was his reading of Martin Buber's *Paths In Utopia*, a work which sought to identify and defend a tradition of pluralist, voluntaristic, grassroots socialism rooted in early socialist and anarchist sources. Another link with utopianism in Ward's work was his connection with the persistent utopian impulse in architecture and in town and country planning. Ward made a series of self-conscious identifications with this current of utopian thought, depicting it as the creative design of human environments. Through these connections Ward's work drew attention to utopian emphases on immediacy, agency and immanence. These served as important underpinning elements to his efforts to defend vital and dynamic conceptions of freedom. This was particularly evident in his reflections on British traditions of rural idealism and their relationship with urban utopianism.

Anarchism was for Ward a philosophy that prompted freedom-engendering responses to temporally and spatially proximate contexts. This was premised on his view that 'an anarchist society, like a seed beneath the snow . . . is always in existence'.[52] In a characteristically Wardian set of reflections, he mused: 'Suppose our future in fact lies, not with a handful of technocrats pushing buttons to support the rest of us, but with a multitude of small activities, whether by individuals or groups, doing their own thing? . . . making their own niche in the world of ordinary needs and their satisfaction. Wouldn't that be something to do with anarchism?'[53] His advocacy of active engagement with social change and the immediate physical environment formed a central component of his ideal of individual freedom and was part of the way that Ward interpreted the utopian tradition. At the root of Ward's interpretation of anarchism was the view that 'it is a description of everyday life, which operates side by side with, and in spite of, the dominant authoritarian trends of our society'.[54] Ward's utilization of utopian currents of thought, especially his conceptual and practical concerns with immediacy and proximity, supported and developed direct action and DiY approaches to social engagement and radical change in Britain.

One key component of Ward's relationship to utopianism was the influence of Martin Buber's *Paths in Utopia*. Buber featured strongly in Ward's book *Influences* in which he charted a selection of thinkers who had significantly affected his ideas. The brand of socialism presented in Buber's book provides an essential key to Ward's ideological location of anarchism as a political idea. Buber's book was a defence and restatement of the current in socialist thought attacked by Marx and Engels as 'Utopian'. Notably, it focused in particular on figures in the anarchist tradition, Proudhon, Kropotkin and Gustav Landauer, as representatives of that current. Thus, Ward described Buber's book as a 'reassertion of the anarchist tradition in socialist thought'.[55] Buber's argument in his book was that socialism had hit a dead end in following the precepts of Marxian 'Scientific' socialism and that a re-examination of the maligned utopian ideal could contribute to its reinvigoration. As he stated, 'if Socialism is to emerge from the blind-alley into which it has strayed, among other things the catchword "Utopian" must be cracked open and examined for its true content.'[56]

Buber described utopian socialism as concerned with: '[T]he various forms of co-operative society as being the most important cells for social re-structure.'[57] This drew particularly on the utopian socialist view of the universe as an orderly, integrated system and the non-antagonistic social analogy of this view, which led these thinkers to focus on association, community and cooperation. They drew on the small group experiences of village life, workshops, religious groups, friendly societies and trade clubs.[58] Thus their social theory emphasized cooperative communities, experiment, expediency, the social rather than the political aspects of organization, small-scale gradualism, peaceful change, class collaboration and a turn away from comprehensive revolution.[59] Most importantly, the utopian socialists believed that their ideal societies could be established, *without a significant transitory phase*, through constructive human agency according to reason. Buber contrasted this view with what he termed the 'eschatology' of Marxist social goals: 'The vision of rightness in Revelation is realised in the picture of a perfect time – as messianic eschatology; the vision of rightness in the Ideal is realized in the picture of a perfect space – as Utopia.'[60] These subtle distinctions between time and place as the alternative focuses of differing visions of the perfect social order are highly relevant to the intersections between utopianism and anarchism in the work of Ward. In his work utopia is an ideal of community organization of public space *in the present* as the expression of agency and association. Utopian socialism emerged from Buber's book as a pluralist and pragmatic approach. It also emerged as closely related to the thematic concerns of anarchism. Ward was strongly influenced by Buber's interpretation of the relationship between utopianism and anarchism. This built on a strong connection between Ward's anarchism and the utopian impulses of radical architectural and planning traditions.

In general terms utopianism pays consistent attention to the organization of the physical environment and planning for new communities. Accordingly, commentators have noted that 'space and place are fundamental to utopias', and that utopia is a 'spatially organized image' which applies itself to 'formal principles of organization'.[61] It is thus unsurprising to note the persistent utopian impulse in architecture and in town and country planning. Goodwin and Taylor note that 'utopian thinkers passed on some of their key ideas to planners' and that this has 'established a notion of physical design for utopia which overlaps with the literature of social and political theory.' They go on to add that 'Had town planning as a profession not developed rather separately from radical political movements such as socialism, it would probably be rather difficult to separate the two traditions today.'[62] In the twentieth century the overlap between architecture, town planning and radical social thought developed into a key current of anarchist political theory, most notably in the work of Goodman in America and Ward in Britain. Ward focused in particular on the radical importance of individual imaginative engagement with the plans and designs of urban life. In his work the radical significance of design in relation to shared physical environments developed as part of his agency-based, direct and localized approach to social activity. In defence of utopianism, he emphasized the importance for human freedom of engagement in the construction, planning and implementation of ideals in the direct and tangible sphere of public spaces and buildings. The importance of the lived environment for supporting freer individuals and stronger communities was a particularly dominant theme of Ward's work and evidence of his enduring ties to his architectural background. Involved here was a notion of planning as an activity of engagement that was central to the constructive and topical way twentieth-century anarchism interpreted the utopian tradition. It underpinned Ward's interest in ad hoc settlements, the self-building movement and his advocacy of stimulating human environments. The tradition was for Ward one which concerned individual creativity and initiative.

Ward's interest in planning was also related to his interest in romantic traditions of architecture and the utopianism of early thinkers about cities. Associates and disciples of John Ruskin and William Morris, including Philip Webb, W. R. Lethaby, Raymond Unwin and A. J. Penty developed this tradition in the period up to the First World War. The central notion was that architecture should be the expression of the pleasure of work, need and use, and not represent the division of labour underpinning industrial production. Ward absorbed this tradition and it fed into his interests in town planning and housing. An important element of this tradition in architecture and town planning for Ward was Ebenezer Howard's emphasis on the importance of land and its unearned increase in value. This was the basis on which Howard constructed the Garden City idea. The unearned increment would be secured for public rather than private uses and would support communal amenities organized by autonomous, self-governing communities. The actual ideals of self-government when it came to realizing Garden Cities were sadly undermined by the pressure to placate potential shareholders. What transpired was modelled more along the lines of the company towns of Cadbury and Lever than Howard's alternative. The spirit of Howard's original ideals, however, was the drive to fuse private responsibility and public spirit. Howard saw the new social order represented in his plans as a form of social individualism, a model of community that was neither individualistic capitalism nor collectivist socialism.[63] This was reflected in Ward's ideal conception of the individual and society as mutually dependent but under threat from public overarching systems of top-down authority. Ward's relationship to the intellectual traditions of urban utopianism helps explain his nuanced approach to the New Town idea in Britain. Ward's book *New Town, Home Town* charted the betrayal of the New Town idea while at the same time defending the much maligned post-war examples of town planning against the more ferocious of their attackers. Ward remarked:

> The saddest of all the shortcomings of the post-war New Towns programme is one of which residents are hardly aware, even though it affects their futures and the level of social goods their town can provide. This is the failure of the legislators to ensure that the 'unearned increment' in site values that is generated simply by the fact that the residents live, work and shop there, should accrue for the benefit of the town itself.[64]

Ward had a conception of land that was initially reminiscent of romantic conceptions of rural arcadia and pre-industrial social forms. Part of what Ward did in his discussion of the countryside was to reclaim this image of the rural idyll as a element of the popular imagination. Ward sought to claim the anti-urban tradition back from its reactionary image on the political right by pointing to the radical focus on the countryside and land in the work of Morris, Kropotkin and Howard. He also drew attention to the plotlands movement of the early twentieth century. The plotlands were areas of land sold off very cheaply during a period of agricultural depression. This provided the opportunity for poor city dwellers to buy land and build makeshift homes for themselves. Ward saw the plotlands movement as the expression of a deep-seated agrarian current of English revolt. Ward also interpreted the British allotment movement as a similar attempt to reclaim the use of the land that had been appropriated by enclosure. In discussing the plotlands movement in his book *Arcadia for All*, Ward described it in terms of the pioneering, raw democratic quality associated with popular movements onto the land, especially early American frontier settlements.[65] Nonetheless, a major part of Ward's response to the countryside challenged the traditional idyllic rural image. The great danger of rural romanticism, he argued, was that it precluded the imagination of urban idylls, and what he termed 'utopian courage'. Rural romanticism was thus a kind of intellectual laziness: '[A] substitute for the utopian courage of imagining what a true community, in an industrial city, might be – indeed of imagining how far community may have already been attained.'[66]

An edited volume published in 1999 entitled *Town and Country*, to which Ward contributed an essay, explored concerns with a changing society and environment, local distinctiveness, and English identities, from a range of political perspectives. The editors, Anthony Barnett and Roger Scruton, introduced the volume as the result of 'exchanges of a non-partisan kind between people from different political traditions'.[67] Even a cursory glance through this volume would however quickly betray the anti-free-market agenda that united the diverse range of thinkers included. This echoed Ward's own antagonism to market-driven conceptions of society. Ward had several challenging points to make in his contribution to this volume. First was his challenge to the mainstream images of traditional rural idioms and values. Typically, he pointed out the unofficial uses of the countryside outside recognized systems of tenure and use and the devastating blow dealt to these alternatives by enclosure. But, also typically, he blurred ideological categories by pointing out the importance of these uncharted and unregistered communities of activity as the sectors from which the industrial revolution began, and he resisted an over-romanticized nostalgia for past pre-industrial freedoms.[68]

In reclaiming the rural idyll for the popular imagination Ward was asserting the radical importance of access to land. In emphasizing the importance of urban utopianism Ward was concerned with combining the values of radical movements demanding access to land with the plurality and diversity of city life. Ward's interest in cites, utopianism, land-seeking radicalism and planning were parts of his conceptualization of freedom as composed of independence, individuality, responsibility and initiative. He utilized the perspective of Richard Sennett as part of his advocacy of city life, or rather as part of his advocacy of a certain conception of freedom and personal morality which he associated with life in the city. Sennett's core theme in his book on the city, *The Uses of Disorder*, was the notion that direct interpersonal urban negotiation and interaction engendered personal growth. This idea fed into Ward's focus on the virtues of self-responsibility, autonomy, activity, plurality and diversity. He also incorporated an understanding of the city as the unique source of the experience from which these qualities derive.

According to Sennett, the city's vast complexity, disorder and dislocation encourages the positive human values of acceptance of that disorder (the root of the mature individual personality) and the ability to shape life within it (the root of true community). These values offset the irresponsible human desire to impose predictable order through structured simplification as a means to avoid the unpredictability and discomfort of difficult social situations. This simplification involves fixing objects and understandings in advance and a disregard for the realities and experiences of actual social situations. This projection of rigid images through the hierarchically imposed design of public spaces undermines real human diversity. In the parallel effort within the individual to avoid the unknown he voluntarily limits his freedom. As we saw in an earlier chapter, the attempt by the individual to avoid 'responsibility' for his own freedom, as Comfort termed this kind of intellectual and emotional honesty, was the cause of war, totalitarianism and 'asociality'. Thus, the ideas that Ward appropriated from Sennett were already well embedded in the British anarchist tradition that Ward was working within.

In Sennet's work, the effect of imposing predictable order, in order to avoid the difficult and complicated world of social interaction and negotiation, is the withdrawal from participation in community life. The essence of urban life is its diversity and possibilities for complex experience: '. . . an anarchy that will not destroy men, but make them richer and more mature.'[69] This type of experience encourages engagement, responsibility and self-development. The following statement of his view of the utopian potential of the urban environment was indicative of Ward's appropriation of Sennett's agenda: 'The occupants have to attack the environment, to modify it and to make it their own.'[70] Like Sennett, Ward linked this concept of civic virtue developed from urban experience to the American democratic ideal. These ideals are also linked to those of Paul Goodman, especially Goodman's emphasis on the human desire to be useful, and his concern with the requisite environment for enabling children to 'grow up'. Like Goodman, Ward focused on the immediate spatial and temporal environment of human activity, and the habits of responsibility and initiative that develop in relation to immediate contexts. He was concerned with experienced reality, and the environment as a source of experience, belonging and discovery. Ward valued the responsibility, excitement, adventure and exploration that the city offered individuals. His anarchism was fundamentally concerned with the vitality of human responses to the conditions presented by their environment.

A Theory of Pragmatic Idealism

Anarchism is generally perceived as overlapping with utopianism in terms of a shared idealistic approach to change, which disregards the conditions of the present in favour of an image of a perfected future. A focus on the work of Ward illustrates that the overlap actually forms around a developing set of focuses on the immediate environment and the present. This, rather than the image of a perfected future, is the conceptual area in which anarchist and utopian traditions of thought intersect. In the work of Ward the relationship between anarchism and utopianism is based on a focus on the present expressed via emphases on the temporal and spatial immediacy of political change and an anti-determinist focus on agency. The anarchist tradition has supported and developed these present focused-themes by asserting the immanence of desirable social forms in existing social behaviour and emphasizing the importance of congruity between means and ends in strategies for political change. For Ward, anarchism was a philosophy that prompted freedom-engendering responses to temporally and spatially immediate contexts. His advocacy of active engagement with social change and the immediate physical environment formed a central component of his ideal of individual freedom. The balance he presented between radical idealism and gradualist pragmatism was central to the way he interpreted the utopian tradition. This position was in line with his belief, following Goodman, that freedom was achieved through the activity of liberating oneself through the conscious expression of ones own will in relation to current and immediate contexts. This understanding of freedom as related to the exercise of agency was central to Ward's attack on the role of the state in directing and administering social relationships. In particular, Ward's development of twentieth-century anarchist philosophies of direct action and DiY politics were underpinned by the development of a theory of idealistic pragmatism that relied on the utilization of present-focused utopian themes. He saw direct action as the reflection in political behaviour of the anarchist prefigurative ethic. By this he meant that direct action aimed to realize its desired end in respect to a given situation. In this way the principle of direct action represented the attempt to modify one's environment directly.[71]

This present-focused interpretation of utopianism follows Barbara Goodwin's depiction of utopianism as concerned with 'immediate realization in the present'.[72] It also follows Buber's view that utopianism endorses an idea of social change as 'beginning here and now in the given conditions of the present'.[73] A focus on the present in the realm of political ideas is for Karl Mannheim the 'most extreme form of the utopian mentality', displaying 'absolute presentness' and 'tense expectation', and more concerned with 'the present pregnant with meaning' than 'the process of becoming'. Mannheim saw the classical anarchist tradition as linked to the utopian tradition through the belief in the possibility of immediate change in the present. He argued that nineteenth-century anarchism was the epitome of utopian present-focused immediacy. For Mannheim, anarchism preserved the immediacy of the utopian chiliast 'in its purest and most genuine form'.[74]

Kropotkin's emphasis on the importance of a revolutionary focus on the present vindicates Mannheim's identification of classical anarchism's utopian affinities. In 'Modern Science and Anarchism', Kropotkin argued that the rift between anarchism and Marxism in the late nineteenth century centred on their disagreement over the relationship between revolutionary practice and the present. Anarchists were 'compelled to separate' from the Marxists, claimed Kropotkin, when they began to say that 'there is no possibility of *abolishing* capitalist exploitation within the lifetime of our generation'. Against this, he stated, anarchists 'maintain that already now, without waiting for the coming of new phases and forms of the capitalist exploitation of labour, we must work for its *abolition*'.[75] Kropotkin's essay put this sense of immediacy at the centre of the anarchist tradition. He also linked it with a further facet of the utopian focus on the present, the anti-determinist rejection of overarching historical logic. Ward was adhering to the immediacy of the anarchist tradition when he approvingly quoted this passage from the work of Alexander Herzen: 'A goal which is infinitely remote is not a goal at all, it is a deception. A goal must be closer – at the very least the labourer's wage or pleasure in the work performed. Each epoch, each generation, each life has had, or has, its own experience, and the end of each generation must be itself.'[76] As we have seen, Comfort also focused on immediate human goals over distant, abstracted ones, and this was reflected in his discussions concerning direct action, the importance of congruity between means and ends, and the rejection of 'lesser evils' in the struggle for human progress. In Comfort's case this concern was motivated by an acute sense of the boundaries of the human sense of responsibility in an age of mechanical warfare. But he also sought to propound the positive social values alive in immediate, tangible and human-centred endeavours.

Mannheim identified the dispute between Marxism and anarchism as an issue of determinism versus indeterminism. The indeterminist aspect of the chiliastic mentality, argued Mannheim in his critique of anarchism, naively disregarded social evolution and the determinate movement of history. Instead, the chiliast anarchist was 'on the lookout ready to take the leap' from the 'ordinary course of events'. Marxist determinism won out over utopian anarchist indeterminism, argued Mannheim, when 'In place of the unorganised, oscillating experience of the ecstatic utopia, came the well-organized Marxian revolutionary movement' in which 'the road which leads from things as they are to the realization of the idea is already staked out historically and socially'.[77] This argument linked utopian immediacy and indeterminacy to anarchism as parts of a present focused approach to social change. Judith Shklar also asserted the centrality of the anti-determinist character of utopianism and linked this specifically to a focus on agency in the present. For Shklar, utopianism rested on 'the belief that people can control and improve themselves and, collectively, their social environment'. Shklar saw the present as a central feature of utopianism. She saw both Fabian and Marxian forms of socialism as rejecting utopianism in their 'attachment to historical determinism'. In her definition of utopianism she linked a focus on human agency in the present to 'the radical notion that men make their own history'.[78]

The relationship between utopian immediacy and anti-determinism and the anarchist tradition was highlighted particularly in Buber's *Paths in Utopia*. He identified anarchist thinkers, including Proudhon and Kropotkin, as important contributors to the utopian focus on the present. He argued that they added an emphasis on the structural renewal of forms of community and association already present in society. This view of the social ideal as immanent in the present reinforced the imperative for immediacy and agency in the utopian approach to social change. As Buber recognized, Kropotkin's argument in *Mutual Aid* emphasized the natural propensity for spontaneous human cooperation for mutual benefit. Kropotkin's belief in the potential for immediate social change through human agency was premised on this view of the already existing cooperative potential in human association.[79] This view of the immanence of desired social forms has supported and developed the utopian emphasis on immediacy and indeterminacy.

Buber noted that another key feature of the anarchist tradition contributed to the focus on the present in utopian thought. This is the anarchist belief in the importance of congruity between means and ends. Anarchism's view of social change rests on a prefigurative ethic, which states that action in the present must embody its goals for the future. David Miller identifies this ethic as one of the most distinctive differences between anarchism and Marxism. What Miller sees as the essential 'ahistorical' nature of anarchism requires that the non-hierarchical society must be prefigured in the means used in its name in the present. A focus on continuity is necessary under this understanding of anarchism because it lacks an adequate historical basis by which to anticipate the shape of change. As anarchism 'does not fundamentally rest on a theory of historical progress', argues Miller in his critique of anarchism, its means 'must be in conformity with its ends'.[80] This prefigurative ideal is in fact one of the core features of the anarchist critique of Marxism. Anarchists argue that Marxism subverts its own aims of equality and liberty, deferring them indefinitely by focusing on the incongruent means of class dictatorship and an elite leadership. As Ward argued: 'Socialism in the 20th century promised "jam tomorrow" so regularly, and the promise remained so often unfulfilled, that as Herzen insisted, new generations will have to evolve their own more immediate social aims, which, the anarchists hope, will be structured around styles of social organization other that the machinery of the state.'[81] Like Herzen, and in line with the ideas of his anarchist forebear Alex Comfort, Ward argued that moral responsibility must not be abrogated in the name of an unpredictable or abstract future order. This feature of anarchism is linked to its anti-determinist focus on human agency, one of its key connections with utopianism. Buber firmly linked the anarchist prefigurative ethic to utopian theory. He argued that the utopian 'does not believe in the post-revolutionary leap' but, like the anarchist, he does believe in 'revolutionary continuity'.[82]

Ward's development of twentieth-century anarchist philosophies of direct action and DiY politics were underpinned by the development of a theory of idealistic pragmatism that relied on the utilization of utopian present-focused themes. This idealistic pragmatism has much to offer mutualist social policy agendas. Ward's attachment to the present was expressed in the statement that 'If you want to build a free society, the parts are all at hand.'[83] This was a claim which highlighted the ongoing importance of a belief in the immanence of desirable social forms. This claim also highlighted the importance of constructive activity in the present and in relation to the immediate environment. In this way a pragmatic idealism developed within twentieth-century anarchism that drew on and developed a present-focused understanding of utopianism. In Ward's work this was presented as the aim to 'combine immediate aims with ultimate ends'.[84] He approached the present as the relevant locus of experience and emphasized piecemeal activity while advocating radical social ideals. This combination of values presents a challenge to conventional demarcations of socialism as divided between philosophies of idealistic revolutionary upheaval and reformist approaches to social change. Anarchist utopianism rejects the relationship between the present and the future implicit in both of these approaches. It rejects the deferral of social change, the separation of means and ends, and the handing of responsibility for change to elite groups, features which it sees represented in Marxian and social democratic forms of socialism. The influence of this approach, through the work of Ward, has been communicated to movements seeking to develop new approaches to social change.

Ward's anarchism was grounded in the proposition that valuable behaviour occurred only by the free and direct response of individuals or voluntary groups to the conditions presented by their environment. The emphasis on the virtues of engagement with the immediate environment developed the utopian focus on the present alongside the anarchist notion of the freedom of the self-creating individual. These ideas presented a coherent anarchist basis for direct action politics and DiY approaches to political activity. Ward in particular has featured as a significant intellectual source of the DiY phenomenon in British protest politics in George McKay's 1998 study.[85] As David Goodway has stated, 'Ward is indeed one of the great radical figures of the last thirty to forty years, but his impact has been subterranean.'[86] Ward's ideas are one of the influences on new approaches in protest politics despite receiving 'little public recognition or understanding by mainstream political theorists'.[87]

The collection of essays edited by McKay concerning the emergence of a DiY culture in resistance politics in Britain demonstrates the link between this phenomenon and the anarchist tradition. McKay has identified DiY culture as a youth-centred cluster of interests and practices concerned with ecology, anti-road building and animal rights. He argues that the use of direct action tactics is one of DiY culture's strongest affinities with anarchism. He also highlights DiY culture's commitment to Ward's notion of social change as the piecemeal achievement of grassroots association. Demonstrating the significance of Ward's ideas, Mckay introduces a quote from *Anarchy in Action* (concerning anarchist principles of voluntary, temporary, small organizations and their relevance to new protest movements) with the following statement: 'I think it speaks to DiY culture in the 1990s and may signal a route worth pursuing for both historical and theoretical awareness of young or newer activists today.'[88] The edited volume *Richer Futures* also pays sustained tribute to Ward's intellectual connection to emerging styles of resistance politics. George Monbiot's essay in this volume is concerned with the use of land, the importance of direct action protest, the significance of self-building and the self-help tactics of the poor.[89] McKay has also made reference to the DiY concern with reclaiming the countryside, evident in the Land Is Ours campaign group in which George Monbiot is involved, and the questioning of urban/rural binaries evident in the campaigns of groups like Reclaim The Streets.[90] This is expressed particularly in their challenges to the restrictions car culture imposes on the use of civic spaces. In McKay's volume, John Jordan argues that in the DiY approach 'the poetic and the pragmatic join hands'.[91] McKay notes that 'The culture of immediacy is a factor in the continuing rhetoric of newness around DiY.'[92] In these volumes Ward's claim is vindicated that, despite the fact that 'the historians have dismissed anarchism as one of the nineteenth-century also-rans of history', 'it is emerging again as a coherent social philosophy in the guerrilla warfare for a society of participants.'[93] Ken Worpole, the editor of *Richer Futures*, identifies the aims of the volume as follows:

> This book is about a new kind of politics that is emerging . . . [and] to pay tribute to the writer Colin Ward . . . Ward has been one of the most quietly influential commentators on our times . . . In the chapters which follow, many themes first raised by Ward are further developed and elaborated by people who continue to assert the value of the informal, the voluntary, the experimental and the self-sufficient as being amongst the most considered responses to many of the pressing social issues which confront us today.[94]

Ward's connections with utopian styles of political thought were well rooted in his intellectual sources and influences. They were also firmly supported by the themes of his work. The most important product of the relationship between utopianism and anarchism represented by his work is a particular political philosophy of immediacy, or directness, in temporal and spatial terms. In Ward's work, and in the wider twentieth-century anarchist tradition, this valorization of proximity includes focuses on human agency, the immanence of ideal social forms, immediate piecemeal change, and congruence between means and ends. These ideas have had a role to play in the efforts of contemporary protest movements to revise conventional notions of radical praxis. They also have an important role to play in contemporary mutualist thinking about social welfare, which aims to deploy and develop social capital in welfare-dependent communities through reciprocal and self-help programmes of participation and local labour exchange. Ward's DiY approach demonstrates that utopian emphases on immediacy, agency and immanence have served as important underpinning elements to the efforts of twentieth-century anarchists to defend vital and dynamic conceptions of freedom.[95] These efforts have been widely utilized by contemporary protest and social movements. Ward's work could provide these movements with much more in the way of inspiration and self-interrogation, especially in so far as mutualist and co-operative initiatives in the contemporary policy context seek central government support for their plans. As the discussion of the 'informal' economy highlights here, advocacy for local participation in support networks should seek not just the enlargement of community managed social care but also 'the movement of work back into the domestic economy' if it is going to engender self-governing community relationships.[96]

Anarchism and Social Policy

Ward drew out the implications of anarchist political thought not just for contemporary protest movements but also for the critique of the institutions of British post-war public policy. This demonstrates the extent to which he saw anarchism as relevant to mainstream political concerns. Ward applied his libertarian socialist critique to state welfare services including the NHS, education and council housing. His position regarding British social policy was a rejection of both capitalism and state socialism. Ward complained that any protest against the tyranny of government was heard with approval by the free-market right and fiercely attacked by the traditional or mainstream left. He remarked that, regarding the traditions of mutual aid and self-help, 'I cannot imagine how these phrases came to be dirty words for socialists since they refer to human attributes without which any conceivable socialist society would flounder.[97] As Greenleaf noted of the persistent but minority libertarian socialist strand in Britain: 'There has always been a quite contrary tendency or strand of socialist thought that has rested its appeal in good part, and sometimes entirely, on a critical concern about the prospect of big government and centralisation.'[98] Ward aimed to demonstrate that the modern association of the state with social welfare heightened the anarchist case against centralized authority rather than weakened it. Rather than seeing the anarchist antipathy to the state as historically outmoded because of its association with social welfare, Ward focused on this aspect of modern state behaviour as a central component of his critique.

Ward showed that social welfare in Britain did not originate from the state, Labour governments, National Insurance law, or the institution of the National Health Service. Rather, it originated in working class self-help and mutual aid practices in the nineteenth century, which built up a dense network of social and economic initiatives ranging from friendly societies, building societies, coffin clubs and sick clubs to community organized education, healthcare and consumer control, up to trade unions and the Co-operative Movement. 'How did we allow it to ossify?' lamented Ward, 'How on earth did British socialists allow these concepts to be hijacked by the political right, since it is these human attributes, and not the state and its bureaucracies, that actually hold human society together?' He blames the Marxists and the Fabians of course, who starved mutual aid traditions of 'ideological oxygen' by leading the political left into an exclusive investment in the idea of the state. Their model of elite control bolstered the 'undisguised contempt' of the British civil service and professional classes for 'the way ordinary people organised anything.'[99]

A key large-scale illustration of the endemic mutualist welfare practices preceding the institutions of the welfare state, and a radical challenge to the familiar image of inadequate and inconsistent welfare before the intervention of the state, is the Tredegar Medical Society, founded in 1870 in South Wales. Through voluntary levy it provided medical and hospital care for local miners and steelworkers and their dependents, irrespective of contribution or employment status. Ward stressed that this example and others like it demonstrated clearly that a different model of welfare could have evolved in Britain in the post-war era. As he argued: 'There once was the option of universal health provision "at the point of service" if only Fabians, Marxists and Aneurin Bevan had trusted the state and centralised revenue-gathering and policy-making less, and our capacity for self-help and mutual aid more.'[100] The local and federalized approach to medical care was, however, ignored in favour of a centralized model of health provision and, as a result, 'permanent daily need' became 'the plaything of central government financial policy'.[101]

The principle of self-taxation by means of which friendly societies and the like fed their mutual funds contrasts unfavourably with the much larger levies drawn from the income of twentieth- and twenty-first-century workers by the state, in order to support its own institutions and other non-welfare activities over which the contributors have no control. The PAYE taxation system introduced during the war established an effective central government monopoly over revenue gathering, leaving no self-taxable margin in working incomes for the voluntary contributions that had supported local user-controlled initiatives. Ward makes an important point about the superficiality of the celebrated principle of 'universalism' embedded in the British model of welfare, held to be enshrined in the state administration of health and social services and centralized revenue collection. The posited egalitarianism of a universal taxation model of welfare rests on the assumption that, unlike localist and decentralized provision, central control can ensure an impartial and equal service to all, irrespective of locality, class or status. 'The short answer to this is that it doesn't!' retorted Ward, and, as he elaborated, 'universalism is an unattainable idea in a society that is enormously divided in terms of income and access to employment.'[102] He supported this point by also highlighting the differential benefits drawn from state welfare provision by working-class and middle-class families, demonstrating that the middle classes receive a greater degree of state support especially in the areas of health and education. Further to his egalitarian case against the assumed 'universalism' of state provision, the socialist ideal of centralized welfare, by means of which 'nobody except the providers has any actual say about anything' seemed to Ward to be 'a very vulnerable utopia'.[103] Instead of being firmly and permanently embedded in already existing community-governed practices, welfare has become a resource to be administered *or removed* according to the assessments of national needs made by (often billionaire) central government actors. Social support in Britain is delivered via a set of provisions that can be given *or* taken away from above, and according to Ward this conclusively means that 'We took the wrong road to welfare.'[104]

Ward argued that since the late nineteenth century the tradition of fraternal and autonomous associations springing up from below had been displaced by one of authoritarian institutions directed from above. In this way, the tradition of working-class self-help and mutual aid had been disregarded. In the same vein Ward argued that the nineteenth-century dame schools, set up by working-class parents for their children and under their control, were swept away by the board schools of the 1870s. Similarly, the self-organization of patients in working-class medical societies was lost in the creation of the NHS. Ward noted the same dynamic in the housing sector. He argued that self-help building societies were stripped of mutuality by the tradition of municipal housing which was opposed to the principle of dweller control. Ward was adamant that 'We are paying today for confusing paternalistic authoritarianism with Socialism and social responsibility.'[105] One of the most characteristic of Ward's statements concerns the dichotomy between state-administered welfare and welfare services that were established and managed by voluntary organization:

> When we compare the Victorian antecedents of our public institutions with the organs of working-class mutual aid in the same period, the very names speak volumes. On the one side the Workhouse, the Poor Law Infirmary, the National Society for the Education of the Poor in Accordance with the Principles of the Established Church; and the other, the *Friendly* Society, the Sick *Club*, the *Co-operative* Society, the Trade *Union*. One represents the tradition of fraternal and autonomous associations springing up from below, the other that of authoritarian institutions directed from above.[106]

A major part of Ward's project concerning British social policy was the reclamation for the anti-market left of the libertarian terminology adopted by the free-market right. Ward discussed the parallel between his ideas and the libertarian conservatism of figures like David Green, Director of the Health and Welfare Unit at the Institute of Economic Affairs. Green had a parallel interest in the study of working-class self-organization. He would have agreed with Ward's statement that 'The habit of self-help and mutual aid have been deliberately repressed by inducing the habit of reliance on the bureaucratic organisation.'[107] The Institute of Economic Affairs was also responsible for the reprinting in 1996 of the classic text on self-improvement, *Self-Help*, by Samuel Smiles. This is a book which Ward also praised. But Ward, in a typical statement of socialist reclamation, argued that 'Although its chief object unquestionably is to stimulate youths to rely upon their own efforts in life rather than depend upon the help or patronage of others, it will also be found . . . that the duty of helping one's self in the highest sense involves the helping of one's neighbours.' Ward argued: 'Smiles himself was outraged that his book had been regarded as a manual on devil-take-the-hindmost individualism.'[108] Ward's approval for Smiles's work is also significant because it demonstrates the divergent ideological uses that a single work can sustain. Ward rejected the association between voluntaristic self-help and capitalist market-based organization, made by thinkers like Green. For Ward, on the contrary, capitalism maintained the 'ideology of the passive consumer' and reduced individuality and society to mass anonymity.[109] For Ward, 'There is something rather sinister and frightening about the sheer speed with which in so many fields in which relationships based on an ideology of reciprocity and mutual obligation have been replaced by real or simulated market values.'[110] Ward claimed that the concepts of self-help and mutual aid were socialist concepts, and he was incredulous that there should be any doubt about the ideological home of these ideas: 'How on earth did British Socialists allow these concepts to be hijacked by the political right, since it is these human attributes, and not the state and its bureaucracies, that actually hold human society together?'[111]

According to Ward, one of the biggest mistakes of the mainstream socialist movement in Britain was its support for state-owned housing. As he stated: '[B]linded by ideology and ignoring observable facts, we have been so brainwashed as to equate local-authority landlordism with a socialist approach to housing.'[112] The state provision of housing was one of the central values of the Fabian municipal strand of socialism that Ward saw as the tradition that had obscured the libertarian alternative. In the words of Greenleaf, concerning the difference between these strands: '[W]hat the statist aspect of Socialism may entail is suitably represented by the Fabians who believed that the key to the transformation of society was not so much the cultivation and recognition of democracy or individuality but rather wise and authoritative direction from above.'[113] According to Ward, socialist organizations 'instead of conducting a phoney crusade against the right to buy' should concentrate on avoiding the mistakes of 'the era of authoritarian paternalism'.[114] The first step was to recognize that '[T]he whole owner-occupation sector in housing is, though it is very unfashionable to say so except in Conservative circles, a triumphant example of self-help and mutual aid. Building societies originated as working class organisations.'[115]

Ward argued that there was 'nothing necessarily socialist about state-owned social or council housing nor anything necessarily capitalist about owner-occupation'.[116] He advocated home ownership yet attacked capitalist consumerist values. The key to this ideological position lay in the ideas of Proudhon regarding property. Proudhon both attacked and defended private property. The message of his political ideas in this respect was an assertion of the importance of material independence for freedom. When Proudhon attacked property he was attacking the use of it to exploit others. When he defended property he was asserting the importance of personal access to the necessities of house, land and tools as essential components of liberty. The ownership of the means to life, such as land and tools and housing, was central to the independence that he saw as vital for liberty. It was also important for the development of the moral quality of independence of personality that is part of the way anarchists interpret freedom. In his argument for the transfer of municipal housing from the council to its tenants, Ward demonstrated this Proudhonian view of property ownership: 'It would take one third of Britain's households out of the humilities of municipal tutelage into self-determining citizenship, at least as far as their housing is concerned.'[117] Ward emphasized the necessity of direct unalienable access to the necessities of life in order to maintain independence and avoid exploitation and manipulation. In the case of housing this led him to defend private ownership against state ownership. However, in the case of water he argued for national or common ownership. In each case the principle of avoiding dependence was the same and did not entail the market-based model of the free individual as an economically choosing consumer.

If the student of Ward's ideas should be in any doubt over his perspective on the benefits of market-driven social policy, his 1997 publication *Reflected in Water* was more than clear. This book was a fierce attack on the administration of public goods, in this case water, as market commodities. More than once Ward described this development as, using a phrase from the work of Richard Titmuss, 'the philistine resurrection of economic man in social policy'.[118] Ward was morally outraged at the aggressively commercial approach to water supply following privatization which resulted in the cutting of water supply to thousands of poor homes. Ward could not forgive the economic logic behind these experiences. '[I]t is sobering to realise', Ward reflected, 'that, in civilised Britain, the fantasies of wealthy advocates of the logic of the market should reduce us to the brutality of that kind of attitude'.[119] Ward went on to discuss the revealing nature of the difference between public attitudes to water shortages in Britain in 1976, when water was public property and people voluntarily saved water, and 1995, when water came to be understood as a capitalist product. In 1995 there was little public cooperation with attempts to save water such as hosepipe bans. The result of making decisions on important issues like water on economic rather than social grounds was that it led to a frightening decline in public sensibilities and a crisis of social responsibility. Ward argued against the misanthropy of the idea that common ownership was an encouragement to greed and wastefulness. He was arguing in defence of popular and mutual systems and local social institutions: 'if human communities actually achieved control of their own supply and manipulation of water, they would manage fairly and responsibly, recognizing the needs of all, as well as those of their fellow users of the same resource'.[120]

Ward's educational agenda followed his thinking about the damage caused by state authority and market values to local- and community-orientated approaches. His views were linked with the traditional anarchist anti-institutional approach and also with the anti-schooling movement. As he noted: 'This entirely different conception of the school had already been envisaged by Godwin in 1797' and further, 'Goodman peddled his ideas of incidental education in and out of season for most of his writing life'.[121] The result of the Education Act of 1870, the biggest legislative step towards a national system of state education in Britain, Ward argued, was the creation of submissive, apathetic, undifferentiated masses.[122] He stated that 'We no longer cow our children into submission, in fact we indulge them as consumers, with the powerful aid of the advertising industry, but we fail to induct them into a world of adult decision-making, perhaps just because, as adults, we have delegated to others the habit of deciding'.[123] He added that, 'Much of our provision for children seems almost designed to exclude them from the process of providing, so that they are positively obliged to be the listless and ungrateful consumers of services supplied by others'.[124] In relation to these developments, Ward commented in 1970, at the height of the anti-schooling movement, that 'It is a hundred years and more since elementary education became free, compulsory and universal – and we celebrated the anniversary by inventing a new word: de-schooling'.[125] Like Goodman, a pre-eminent influence on anti-schooling philosophy, Ward was concerned that children had an environment that they could interact with and mature in response to in order to properly grow up and develop as confident, creative, social and autonomous beings. He stated that 'our real education is gained from the physical and social environment', and it is this experience that fosters the propensity for active engagement and participation, qualities of citizenship.[126] Ward linked his educational thinking with the citizenship agenda of Bernard Crick, arguing that the 'jug-filling' tradition of education in Britain undermined attempts to direct education towards the values of citizenship. For Ward, children unfolded as individuals and citizens through 'creatively manipulating their surroundings'.[127]

In his approach to education Ward combined two of the strands of influence that acted upon his work. One was an understanding of the relationship between art and individual judgement drawn from the educational philosophy of Herbert Read. This was a view of art as a mode of perception that related the subjectivity of the individual to the exterior world. Art was seen as means of direct experience of the environment. The idea was that art education could be used to develop a critical capacity, including powers of discrimination and judgement. Ward applied this view of art to his prescriptions for education which he presented in his Art and the Built Environment project: 'Art education, with its emphasis on direct experience and personal interpretation, encourages a feeling response which is basic to an understanding of the environment . . . Thus art education has an important role to play in developing awareness and discriminatory skills.'[128] The aim of the Art and the Built Environment project in which Ward was involved was to make children 'aware of conflicts where they exist and to urge them to cultivate the habit of making judgements'.[129] It was proposed that this could be achieved through the use of art in education, which through the direct experience of an environment fostered judgement, perception and engagement. This was alongside the development of an appreciation of particular historical and cultural values and relationships which townscape forms expressed. This also reflected his emphasis on the urban environment as a conducive context for children to develop social skills and individual perception. In the following statement from Art and the Built Environment, Ward expressed the convergence of his art-based and participation-based agendas in education: 'Our long term aim is that people should be better prepared to play a more creative and participatory role in shaping their environment. But participation demands higher levels of awareness, interest, concern for and understanding of the environment.'[130]

The Art and the Built Environment project was related to the publication of a government report in the late 1960s under Sir Arthur Skeffington entitled *People and Planning*. This report, Ward noted, was the government's response to public dissatisfaction with the results of planning policy on British towns and cities and the pressure for more public participation. The report recommended that education about town planning should be part of the way in which all secondary schools make children conscious of their future civic duties. The Skeffington Report was the incentive for the Town and Country Planning Association to set up its education unit. In 1971 Colin Ward and Anthony Fyson were appointed to create that unit. This resulted in a collaborative book *Streetwork: The Exploding School*, which presented an agenda in education closely related to the ideas of Goodman and the anti-schooling movement. This included the emphasis on the importance of participation which Ward shared with Sennett and Crick. This area of thought, drawing on both anarchist and non-anarchist sources, was the second strand of influence that acted on his educational thinking.

Ward identified his perspective with that of the educational pressure group headed by Crick at the Politics Association. For Crick the task was to re-establish 'a popular tradition of political discourse both critical and aspirant.'[131] In this vein Ward argued that 'Civic education must be aimed at creating citizens.'[132] He stated that education should revolve around community contact, community problems, and what the individual 'as a citizen can do about them'.[133] According to Ward, Crick was arguing that if we want a society in which all people feel able and motivated to participate then we need to 'avoid presenting the system and the consensus as some kind of universal truth'. Introducing his own agenda as parallel with Crick's, Ward added that in order to achieve this aim, 'we have to devise a framework for environmental education which really engages the ordinary school student'.[134] This was the vital contribution which he felt that the anarchist tradition could make to educational policy agendas like Crick's. For Ward, 'real education' was 'self education' and came from 'self directed activity', 'taking your own decisions' and 'assuming your own responsibilities'.[135] Ward's work in relation to educational policy applied anarchism to mainstream concerns about political engagement and the state of public education.

Employment, Work and the 'Informal' Economy

What can Colin Ward tell us about the future of mutualism and anarchism in Britain as welfare state provision atrophies into a minimal safety net for the poorest and most ostracized, given the sacrifices that have been made in terms of local and voluntary habits and organizations? In a pertinent piece of rhetoric, Ward asked, 'what is to happen when, as long-term, large-scale unemployment grows, the privileged, employed section of the population shrugs off the responsibility of providing an income for those who cannot get a job and are never likely to have one?'[136] The beginnings of this 'tax-payers' revolt' were already evident in the late 1970s, he argued, with the election of a 'crudely fundamentalist Conservative government' and the subsequent periodic endorsement of 'welfare-bashing' in Britain.[137] As he asked, given that Building Societies have become banks and co-operative retail movements have succumbed to market practices, 'how we get back on the mutual aid road *instead* of commercial health insurance and private pension schemes.'[138] The ideas Ward developed about labour and the 'informal economy' of real human social life provide a basis for conceptualizing an alternative route to work and welfare, and they have a vital part to play in contemporary movements to regenerate the social capital upon which mutual, reciprocal and self-help practices depend. If there is hope, he argues, it lies in the 'so-called underclass' of people outside the economy in alliance with 'those déclassé people who just can't stomach current economic and social values.'[139] Ward detected a renewal of self-help and mutual aid practices in the emergence of 'marginal activities' such as food co-operatives, credit unions, tenant self-management, and LETS. As he stated, 'Huge welfare networks were built up by the poor in the rise of industrial Britain. Perhaps they will be rebuilt, out of the same sheer necessity during its decline.'[140] Ward's writings, including the full scope of their utopian, anti-militarist anarchist underpinnings, have a role to play in the revival and regeneration of mutualist solutions to the dilemmas of sustainable social welfare provision, especially his perspective on the importance of informal working practices and the principles of self-employment. The challenge for those contemporary initiatives seeking to support mutuality and reciprocity in marginalized communities, especially through engagement in welfare practices, is to adhere to the spirit of Ward's insight: 'The only way to banish the spectre of unemployment is to break free from our enslavement to the idea of employment.'[141] Dominant economic arrangements lead to conditions of widespread cyclical unemployment and working people struggle with the attempts of employers to reduce wage costs and raise productivity. This particularly affects young people attempting to enter the labour market. So, Ward argues, 'It *does* in fact make sense to help people on the way to employing themselves.'[142] The answer, for the healthy functioning of cooperative, well-cared for, self-governing communities is, 'the movement of work back into the domestic economy'.[143]

In 1986, in the first edition of the Freedom Press quarterly *The Raven*, writing in a policy context in Britain with distinct parallels to that of the early twenty-first century, Colin Ward reflected on the threats to life and well-being in an age of 'government by technocrats, theologians and ide-ologists' under the 'military and governmental establishments of the great powers'. In a consistent and coherent development of the anti-militarism of the British anarchist tradition he tackled military and social policies together, as the two faces of centralized governmental organization. In this article Ward argued that the spectres 'haunting us all' are nuclear war and unemployment. 'War is the ultimate weapon of governments against peoples,' he writes, 'and it doesn't matter whether we are thinking of our own or other nations' people.' In this he emphasizes the anarchist understanding of war, expressed in the work of Herbert Read and Alex Comfort, as central to the statist mode of domestic social order. The more immediate lived experience of the threats to human well-being presented by the state-or-dered society, argued Ward, was 'the spectre of mass unemployment', which 'In most countries of the world . . . is the ordinary condition that people live in all their lives.'[144] In his exploration of the individual means and social resources that make life and work possible under these circumstances, Ward focused on the self-help and reciprocal domestic arrangements endemic in society. His discussion of what he called the 'informal economy', the sphere of private, social and economic arrangements constituted by these self-help and mutual aid practices, reconceptualized the notion of 'work' to include all human activities that address social needs and demands, whether or not they are included in official employment statistics or formal remu-nerative arrangements. This wider conceptualization of human labour, which highlights the significance of social relationships and reciprocal practices for the quality of human life, is a vital component of an alterna-tive approach to human welfare that depends on neither the vagaries of states nor markets. Recent work emphasizes the importance of informal social care embedded in domestic and family relationships by referring to this private caring labour as the 'core economy', acknowledging the extent to which this informal work supports the formal economy.[145] These ideas feed into social policy prescriptions which draw citizens into reciprocal and mutual exchange practices in various spheres of medical and social care.[146] The conceptual affinities between contemporary thinking about the productive delivery of welfare services and the anarchist social ontology, particularly as deployed and developed in the work of Colin Ward, high-light ways in which anarchism can inform and interrogate thinking about social policy in Britain in the twenty-first century.

One of the first myths to be addressed, Ward implicitly observes, is that economic growth is going to solve the problem of welfare, and his insights in this respect support wider recent doubts about the real social benefits of 'growth' in a formal economic sense. 'We don't really believe that British or American manufacturing industries are going to recover lost markets', wrote Ward, and he continued, 'We don't really believe that big business has any answers for us. Even our faith that the tertiary or service economy is bound to expand to replace the jobs lost in the productive sector has been shattered.' But what Ward considers might prove to be of much greater significance is the growth of a '*self*-service economy', claiming that a positive alternative to the market economy can be effected by household, family and neighbourhood relationships 'revitalised' as 'powerful and relatively autonomous productive' units. According to Ward's reading of the history of the Industrial Revolution, which closely follows the Marxist understanding, it was only under duress that labour moved out of the domestic sphere into the realm of formal employment in the first place. As Ward notes, 'the old American phrase for an employee, a "hired man" carries with it the notion that he was something less than a free citizen, as does the old socialist definition of the working class as those with nothing to sell but their labour power.'[147] Paid employment represents the relationship between employer and employee that Marx referred to as 'alienation', and this condition was the product of the worker's lack of ownership over his time, his tools and the product of his labour. 'Any account of the Industrial Revolution in this country', writes Ward, 'tells how workers were driven by starvation to accept the disciplines of employment.' Home workers in domestic industry worked long hours, but they worked alongside family, in environments shaped by their own movements and habits, determining their own hours and patterns of rest and work. In the words of J. L. and Barbara Hammond in their book *The Town Labourer*, which Ward quotes with approval, 'The forces that ruled his fate were in a sense outside his daily life.' Ward highlights the emphasis that these authors place on the 'strain and violence' that a worker experienced when they were forced from a working environment 'in which he could smoke or eat or dig or sleep as he pleased' to an employment relationship in which 'someone turned the key on him, and for fourteen hours he had not even the right to whistle'. It is a 'moral sacrifice', they argue, that makes sense of the resistance of the hand-loom weavers to go into the power-loom factories, where wages were higher.[148]

Ward made a direct comparison between these insights into early factory life and the sociological research undertaken by Ferdinand Zweig among car workers in Coventry, published in *The Worker in the Affluent Society* in 1961. Zweig noted that workers engaged in intensive 'do-it-yourself' labour at weekends, often returning to the factory on Monday exhausted from their leisure activities. This led Ward to ask 'what *is* work and what *is* leisure, if we work harder at our leisure than at our work.' The first point he makes in relation to this question is to argue that while jobs may be scare, there is never a shortage of work, an insight he traces to William Morris's distinction between useless toil and useful labour. As Ward stated, 'There will never be a shortage of *work* in the sense of coping with useful tasks.'[149] The second point he makes in relation to the distinction between work and employment is to highlight the existing economy of work which is not formal employment, in the sense of the visible, measurable official economy. This covers all the effort people expend in addressing the needs of others, from fixing a tap to babysitting, and under an even wider understanding of the informal economy this extends to meeting the social needs of others. Ward draws examples of informal economic transactions from the work of sociologist Ray Pahl, using his example of a broken window to outline the familiar range of responses to an everyday need. Informal solutions would include paying someone privately in cash who is known to be able to mend windows, asking a friend or neighbour to do it in return for reciprocal goods or services, including reciprocated good will, or undertaking the repair oneself using one's own tools and labour. Ward uses the notion of the 'informal economy' to refer to 'all the possible conceptions of alternative economies', including 'ordinary self-employment' and 'that multitude of mutual services where money doesn't change hands at all', and 'the communal economy of joint use of expensive equipment'. These activities, he notes, 'add up to an enormous range of human activities without which life on this planet would be impossible'.[150] He notes that the language usually employed to describe this sphere of activity includes the terms '*Irregular*', '*peasant*', '*subsistence*', '*natural*', '*domestic*', '*household*', '*communal*', '*cottage*' and '*ghetto*', as well as '*hidden*', '*black*', '*underground*' and '*subterranean*'.[151]

As we have seen, Ward is infinitely better disposed toward the principle of self-taxation, in the accumulation of mutual funds for insurance, credit and welfare provision for example, than he is to the model of universal state taxation. This is reflected in his assessment of that section of the 'informal' economy which entails 'black' economic practices that avoid taxation. His first response to the problem of tax evasion is to point out that 'the greater part of activities and transactions outside the measurable economy have no tax-evasion aspect'.[152] Further to this, he argues that the very concept of a 'black' economy is merely the creation of fiscal policy and has no moral dimension at all. PAYE and purchase tax arrangements were introduced in the Second World War, he argues, in order to 'mop up consumer demand for non-existent goods'. Before this time no one would have understood the notion of a 'black' economy, other than 'boot-leggers' during the Prohibition period in America, or 'the entire citizenship of the Soviet Union', who depended on informal economic arrangements for their survival. He acknowledges the critiques of his position, noting that tax evasion is generally associated in the public mind with a selfish individualism which seeks to avoid the independent obligations attendant upon the individual to contribute towards social goods.[153] Ward of course endorses *self*-taxation to meet social needs and resists the starkly individualist understanding of the self-taxing social model advanced by his detractors. 'Let me repeat,' states Ward, 'the Black economy is the creation of fiscal policy and is not a moral issue.' If we make tax an issue of citizen morality, he adds, we must address the large portion of tax revenue expended on war preparations, armaments and the armed forces. 'Was this what their citizens wanted?' he asks.[154]

Ward does address the other big concern about home working practices, which is its traditional relationship to sweated labour arrangements. First he notes a number of examples of effective liberating home work, drawing on the work of Sebastino Brusco on the informal economy in the manufacture of industrial components in Italy in the 1970s and Peggy Edwards and Eric Flounders account in Frank Field's book *Are Low Wages Inevitable?* of the material gains of home workers in the Nottingham lace industry in the same decade. In both cases an informal sector of small workshops saved the industries from decline and improved the quality of life and work for those involved.[155] Secondly, Ward makes a clear Proudhonian distinction between the material conditions for free home work and those of sweated labour. The difference between owning the relevant means of production, relying on an employer for access to them, or doing without them and 'sweating' over output 'is of course', he argues, 'a matter of access to a very modest amount of credit'. The crucial difference between self-employment and sweatshop labour is access to a basic credit infrastructure for the poor, and some security of tenure for home workers. Ward adds that 'This is the lesson of the Informal Economy in the exploding cities of the Third World too.'[156] Self-employment is a virtue and a necessity, he notes, people in the world's poor cities engage in it in order to survive, and the securely employed in rich countries aspire to it. Marxism and capitalism both deride this truth, regarding self-employment practices as 'petty' or 'primitive', unless, in the capitalist view, the small enterprise is likely to become a big business.[157] 'The obstacle' to self-employment for workers in both rich and poor countries is the same, Ward argues, 'lack of access to capital or credit, lack of security, since in all countries social security is geared to the employed controllable worker, not to the self-employed, and the absence of an infrastructure which could automatically favour the small, local provider.'[158]

Ward resists the association of terms like 'enterprise', 'initiative' and 'self-help' with the political right and the defence of capitalism, and he similarly rejects the identification of socialism with 'a Big Brother State with a responsibility to provide a pauper's income for all and an inflation-proof income for its own functionaries'. He draws on an older socialist image of federated craftsmanship based on the model of a radical self-employed individual 'sitting in his shop with a copy of William Morris's *Useful Work versus Useless Toil* on the workbench, his hammer in his hand, and his lips full of brass tacks. His mind full of notions of liberating his fellow workers from industrial serfdom in a dark satanic mill.' He contrasts this approach to the liberation of work unfavourably with the more familiar contemporary socialist image 'of a university lecturer with a copy of *The Inevitable crisis of Capitalism* in one hand, and a banner labelled "Fight the Cuts" in the other, while his mind is full of strategies for unseating the sitting . . . candidate in the local pocket borough.'[159] The decentralist, anarchist vision of humanized work is achieved via the rejection of employment and the growth of the informal, self-employed economy, not the conquest of the state by a 'proletarian' party. Ward illustrates his argument in this respect with this aside, 'Communism, as some Polish wit said, is a conspiracy by the unemployed intelligentsia to complete the enslavement of the workers.'[160] We learn from Colin Ward's reflections on the anarchist view of liberated work that part of a mutualist set of aspirations, and part of an anti-militarist agenda, must be to 'question the legitimacy of the employing institutions, and the monopoly we ascribe to them of creating wealth'.[161]

Conclusion

Ward was concerned to frame anarchism as a relevant, constructive approach to contemporary political dilemmas. He bought anarchism to bear on new themes and brought new areas of enquiry into the remit of anarchist analyses. Ward's editorship of *Anarchy* and his body of anarchist writing was an attempt to renew the anarchist tradition, to update it with contemporary sources, and to highlight its relevance with modern applications. This was the basis for his contact with mainstream policy agendas including council housing, water privatization and education for citizenship. In Ward's work anarchism was an anti-authoritarian, libertarian and socialist political tradition. It was directed towards the creation of self-governing communities and independent, autonomous individuals. In fact, as Ward showed, all societies are to some extent already pluralistic and problem solving, employing whatever mutual, reciprocal and cooperative techniques are at hand in order to meet their needs. Anarchism is represented by mutual aid practices, and these anarchist social relationships already underpin healthy functioning societies, in spite of the bureaucratic, legislated harms to freedom and equality imposed by centralized elite forms of government. Ward's experience of governmental authority and the growth of the British State during and after World War Two contributed to the appeal of the anarchist tradition. His experiences during the war were a significant catalyst in his development of the anarchist system of thought beyond its eighteenth- and nineteenth-century sources. His anarchism was also a reaction to post-war social administration, specifically welfare institutions.

Ward's argument, following Kropotkin, was that anarchism was in keeping with existing tendencies in nature and society. This basic premise led Ward away from the notion of revolution in the process of social change. The result was a political philosophy which combined idealistic and pragmatic elements. The result of Ward's efforts to revive and update anarchism was a set of 'quietly influential' deployments of the tradition.[162] This is most notable in the field of unofficial political movements concerning civic participation and public space. Ward's anarchist-driven reflections on self-activity and the material and spatial aspects of social theory developed a distinctive emphasis on constructive activity and immediate forms of change. This valued directness as a principle of individual engagement alongside the firmly anarchist adherence to the congruity between the means and the ends of activity directed towards social change. Ward's thinking in this direction emphasized immediacy, proximity and directness in spatial and temporal terms as key representations of the anarchist privileging of agency and self-creation. His ideas suggested a theory of pragmatic idealism which valued constructive activity in the present and in relation to immediate contexts as the deployment of anarchist ideals of self-government.

There is an erroneous under-emphasis on the role of anarchist political theory in the twentieth century, especially in the British context. This means that this important source of ideas about mutuality, reciprocity and self-government in the spheres of work, leisure and well-being has been overlooked in more recent radical debates about social policy that seek to employ and apply some of these themes in a British context. As such they have a disappointingly shallow sense of the anarchist heritage of these themes in Britain and they miss important synergies with anarchist ideas.[163] Ward's anarchism is important for understanding what mutualism really entails, especially in the sphere of welfare provision. For one thing, he shows that it does not have to be legislated for by government, and further, he demonstrates that it must be based on the economic freedoms of self-employment and the credit provisions envisaged by Proudhon. Colin Ward gives us a much clearer picture of what social forms might flourish in a de-militarized society, where welfare and work are immanent features of human society and not manna to be bestowed or withheld.

Notes

1. Colin Ward, 'Witness for the Prosecution', *The Raven Anarchist Quarterly* 29, 8 (1), Spring, 1995, p. 59.

2. Ward, 'Witness for the Prosecution', p. 60.

3. Colin Ward, 'Anarchism and the Informal Economy', in *The Raven*, 1, 1986, pp. 25–37, p. 35.

4. Alex Comfort, 'Imagination or Reportage?' (1946), in *Readers News*, January, reproduced in Goodway (ed.), *Writings against Power and Death. The Anarchist Articles and Pamphlets of Alex Comfort* (London: Freedom Press, 1994), pp. 91–2.

5. Colin Ward, *Anarchy in Action* (London: Freedom Press, 1982), p. 19.

6. Ward, *Anarchy in Action*, pp. 19–20.

7. Colin Ward, with David Goodway, *Talking Anarchy* (Nottingham: Five Leaves Publications, 2003), p. 47.

8. Colin Ward (ed.), *A Decade of Anarchy (1961–1970)* (London: Freedom Press,1987), p. 12.

9. Colin Ward, 'Cheer Up!' (1987), *New Society* (June), p. 26.

10. Ward, *Anarchy in Action*, p. 39.

11. Ward, *Anarchy in Action*, p. 8.

12. Ward, *Anarchy in Action*, p. 109.

13. Colin Ward, *Influences. Voices of Creative Dissent* (Devon: Green Books, 1991), p. 88.

14. Ward, *Anarchy in Action*, p. 26.

15. Ward, *Anarchy in Action*, p. 8.

16. Ward, *Anarchy in Action*, pp. 8–9.

17. Ward, *Anarchy in Action*, p. 19.

18. Ward, *Anarchy in Action*, p. 20.

19. Ward, *Anarchy in Action*, p. 19.

20. Ward, *Anarchy in Action*, p. 20. Stuart White examines the pragmatic and respectable presentation of Ward's anarchism in 'Making anarchism respectable?

The Social Philosophy of Colin Ward', *Journal of Political Ideologies*, 12 (1), 2007, pp. 11–28.

21. Colin Ward, 'Conversations about Anarchism', pp. 11–23 in Ward (ed.), *A Decade of Anarchy*, p. 23.

22. Ward, *Anarchy in Action*, p. 25.

23. For more detailed discussion of Ward's ideas in relation to those of Goodman, see Carissa Honeywell 'Utopianism and Anarchism', *Journal of Political Ideologies*, 12 (3), 2007, pp. 239–54. For more detailed discussion of the ideas of Paul Goodman in particular, see Carissa Honeywell, 'Paul Goodman: Finding an Audience for Anarchism in 20th Century America', *Journal for the Study of Radicalism* 5 (2), 2011.

24. Colin Ward, 'Foreword', pp. 7–10, in Ward (ed.), *A Decade of Anarchy*, p. 8.

25. Colin Ward, 'After a Hundred Issues', pp. 276–9, in Ward (ed.), *A Decade of Anarchy*, p. 279.

26. Ward, 'Conversations about Anarchism', in Ward (ed.), *A Decade of Anarchy*, p. 13.

27. Ward, 'After a Hundred Issues', in Ward (ed.), *A Decade of Anarchy*, p. 277.

28. Colin Ward, quoted in David Goodway, 'The Anarchism of Colin Ward', pp. 3–20, in Ken Worpole (ed.), *Richer Futures. Fashioning a New Politics* (London: Earthscan Publications, 1999), p. 7.

29. Ward, in 'Conversation about Anarchism', in Ward (ed.), *A Decade of Anarchy*, p. 13.

30. Ward, *Anarchy in Action*, p. 22.

31. Ward, *When We Build Again, Let's Have Housing That Works*,(London: Pluto Press, 1985), p. 67.

32. Edgar Cahn, 'foreword' in 'Co-Production. A Manifesto for Growing the Core Economy' (new economics foundation, 2008).

33. Edgar Cahn, 'foreword' in 'Co-Production. A Manifesto for Growing the Core Economy'.

34. Colin Ward, *Tenants Take Over* (London: The Architectural Press,1974), p. 12.

35. Colin Ward, *Social Policy. An Anarchist Response* (London: Freedom Press, 2000, first published by the London School of Economics, 1996), pp. 10–11.

36. Colin Ward, 'Orwell and Anarchism' (1955), printed in *George Orwell at Home* (London: Freedom Press, 1998), p. 37.

37. George Orwell, 'Inside the Whale' (1940), quoted in Colin Ward, 'Orwell and Anarchism' (1955), printed in *George Orwell at Home*, p. 33.

38. Colin Ward, 'Big Brother Drives a Bulldozer', in Paul Chilton and Crispin Aubrey (eds) *Nineteen Eighty-Four in 1984* (London: Comedia Publishing Group, 1984), p. 94.

39. W. H. Greenleaf, *The British Political Tradition Volume II. The Ideological Heritage* (London and New York: Methuen, 1983), p. 541.

40. Colin Ward, *When We Build Again, Let's Have Housing That Works*, p. 112.

41. Ward, in 'Conversation about Anarchism', in Ward (ed.) *A Decade of Anarchy*, p. 14.

42. Ward, *Anarchy in Action*, p. 72.

43. Paul Goodman, quoted in Colin Ward, *Influences. Voices of Creative Dissent* (Devon: Green Books, 1991), p. 79.

44. Steven Lukes, *Individualism* (Oxford: Blackwell, 1973), p. 52.

45. Isaiah Berlin, *Four Essays on Liberty* (Oxford: Oxford University Press, 1969), p. 131, quoted in Lukes, *Individualism*, p. 55.

46. Lukes, *Individualism*, p. 56.

47. Lukes, *Individualism*, p. 12.

48. Lukes, *Individualism*, p. 12.

49. Lukes, *Individualism*, pp. 71–2.

50. Lukes, *Individualism*, pp. 136–7.

51. Colin ward, *Talking Anarchy*, pp. 26–7.

52. Ward, *Anarchy in Action*, p. 18.

53. Ward, *Anarchy in Action*, p. 17.

54. Ward, *Anarchy in Action*, p. 18.

55. Ward, *Influences*, p. 79.

56. Martin Buber, *Paths in Utopia* (Boston: Beacon Books, 1958), p. 6.

57. Buber, *Paths in Utopia*, p. 81.

58. Keith Taylor, *The Political Ideas of the Utopian Socialists* (UK: Frank Cass, 1982), pp. 4–9.

59. Taylor, *The Political Ideas of the Utopian Socialists*, pp. 14–19, 34.

60. Buber, *Paths in Utopia*, p. 8.

61. Gibson Burrell and Karen Dale, 'Utopiary: Utopias, gardens and organization', pp. 106–27, in Martin Parker (ed.), *Utopia and Organization* (Oxford: Blackwell Publishing, 2002), pp. 106, 110.

62. Barbara Goodwin and Keith Taylor, *The Politics of Utopia. A Study in Theory and Practice* (London: Hutchinson, 1982), p. 201.

63. For a discussion of Ebenezer Howard's ideas, see Robert Beevers, *The Garden City Utopia. A Critical Biography of Ebenezer Howard* (Basingstoke: Macmillan, 1988).

64. Colin Ward, *New Town, Home Town* (London: Calouste Gulbenkian Foundation, 1993), p. 147.

65. Colin Ward and Dennis Hardy, *Arcadia for All. The Legacy of a Makeshift Landscape* (London and New York: Mansell Publishing Ltd., 1984), pp. vii, 4.

66. Colin Ward, *Housing. An Anarchist Approach* (London: Freedom Press. London, 1976), pp. 87–8.

67. Anthony Barnett and Roger Scruton, 'Introduction'. in Anthony Barnett and Roger Scruton (eds), *Town and Country* (UK: Vintage, Random House, 1999), p. xi.

68. Colin Ward, 'The Unofficial Countryside', in Anthony Barnett and Roger Scruton (eds), *Town and Country*, pp. 190–8.

69. Richard Sennett, *The Uses of Disorder. Personal Identity and City Life* (London: Faber and Faber, 1996), p. 108.

70. Ward, *Housing*, p. 55.

71. Ward, *Anarchy in Action*, pp. 26–7.

72. Goodwin and Taylor, *The Politics of Utopia*, p. 26.

73. Buber, *Paths in Utopia*, p. 16.

74. Karl Mannheim, *Ideology and Utopia. An Introduction to the Sociology of Knowledge* (London: Routledge and Kegan Paul Ltd., 1960), pp. 191, 193, 195, 202.

75. Peter Kropotkin, 'Modern Science and Anarchism', pp. 57–93, in Emile Capouya ad Keitha Tompkins (eds), *The Essential Kropotkin* (New York: Liveright, 1975), pp. 74–5.

76. Quoted in Colin Ward, *Anarchy in Action*, p. 136.

77. Mannheim, *Ideology and Utopia*, pp. 195, 219, 220.

78. Judith Shklar, *After Utopia. The decline of Political Faith* (Princeton: Princeton University Press, 1957), pp. 219, 257–265, p. 258.

79. Buber, *Paths in Utopia*, pp. 38–45.

80. David Miller, *Anarchism* (London: J. M. Dent and Sons Ltd.,1984), pp. 93, 150.

81. Colin Ward, *Anarchism. A Very Short Introduction* (Oxford: Oxford University Press, 2004), p. 32.

82. Buber, *Paths in Utopia*, p. 13.

83. Ward, *Anarchy in Action*, p. 20.

84. Ward, *Anarchy in Action*, p. 30.

85. George McKay, 'DiY Culture; Notes Towards and Introduction', pp. 1–53, in George McKay (ed.), *DiY Culture. Party and Protest in Nineties Britain* (London: Verso, 1998), pp. 20, 34, 51–2.

86. Goodway, 'The Anarchism of Colin Ward', pp. 3–20, in Worpole (ed.), *Richer Futures*, p. 3.

87. Worpole, 'Introduction', in Worpole (ed.), *Richer Futures*, p. xi.

88. McKay, in McKay (ed.), *DiY Culture*, p. 51.

89. George Monbiot, 'The Land is Ours', pp. 100–8, in Worpole (ed.), *Richer Futures*.

90. McKay, in McKay (ed.), *DiY Culture*, p. 32.

91. John Jordan, 'The Art of Necessity: The Subversive Imagination of anti-Road protest and Reclaim the Streets', pp. 129–51, in McKay (ed.), *DiY Culture*, p. 132.

92. McKay, in McKay, *DiY Culture*, p. 13.

93. Ward, *Anarchy in Action*, p. 29.

94. Worpole, 'Introduction', in Worpole (ed.), *Richer Futures*, p. xi.

95. See Honeywell, 'Utopianism and Anarchism'.

96. Colin Ward, 'Anarchism and the Informal Economy', pp. 25–37, p. 31.

97. Ward, *When We Build Again, Let's Have Housing That Works*, p. 15.

98. Greenleaf, *The British Political Tradition Volume II*, p. 411.

99. Ward, *Social Policy. An Anarchist Response*, pp. 10–11.

100. Ward, *Social Policy. An Anarchist Response*, p. 16.

101. Ward, *Anarchism*, p. 28.

102. Ward, *Social Policy. An Anarchist Response*, p. 16.

103. Ward, *Social Policy. An Anarchist Response*, p. 12.

104. Ward, *Social Policy. An Anarchist Response*, p. 17.

105. Ward, *When We Build Again, Let's Have Housing That Works*, pp. 9–10.

106. Ward, *Social Policy. An Anarchist Response*, p. 9.

107. Ward, *When We Build Again, Let's Have Housing That Works*, p. 35.

108. Ward, *When We Build Again, Let's Have Housing That Works*, p. 28.

109. Ward, *Housing*, p. 8.

110. Ward, *Social Policy. An Anarchist Response*, p. 76.

111. Ward, *Social Policy*, p. 11.

112. Ward, *When We Build Again, Let's Have Housing That Works*, p. 15.

113. Greenleaf, *The British Political Tradition Volume II*, p. 359.

114. Ward, *When We Build Again, Let's Have Housing That Works*, p. 56.

115. Ward, *When We Build Again, Let's Have Housing That Works*, p. 29.

116. Ward, *When We Build Again, Let's Have Housing That Works*, p. 45.

117. Colin Ward, *Tenants Take Over* (London: The Architectural Press, 1974), p. 8.

118. Richard Titmuss, *The Gift Relationship: From Human Blood to Social Policy* (London: Allen and Unwin, 1970), p. 4, quoted in Colin Ward, *Reflected in Water. A Crisis of Social Responsibility* (London and Washington: Cassell, 1997), p. viii.

119. Ward, *Reflected in Water*, p. 12.

120. Ward, *Reflected in Water*, p. 131.

121. Ward, *Anarchy in Action*, pp. 82, 84.

122. Ward, *Anarchy in Action*, p. 118.

123. Colin Ward, *The Child in the City* (London: Bedford Square Press, 1990, first Published 1978), p. 178.

124. Ward, *The Child in the City*, p. 181.

125. Colin Ward and Anthony Fyson, *Streetwork: The Exploding School* (London: Routledge and Kegan Paul, 1973), p. 2.

126. Colin Ward, *The Child in the Country* (London: Bedford Square Press, 1990, first Published 1988), p. 18.

127. Ward, *The Child in the City*, p. 182.

128. Colin Ward and Eileen Adams, *Art and the Built Environment. A Teachers Approach* (Essex: Longman,1982), p. 9.

129. Ward and Adams, *Art and the Built Environment. A Teachers Approach*, p. 17.

130. Ward and Adams, *Art and the Built Environment. A Teachers Approach*, p. 21.

131. Bernard Crick, 'A Subject at Last!' in Crick, *Essays on Citizenship* (London and New York: Continuum, 2000), p. 33.

132. Ward and Adams, *Art and the Built Environment. A Teachers Approach*, pp. 13–14.

133. Ward and Fyson, *Streetwork*, p. 88.

134. Ward, *Housing*, p. 122.

135. Ward, *Anarchy in Action*, p. 86.

136. Colin Ward, 'Anarchism and the Informal Economy', pp. 25–37, p. 26.

137. Ward, 'Anarchism and the Informal Economy', p. 26.

138. Ward, *Social Policy*, p. 17.

139. Ward, *Social Policy*, p. 17.

140. Ward, *Social Policy*, p. 17.

141. Ward, 'Anarchism and the Informal Economy', p. 27.

142. Ward, 'Anarchism and the Informal Economy', p. 31.

143. Ward, 'Anarchism and the Informal Economy', p. 31.

144. Ward, 'Anarchism and the Informal Economy', pp. 25–37, p. 25.

145. The idea of the 'core economy' is associated with the work of Neva Goodwin.

146. Particularly in the work of Elinor Ostrom, Anna Coote and Edgar Cahn.

147. Ward, 'Anarchism and the Informal Economy', p. 27.

148. J. L. and Barbara Hammond, *The Town Labourer: 1760–1832* (Sutton; Reprint edition, 1995).

149. Ward, 'Anarchism and the Informal Economy', p. 34.

150. Ward, 'Anarchism and the Informal Economy', p. 30.

151. Ward, 'Anarchism and the Informal Economy', p. 29.

152. Ward, 'Anarchism and the Informal Economy', p. 29.

153. Ward, 'Anarchism and the Informal Economy', p. 35.

154. Ward, 'Anarchism and the Informal Economy', p. 30.

155. Ward, 'Anarchism and the Informal Economy', p. 31.

156. Ward, 'Anarchism and the Informal Economy', p. 32.

157. Ward, 'Anarchism and the Informal Economy', p. 32.

158. Ward, 'Anarchism and the Informal Economy', p. 33.

159. Ward, 'Anarchism and the Informal Economy', p. 33.

160. Ward, 'Anarchism and the Informal Economy', pp. 34–5.

161. Ward, 'Anarchism and the Informal Economy', p. 37.

162. Worpole, 'Introduction', in Worpole (ed.), *Richer Futures*, p. xi.

163. See for example 'Co-Production. A Manifesto for Growing the Core Economy' (new economics foundation, 2008).

5

Concluding Reflections

Anarchism, as presented by the writers of the British tradition explored here, inveigles its audiences into a singular and inescapable awareness of themselves, their inner lives and their relationships. At times it is an uncomfortable encounter. The authors presented here make no provision for a discrete, self-contained sphere of 'political' dilemmas, prompting readers of their work to interrogate even their most interior experiences for evidence of regimented social ordering. Dangers lurk, these anarchists warn us, in inherited assumptions about the limits of the human capacity for self-governed social order, evident but disguised in popular notions such as 'lesser evils', 'necessary means', 'the greater good', 'representation', 'nationhood', 'universal welfare' and 'full employment'. The dangers manifest themselves not just in limitations on freedom and heightened experience, or in the loss of civilian identity, but in the breakdown of social relation-ships, the atomization of individual life, the threat of mass warfare and the retraction of adequate social care. Yet the process of interrogation reveals inherent human tendencies for robust individual creativity and initiative, and hardy, deep-rooted social bonds based not just on needs and sociable instincts, but also on the expressive and inquisitive qualities of the human personality. These anarchists celebrated the transformative potential of human experience. Freedom is not passive but active, they argued. It is cre-ated and designed as part of the human engagement with his environment, particularly through the sensations of the body. The experiences of the dynamically creative and self-aware human mind extend human knowl-edge and consciousness, expanding sensibilities and leading to greater social awareness. In the work of these anarchists, freedom is a sort of inte-gration of the personality, which is developed in qualities of confidence and self-awareness and alive to the material and human environments that make that freedom possible. In short, undeveloped selves live in undeveloped communities.

Utopia features heavily in the work of these authors, a singular utopia premised on a faith in human social, biological, aesthetic and problem-solving instincts. Anarchism is often charged with a blind and unrealistic confidence in the moral capacities of unfettered individuals, but in fact, as these authors show, the conviction actually reflected in anarchist thought and practice is that individuals and social groups are effective and creative in their attempts to secure their needs and interests. It is not really a moral point. In fact, throughout the work presented here, the anarchists have demonstrated an acute awareness of the limited human capacities for moral reasoning at a distance, either in terms of time or space, from the potential subjects of actions or decisions. Human psychology means, they argue, that individuals cannot retain a sense of the human subjectivity of others in the absence of direct and personal relationships with them. These limitations thus underpin the mass killing of war and the harm caused by centralized political leadership. A key point in this analysis is that abstract unities, endowed with personalized attributes, such as 'the nation', cannot exercise the moral reasoning, creative capacity or self-awareness that is distinctive to the human individual. These anarchists responded to what they saw as the need to recover human experience and explore human purposes, via immediate and tangible connections between individuals, in the face of a collectivizing, soulless modernity. In their work utopia is thus linked with immediacy and directness in social experience, the rejection of deferred conceptions of 'the good', and a suspicion towards abstract impersonal goals. This is alongside a focus on association, community, cooperation, experiment, expediency, social organization and small-scale gradualism. For these authors, utopia is an ideal of community transformation of public space in the present as the expression of agency and association.

Anarchism as a political tradition in Britain has made firm and coherent contributions to debates about the importance of human connectedness that go to the heart of understanding the success or failure of democracy, the roots of human freedom, health and well-being, and the social experience of war. The centrality of voluntary, spontaneous social connectedness in the work of anarchists like those examined in this volume thus has parallels in more mainstream political and social science with the recognition of the importance of what has, especially since the work of Robert Putnam, been referred to as 'social capital'. As used by social scientists, in the words of Putnam, the term refers to 'social networks, norms of reciprocity, mutual assistance, and trustworthiness'. The concept is used to demonstrate the value of social networks for the people within them and for society at large. Putnam himself highlights 'the extraordinary power and subtlety of social networks to enable people to improve their lives'.[1] Putnam framed social capital as an attribute of societies and, as such, a broad societal measure of communal health. According to Putnam and his followers, social capital is reflected in the membership of social groups, including non-political organizations, which facilitate co-operation and mutually supportive relations in communities by building trust and shared values. It is thus a vital resource for combating the social disorders prevalent in modern society, such as crime, and a key component in building and maintaining democracies.[2] The anarchists studied here also aimed to advocate and support the development and survival of vibrant, participatory communities embedded in face-to-face contact between individuals. In their terminology, this was in defence of a 'social' as opposed to a 'political' principle of human organization, and it was represented in voluntary organization and grassroots association. Recent academic and policy debates, from discussions about social capital to social policy initiatives which advance the idea of 'co-production', demonstrate a swell of interest in reciprocity and mutualism in social connections, and individual involvement in the public life of the community.[3] These approaches emphasize the importance of person-to-person contact over time for building trust and mutuality, as Putnam describes it 'defined by connections among people who know each other'.[4] There are clear synergies to be explored between anarchist and non-anarchist attempts to redefine the relationships between the social and the political, informal work and formal economic activity, and individual confidence and social connectedness. The anarchist figures in this book highlight the resources of British intellectual culture for debates such as these, in particular for thinking about a model of social policy that separates the public sphere from top-down ideologies of social provision. For the anarchists, however, any agenda is suspect unless it immediately and tangibly aims to diminish homogeneity, hierarchy, dependence (as opposed to independence), war and poverty. Alongside the more positive contributions to social dilemmas made by anarchist writers, these suspicions could have a role to play in the anarchist interrogation of ongoing debates. For example, Colin Ward demonstrates that any attempt to fuse private responsibility and public spirit needs to recognize the economic underpinning necessary for community self-management, such as reliable tenure and small-scale credit facilities.

The anarchists examined here demonstrated through their work the rich native set of resources available in British social and intellectual traditions for imagining and employing an appropriately socially focused mode of human organization. They also highlighted the particular threats to human social order as they perceived them in state policies of war, and in centralized economic and social policies. The ideas of these three thinkers were radically anti-militarist, linking warfare with the hierarchical and centralized practices of domestic government. The anarchist distinction between state and society made them particularly sensitive to the infiltration of military concerns in civilian spheres. In this sense the distinction between 'politics' and 'society', which underpinned much of their analysis, was reflected in the dichotomies they presented between war and community, or militarism and civilianism: Read posited regimentation as the enemy of shared human sensibilities, Comfort defined 'fascism' as a wider militaristic social dynamic which undermined 'responsibility', and Ward conflated war and unemployment on the one hand as the opposing structures to mutual aid and self-employment on the other. These authors perceived a close relationship between the growing domestic scope of the state, the emergence of total, industrialized warfare, and the erosion of both vibrant individuality and social responsibility. In various ways they blurred the distinction between the politics of warfare and conscription and the dynamics of interpersonal relations. Alex Comfort in particular condemned the national militarization of civilian life and the rapid development of technologies for killing during and after the Second World War and he related the experiences of civilians in wartime to the breakdown of social relationships in post-war society. Ward also pointed out that the lack of democratic public influence on the development of the atomic bomb reflected the impotence experienced by society in regard to all governmental decisions, and he extended this into his critique of the principles of state welfare. The anarchist anti-militarist agenda condemned the imposition of military purposes on civilian life during the war and saw it as an authoritarian sociological phenomenon associated with centralized government even in peacetime. What is clear is that British anarchists have long argued that immediate interpersonal contact is a vital social resource and their particular insight in this regard is fed by the anti-militarism which imbues this tradition.

Just as anarchists did not accept the 'welfarist' accounts of the social changes precipitated by total warfare in Britain, anarchist ideological commitments regarding social relationships, war and the state also mean that anarchism is unlikely to be 'captured' by any free-market libertarian interpretations of early twenty-first-century history regarding the virtue of cutting back excessive state responsibility for social welfare. This is despite a glancing and superficial coincidence of terminology: Read mounted an attack on the state in defence of individual uniqueness and creativity; Comfort abhorred collectivist rhetoric, urging the individual to take responsibility for his actions; and Ward advocated self-build movements in housing in terms that sometimes sounded like a defence of unregulated private enterprise for personal use. Despite these individualist themes, these three writers were also urging radical changes in the distribution of social and economic power. Drawing on romantic celebrations of creative individuality, shared cultural anxieties about the morally desensitizing impact of mass administration, British traditions of mutualism and self-help, and embedded sources of anti-militarism, the anarchist authors discussed here presented programmes for radical social change that deployed and liberated natural social instincts. These programmes included virulent rejections of war, universal opportunities for aesthetic expression, experimental student-led techniques in education, the devolution of political and economic control to the lowest possible community level in various spheres, popular control over the use of technology and land, and the re-evaluation of social mores according to their individual and social benefit and authenticity. This list demonstrates just what a genuinely enlarged social or civil sphere might look like according to this anarchist tradition, and it gives its adherents a measure by which to assess any top-down administrative claims to be encouraging voluntarism, empowering communities, building social relationships, or supporting liberating opportunities for self-help.

Notes

1. Robert Putnam, 'Introduction' to Robert Putman and Lewis Feldstein, *Better Together: Restoring the American Community* (New York: Simon & Schuster Paperbacks, 2004), p. 4.

2. Robert D. Putnam, Robert Leonardi, Raffaella Y. Nanetti, *Making Democracy Work: Civic Traditions in Modern Italy* (Princeton: Princeton University Press, 1994).

3. See for example 'Co-Production. A Manifesto for Growing the Core Economy' (new economics foundation, 2008).

4. Robert Putnam, 'Introduction' to Robert Putman and Lewis Feldstein, *Better together: Restoring the American Community*, p. 9.

Bibliography

Adams, Ian, *Political Ideology Today* (Manchester: Manchester University Press, 1993)

Addison, Paul, *The Road to 1945: British Politics and the Second World War* (London: Cape, 1975)

Anderson, Benedict, *Under Three Flags: Anarchism and the Anti-Colonial Imagination* (London: Verso, 2005)

Antliff, Alan, *Anarchy and Art: From the Paris Commune to the Fall of the Berlin Wall* (Vancouver: Arsenal Pulp Press, 2007)

Apter, David E., 'The Old Anarchism and the New – Some Comments', pp. 1–13, in Apter and Joll (eds), *Anarchism Today* (London and Basingstoke: Macmillan, 1971)

Apter, David E., and James Joll (eds), *Anarchism Today* (London and Basingstoke: Macmillan, 1971)

Barker, Rodney, *Political Ideas in Modern Britain* (London: Methuen and Co. Ltd, 1978)

Barnett, Anthony, and Roger Scruton (eds), *Town and Country* (UK: Vintage, Random House, 1999)

Beevers, Robert, *The Garden City Utopia. A Critical Biography of Ebenezer Howard* (Basingstoke: Macmillan, 1988)

Berdyaev, Nikolai, *Slavery and Freedom* (London: Geoffrey Bles, 1943)

Berlin, Isaiah, 'Two Concepts of Liberty', pp. 118–72, in *Four Essays on Liberty* (Oxford: Oxford University Press, 1969)

—, *Four Essays on Liberty* (Oxford: Oxford University Press, 1969)

Berry, Francis, *Herbert Read* (London: Longmans, Green, and Co., 1953)

Bourne, Randolph S., 'The State' (1919), in *War and the Intellectual: Essays, 1915–1919* (New York: Harper Torchbooks, 1964)

Brittain, Vera, *Seeds of Chaos* (London 1944. Published for the Bombing Restriction Committee by New Vision Press)

Brock, Peter, *Twentieth Century Pacifism* (New York: Van Nostrand Reinhold Company, 1970)

Brooke, Stephen, *Reform and Reconstruction. Britain after the War 1945–51* (Manchester and New York: Manchester University Press, 1995)

Buber, Martin, *Paths in Utopia* (Boston: Beacon Books, 1958)

Buchanan, Tom, *Britain and the Spanish Civil War* (Cambridge: Cambridge University Press, 1997)

Bull, Malcolm (ed.), *Apocalypse Theory and the Ends of the World* (Oxford: Wiley-Blackwell, 1995)

Burdon, Christopher, *The Apocalypse in England Revelation Unravelling, 1700–1834* (Basingstoke: Macmillan, 1997)

Burrell, Gibson, and Karen Dale, 'Utopiary: Utopias, gardens and organization', pp. 106–27, in Martin Parker (ed.), *Utopia and Organization* (Oxford: Blackwell Publishing, 2002)

Calder, Angus, *The People's War* (London: Cape, 1969)

—, *The Myth of the Blitz* (London: Jonathan Cape, 1991)

Call, Lewis, *Postmodern Anarchism* (Lanham, MD; Oxford: Lexington, 2002)

Camus, Albert (with foreword by Herbert Read), *The Rebel* (London: Penguin, 1965)

Capouya, Emile, and Keitha Tompkins (eds), *The Essential Kropotkin* (New York: Liveright, 1975)

Carter, Alan, 'Review of George Crowder, *Classical Anarchism. The Political Thought of Godwin, Proudhon, Bakunin, and Kropotkin* (Oxford: Clarendon Press, 1991)' (1995), in *Political Studies* (vol. 43, no. 1)

Carter, April, 'Anarchism and Violence', in J. Rowland Pennock and John W. Chapman (eds) *Anarchism (NOMOS XIX)* (New York: New York University Press, 1978)

—, *The Political Theory of Anarchism* (London: Routledge & Kegan Paul, 1979)

Ceadel, Martin, *Pacifism in Britain 1914–1945* (Oxford: Clarendon Press, 1980)

—, *Thinking about Peace and War* (Oxford: Oxford University Press, 1987)

Cesarani, David, 'Lacking in Conviction: British War Crimes Policy and National Memory of the Second World War', pp. 27–44, in Martin Evans and Ken Lunn (eds) *War and Memory in the Twentieth Century* (Oxford: Berg, 1997)

Chilton, Paul, and Crispin Aubrey (eds) *Nineteen Eighty-Four in 1984* (London: Comedia Publishing Group, 1984)

Clark, Samuel, *Living without Domination : The Possibility of an Anarchist Utopia* (Aldershot: Ashgate, 2007)

Comfort, Alex, 'An Exposition of Irresponsibility' (1943), *Partisan Review* (October)

—, 'Bombing Policy', *Tribune*, 2 April 1943

—, 'October, 1944' (1944), *NOW*.

—, *The Power House* (London: Routledge, 1944)

—, 'War Criminals', Correspondence, *Tribune*, 6 Oct 1944

—, 'An Anarchist View: The Political Relevance of Pacifism' (1945), *Peace News* (7 December)

—, 'Criminal Lunacy Exposed' (1945), *War Commentary* (25 August)

—, *Art and Social Responsibility* (London: The Falcon Press Limited, 1946)

—, 'Imagination or Reportage?' (1946), in *Readers News* (January)

—, 'Peace and Disobedience' (1946), *Peace News* Pamphlet

—, 'The Kinsey Report' (1948), *Freedom* (1 May)

—, *The Novel and Our Time* (London: Phoenix House Limited, 1948)

—, 'The Right Thing to Do' (1948), BBC talk, December 1948, published as a *Peace News* Pamphlet and in *Freedom* (24 December 1948)

—, 'Keep Endless Watch' (c. 1949), *Readers News*

—, *On This Side Nothing* (New York: Viking, 1949)

—, *The Pattern of the Future* (London: Routledge and Kegan Paul, 1949)

—, *Authority and Delinquency in the Modern State* (London: Routledge and Kegan Paul, London, 1950)

—, 'Psychopaths in Power' (1950), *Freedom* (14 October)

—, 'Social Responsibility in Science and Art' (1951), BBC talk, published as a *Peace News* Pamphlet (1952), and in *Freedom* (1 and 8 December 1951)

—, 'What Can We Do To Stop Them? (1951)', Speech at Public meeting organised by the London Anarchist Group, 28 March 1951, printed in *Freedom* (14 April 1951)

—, 'The Individual and World Peace' (1954), *Resistance* (New York, June)

—, *Sex in Society* (London: Gerald Duckworth, 1963)

—, *Sexual Behaviour in Society* (London: Gerald Duckworth and Co. Ltd, 1950, reprinted as *Sex in Society*, 1963)

—, *Nature and Human Nature* (London: Weidenfeld and Nicolson, 1966)

—, (edited with an introduction by David Goodway), *Writings against Power and Death. The Anarchist Articles and Pamphlets of Alex Comfort* (London: Freedom Press, 1994)

—, 'Preface' in Harold Barclay *People without Government* (London: Kahn and Averill, 1996)

Crick, Bernard, *George Orwell. A Life* (London: Penguin, 1992)

—, 'A Subject at Last!' in Crick, *Essays on Citizenship* (London and New York: Continuum, 2000)

Critchley, Simon, *Infinitely Demanding: Ethics of Commitment, Politics of Resistance* (London: Verso, 2007)

Crowder, George, *Classical Anarchism. The Political Thought of Godwin, Proudhon, Bakunin, and Kropotkin* (Oxford: Clarendon Press, 1991)

Currey, R. N., *Poets of the 1939–1945 War* (London: Longmans, Green & Co Ltd, 1967)

Darwin, C., *The Descent of Man* (Oxford: Oxford University Press, 1909)

Davey, Kevin, 'Herbert Read and Englishness', pp. 270–86, in David Goodway (ed.), *Herbert Read Reassessed* (Liverpool: Liverpool University Press, 1988)

Day, Richard, *Gramsci is Dead: anarchist Currents in the Newest Social Movements* (London: Pluto Press, 2005)

Edgerton, David, *Warfare State: Britain, 1920–1970* (Cambridge: Cambridge University Press, 2006)

Evans, Martin and Ken Lunn (eds) *War and Memory in the Twentieth Century* (Oxford: Berg, 1997)

Ferguson, Robert, *The Short Sharp Life of T.E.Hulme* (London: Penguin, 2002)

Fowler, R. B., 'The Anarchist Tradition of Political Thought' (1972), *The Western Political Quarterly* (vol. 25, no.4, Dec.), pp. 738–52

Franks, Benjamin, *Rebel Alliances: The Means and Ends of Contemporary British Anarchisms* (Edinburgh: AK, 2006)

Freedom Press, *George Orwell at Home* (London: Freedom Press, 1998)

French, Warren, (ed.), *The Forties: Fiction, Poetry, Drama* (Deland, FL, Everett/ Edwards, 1969)

Gardner, Brian (ed.), *The Terrible Rain: The War Poets 1939–45* (London: Methuen, 1968)

Goodin, Robert, and Philip Pettit, *A Companion to Contemporary Political Philosophy* (Oxford: Blackwell, 1993)

Goodway, David, 'The Politics of Herbert Read', pp. 177–95, in David Goodway (ed.), *Herbert Read Reassessed* (Liverpool: Liverpool University Press, 1988)

— (ed.), *For Anarchism: History, Theory and Practice* (London: Routledge, 1989)

— (ed.), *Herbert Read. A One-Man Manifesto and Other Writings for Freedom Press* (London: Freedom Press, 1994)

— (ed.), *Writings against Power and Death. The Anarchist Articles and Pamphlets of Alex Comfort* (London: Freedom Press, 1994)

— (ed.), *Herbert Read Reassessed* (Liverpool: Liverpool University Press, 1998)

—, 'The Anarchism of Colin Ward', pp. 3–20, in Ken Worpole (ed.), *Richer Futures. Fashioning a New Politics* (London: Earthscan Publications, 1999)

—, *Anarchist Seeds beneath the Snow* (Liverpool: Liverpool University Press, 2006)

Goodway, David, and Colin Ward, *Talking Anarchy* (Nottingham: Five Leaves Publications, 2003)

Goodwin, Barbara, *Using Political Ideas* (Chichester: John Wiley & Sons, 1997)

Goodwin, Barbara, and Keith Taylor, *The Politics of Utopia. A Study in Theory and Practice* (London: Hutchinson, 1982)

Gordon, Uri, 'Anarchism Reloaded', *Journal of Political Ideologies* 12 (1), 2007, pp. 29–48

—, *Anarchy Alive: Anti-Authoritarian Politics from Practice to Theory* (London: Pluto Press, 2008)

Graeber, David, 'For a New Anarchism' (2002), *New Left Review* (12 Jan/Feb), pp. 61–73

—, *Fragments of an Anarchist Anthropology* (Chicago: Prickly Paradigm Press, 2004)

Grayling, A. C., *Among the Dead Cities* (London: Bloomsbury Publishing, 2006)

Green, David, *Reinventing Civil Society: The Rediscovery of Welfare without Politics* (London: IEA Health and Welfare Unit, 1993)

Greenleaf, W. H., *The British Political Tradition Volume II. The Ideological Heritage* (London and New York: Methuen, 1983)

Guérin, Daniel, *Anarchism* (New York and London: Monthly Review Press, 1970)

Hammond, J. L. and Barbara, *The Town Labourer*: 1760–1832 (Sutton; Reprint edition, 1995)

Harrison, Charles, *English Art and Modernism 1900–1939* (New Haven and London: Yale University Press, 1981)

Hendry, J. F., and Henry Treece, *The White Horseman. Prose and Verse of the New Apocalypse* (London: Routledge, 1941)

—, *The Crown and the Sickle. An Anthology* (London: P.S. King and Staples Limited, 1945)

Hennessy, Peter, and Anthony Seldon (eds) *Ruling Performance: British Governments from Attlee to Thatcher* (Oxford: Basil Blackwell, 1987)

Heywood, Andrew, *Political Ideologies. An Introduction* (Basingstoke: Macmillan, 1998)

Hinton, James, *Protests and Visions. Peace Politics in 20th Century Britain* (London: Hutchinson Radius, 1989)

Hobsbawm, E. J., 'Reflections on Anarchism', pp. 82–91, in *Revolutionaries. Contemporary Essays* (London: Quartet Books, 1977)

Honeywell, Carissa, 'Paul Goodman: Finding an Audience for Anarchism in 20th Century America', *Journal for the Study of Radicalism* 5 (2), 2011

Honeywell, Carissa, 'Utopianism and Anarchism', *Journal of Political Ideologies* 12 (3), 2007, pp. 239–54

Hulme, T. E., *Speculations. Essays on Humanism and the Philosophy of Art,* edited by Herbert Read (London: Kegan Paul, Trench, Trubner and Co., Ltd, 1924)

Joll, James, *The Anarchists* (London: Methuen and Co. Ltd, 1969)

—, 'Anarchism – a Living Tradition', pp. 212–25, in David E. Apter and James Joll (eds) *Anarchism Today* (London and Basingstoke: Macmillan, 1971)

Kennedy, Pagan, *The Dangerous Joy of Dr. Sex and Other True Stories* (Santa Fe: Santa Fe Writers project, 2008)

King, James, *The Last Modern. A Life of Herbert Read* (New York: St. Martin's Press, 1990)

Kinna, Ruth, *Anarchism: A Beginners Guide* (Oxford: Oneworld, 2005)

Kropotkin, Peter, *Ethics: Origin and Development* (Dorchester: Prism Press, 1924)

—, *Mutual Aid* (London: Allen Lane, Penguin, 1972)

—, edited by Emile Capouya and Keitha Tompkins, *The Essential Kropotkin* (New York: Liveright, 1975)

—, 'Modern Science and Anarchism', pp. 57–93, in Emile Capouya and Keitha Tompkins (eds), *The Essential Kropotkin* (New York: Liveright, 1975)

Laslett, Peter, and W. G.Runciman (eds), *Philosophy, Politics and Society*, Second Series (Oxford: Blackwell, 1972)

Lawrence, D. H. (ed. Mara Kalnins) *Apocalypse and the Writing on Revelation* (Cambridge: Cambridge University Press, 1980)

Lukes, Steven, *Individualism* (Oxford: Blackwell, 1973)

Mannheim, Karl, *Ideology and Utopia. An Introduction to the Sociology of Knowledge* (London: Routledge and Kegan Paul Ltd, 1960)

Marshal, Peter, *Demanding the Impossible: A History of Anarchism* (London: Fontana Press, 1993)

Martin, David A., *Pacifism: An Historical and Sociological Study* (London: Routledge and Kegan Paul, 1965)

Marwick, Arthur, *The Sixties. Cultural Revolution in Britain, France, Italy and the United States c.1958–c.1974* (Oxford: Oxford University Press, 1998)

May, Todd, *The Political Philosophy of Poststructuralist Anarchism* (Pennsylvania: Pennsylvania State University Press, 1994)

McGinn, Bernard, 'The End of the World and the Beginning of Christendom', pp. 58–89, in Malcolm Bull (ed.), *Apocalypse Theory and the Ends of the World* (Oxford: Wiley-Blackwell, 1995)

McKay, George, *DiY Culture. Party and Protest in Nineties Britain* (London: Verso, 1998)

McLaughlin, Paul, *Anarchism and Authority: A Philosophical Introduction to Classical Anarchism* (Aldershot: Ashgate, 2007)

Mellor, David, *A Paradise Lost. The Neo-Romantic Imagination in Britain 1935–55* (London: Lund Humphries in association with the Barbican Art Gallery, 1987)

Miller, David, *Anarchism* (London: J.M. Dent and Sons Ltd, 1984)

Moorehead, Caroline, *Troublesome People. Enemies of War 1916–1986* (London: Hamish Hamilton, 1987)

Morgan, Kenneth, *The People's Peace: British History 1945–1989* (Oxford: Oxford University Press, 1990)

New economics foundation, 'Co-Production. A Manifesto for Growing the Core Economy', (new economics foundation, 2008)

Newman, Saul, *From Bakunin to Lacan: Anti-Authoritarianism and the Dislocation of Power* (London: Lexington, 2001)

Novak, D., 'The Place of Anarchism in the History of Political Thought' (1958), *Review of Politics* 20 (3), July, pp. 307–29

Orwell, George, edited by Sonia Orwell and Ian Angus, *The Collected Essays, Journalism and Letters of George Orwell, Volume 3, As I please, 1943–1945* (New York: Secker & Warburg, 1968)

—, edited by Sonia Orwell and Ian Angus, *The Collected Essays, Journalism and Letters of George Orwell, Volume 4, In Front of Your Nose, 1945–1950* (Harmondsworth: Penguin, 1970)

Ostergaard, Geoffrey, 'Resisting the Nation-State: The Pacifist and Anarchist Traditions', pp. 171–96 in Leonard Tivey (ed.), *The Nation-State. The Formation of Modern Politics* (Oxford: Martin Robertson, 1981)

Paine, T., *The Rights of Man* (1792; London: Watts, The Thinkers Library, 1939)

Paley, Morton D., *Apocalypse and Millennium in English Romantic Poetry* (Oxford: Oxford University Press, 1999)

Paraskos, Michael, 'Introduction' to Herbert Read, *To Hell with Culture* edited by Michael Paraskos (London and New York: Routledge, 2002, first published 1963)

—, 'The Curse of King Bomba: or how Marxism stole Modernism', pp. 44–57, in Michael Paraskos (ed.), *Re-Reading Read: New Views on Herbert Read* (London: Freedom Press, 2007)

Paraskos, Michael (ed.), *Re-Reading Read: New Views on Herbert Read* (London: Freedom Press, 2007)

Parker, Martin (ed.), *Utopia and Organization* (Oxford: Blackwell Publishing, 2002)

Pennock, J. Roland, and John W. Chapman (eds), *Anarchism*, Nomos XIX (New York: New York University Press, 1978)

Pierson, Stanley, *British Socialists. The Journey from Fantasy to Politics* (Cambridge, Massachusetts and London: Harvard University Press, 1979)

Piette, Adam, *Imagination at War: British Fiction and Poetry 1939–1945* (London and Basingstoke: Papermac/Macmillan, 1995)

Pike, Derrick, 'Conscientious Objectors in World War Two', *The Raven: Anarchist Quarterly*, 29, 8 (1), Spring 1995

Poggioli, Renato, *The Theory of the Avant-Garde* (London and Cambridge, MA: Oxford University Press; Harvard University Press, 1968)

Putman, Robert, and Lewis Feldstein, *Better Together: Restoring the American Community* (New York: Simon & Schuster Paperbacks, 2004)

Putnam, Robert, Robert Leonardi and Raffaella Y. Nanetti, *Making Democracy Work: Civic Traditions in Modern Italy* (Princeton: Princeton University Press, 1994)

Read, Benedict, and David Thistlewood (eds) *Herbert Read. A British Vision of World Art* (Leeds: Leeds City Art Galleries, 1993)

Read, Herbert, *Wordsworth* (London: Faber and Faber, 1930)

—, *The Meaning of Art* (London: Faber and Faber, 1931)

—, *Art Now. An Introduction to the Theory of Modern Painting and Sculpture* (London: Faber and Faber, 1933)

—, *Henry Moore, Sculptor: An Appreciation* (London: Zwemmer, 1934)

—, *In Defence of Shelley and Other Essays* (London: Heinemann, 1936)

— (ed.), *Surrealism* (London: Faber and Faber, 1936)

—, 'The Method of Revolution' (1938), in *Spain and the World* (16 September)

—, 'The Method of Revolution: An Answer' (1938), *Spain and the World* (12 November)

—, *Poetry and Anarchism* (London: Faber and Faber, 1938)

—, 'The Prerequisite of Peace' (1938), *Spain and the World* (Supplement, May)

—, *The English Vision. An Anthology* (London: Routledge, 1939)

—, *Education through Art* (London: Faber and Faber, 1943)

—, *The Education of Free Men* (London: Freedom Press, 1944)

—, 'After the Trial' (1945), speech after the trial of the editors of *War Commentary*, printed in *Freedom: Is It a Crime?* (London: Freedom Defence Committee, 1945)

—, 'Before the Trial' (1945), speech before the trial of the editors of *War Commentary*, printed in *War Commentary* (21 April 1945), and *Freedom: Is it a Crime?* (London: Freedom Defence Committee, 1945)

—, *Annals of Innocence and Experience* (London: Faber and Faber, 1946, first published 1940)

—, 'Anarchism: Past and Future' (1947), lecture to the London Anarchists, printed in *Freedom* (17 May 1947)

—, 'Neither Communism nor Liberalism' (1947), BBC talk, printed in *Freedom* (4 January)

—, 'The Problem of War and Peace' (1947), BBC talk, printed in *Freedom* (20 September 1947)

—, *Coleridge as Critic* (London: Faber and Faber, c.1948)

—, 'The End of an Age' (1948), *Freedom* (13 November)

—, 'Culture and Religion' (1949), BBC talk, printed in *Freedom* (23 July and 6 August 1949)

—, 'Americanism' (1950), *Freedom*, (1ˢᵗ April)

—, 'Art and Evolution of Man' (1951), Freedom Press, Conway Memorial Lecture (10 April 1951)

—, 'A One-Man Manifesto' (1951), *Freedom* (3ʳᵈ March)

—, 'A statement' (1953), *Freedom* (17 January)

—, 'The Centenary of *The Ego and His Own*' (1946), *Freedom* (27 July), reprinted in *The Tenth Muse: Essays in Criticism* (London: Routledge & Kegan Paul, 1957)

—, 'In Defence of Shelley' (1936), in Herbert Read, *Selected Writings. Poetry and Criticism* (London: Faber and Faber, 1963)

—, 'Psycho-analysis and Literary Criticism' (1924), in Herbert Read, *Selected Writings. Poetry and Criticism* (London: Faber and Faber, 1963)

—, *Selected Writings of Herbert Read* (London, Faber and Faber, 1963)

—, 'Surrealism and the Romantic Principle' (1936), in Herbert Read, *Selected Writings. Poetry and Criticism* (London: Faber and Faber, 1963)

—, *The Philosophy of Modern Art* (London: Faber and Faber, 1964, first published New York: Horizon Press, 1953)

—, *Henry Moore. A Study of His Life and Work* (London: Thames and Hudson, 1965)

—, *The Origins of Form in Art* (London: Thames and Hudson, 1965)

—, *Art and Alienation. The Role of the Artist in Society* (London: Thames and Hudson, 1967)

—, 'Education in Things', in *The Redemption of the Robot* (London: Faber and Faber, 1970)

—, *The Contrary Experience. Autobiographies* (New York: Horizon Press, 1973, first published 1963)

—, *Anarchy and Order* (London: Souvenir Press (Educational and Academic) Ltd, 1974)

—, 'The Grass Roots of Art' (1955), in George Woodcock (ed.) *The Anarchist Reader* (London: Fontana, 1977)

— (ed. David Goodway), *Herbert Read. A One-Man Manifesto and Other Writings for Freedom Press* (London: Freedom Press, 1994)

—, *To Hell with Culture* edited by Michael Paraskos (London and New York: Routledge, 2002, first published 1963)

Reichert, William O., 'Anarchism, Freedom, and Power' (1969), *Ethics* (vol. 79.2), pp. 139–49

Remy, Michel, *Surrealism in Britain* (Aldershot: Ashgate Publishing Limited, 1999)

Ritter, Alan, *Anarchism. A Theoretical Analysis* (Cambridge: Cambridge University Press, 1980)

Robertson, Alexander, Michel Remy, Mel Gooding, and Terry Friedman, *Angels of Anarchy and Machines for Making Clouds: Surrealism in Britain in the Thirties* (Leeds: Leeds City Are Galleries, 1986)

Rowland, Christopher, ' "Upon Whom the Ends of the Ages have Come": Apocalyptic and the Interpretation of the New Testament', pp. 38–57, in Malcolm Bull (ed.), *Apocalypse Theory and the Ends of the World* (Oxford: Wiley-Blackwell, 1995)

Runkle, Gerald, *Anarchism Old and New* (New York: Dell Publishing 1972)

Salmon, Arthur E., *Alex Comfort* (Boston: Twayne Publishers, 1978)

Savage, D. S., George Woodcock, Alex Comfort, and George Orwell, 'Pacifism and the War. A Controversy'(1942), *Partisan Review* (September–October), pp. 414–21

Sennett, Richard, *The Uses of Disorder. Personal Identity and City Life* (London: Faber and Faber, 1996)

Shaffer, Elinor, 'Secular Apocalypse: Prophets and Apocalyptics at the End of the Eighteenth Century', pp. 138–58 in Malcolm Bull (ed.), *Apocalypse Theory and the Ends of the World* (Oxford: Wiley-Blackwell, 1995)

Sheehan, Seán M., *Anarchism* (London: Reaktion Books, 2003)

Shires, Linda M., *British Poetry of the Second World War* (London and Basingstoke: Macmillan, 1985)

Shklar, Judith, *After Utopia. The Decline of Political Faith* (Princeton: Princeton University Press, 1957)

Sillars, Stuart, *British Romantic Art and the Second World War* (New York: St. Martin's Press, 1991)

Skelton, Robin, (ed.) *Herbert Read, A Memorial Symposium* (London: Methuen and Co. Ltd, 1970)

Skinner, Quentin, *Liberty before Liberalism* (Cambridge: Cambridge University Press, 1998)

Smith, Michael P., *The Libertarians and Education* (London: George Allen & Unwin, 1983)

Spalding, Frances, *British Art since 1900* (London: Thames and Hudson, 1986)

Spring, Joel, *Wheels in the Head: Educational Philosophies of Authority, Freedom, and Culture from Socrates to Human Rights* (USA: McGraw-Hill, 1999)

Stafford, David, 'Anarchists in Britain Today', pp. 84–104, in David E. Apter and James Joll (eds), *Anarchism Today* (London and Basingstoke: Macmillan, 1971)

Stanford, Derek, *Inside the Forties. Literary Memoirs 1937–1957* (London: Sidgwick and Jackson, 1977)

Stansky, Peter, and William Abrahams *London's Burning. Life, Death and Art in the Second World War* (London: Constable, 1994)

Steele, Tom, *Alfred Orage and The Leeds Arts Club* (Hants: Scolar Press,1990)

Swenarton, Mark, *Artisans and Architects. The Ruskinian Tradition in Architectural Thought* (Basingstoke and London: Macmillan, 1989)

Sylvan, Richard, 'Anarchism', pp. 215–43, in Robert Goodwin and Philip Pettit (eds), *A Companion to Contemporary Political Philosophy* (Oxford: Blackwell, 1993)

Taylor, Keith, *The Political Ideas of the Utopian Socialists* (UK: Frank Cass, 1982)

Taylor, Keith, and Barbara Goodwin, *The Politics of Utopia. A Study in Theory and Practice* (London: Hutchinson, 1982)

Taylor, Richard, *Against the Bomb. The British Movement 1958–1965* (Oxford: Clarendon Press, 1988)

Taylor, Richard, and Nigel Young, *Campaigns for Peace: British Peace Movements in the Twentieth Century* (Manchester: Manchester University Press, 1987)

Teichman, Jenny, *Pacifism and the Just War* (Oxford: Basil Blackwell, 1986)

Thistlewood, David, 'Herbert Read's Paradigm: A British Vision of Modernism', pp. 76–94, in Benedict Read and David Thistlewood (eds), *Herbert Read. A British Vision of World Art* (Leeds: Leeds City Art Galleries, 1993)

Thomas, Paul, *Karl Marx and the Anarchists* (London, Boston and Henley: Routledge and Kegan Paul, 1980)

—, 'Review of Alan Ritter, *Anarchism: A Theoretical Analysis* (Cambridge: Cambridge University Press, 1980)' (1982), in *Political Theory* (Volume 10, Issue 1, Feb)

Titmuss, Richard, *Problems of Social Policy* (Connecticut: Greenwood Press, 1971, originally published in 1950 by His Majesty's Stationary Office and London: Longmans, Green and Company)

Tivey, Leonard (ed.), *The Nation-State. The Formation of Modern Politics* (Oxford: Martin Robertson, 1981)

Treece, Henry, (ed.) *Herbert Read, An Introduction to His Work by Various Hands* (London: Faber and Faber, 1944)

—, *How I See Apocalypse* (London: Lindsay Drummond, 1946)

Walter, Nicolas, 'Nonviolent Resistance: Men against War', *Nonviolence*, 63, 1963

—, 'Anarchism in Print Yesterday and Today', pp. 127–44, in David E. Apter and James Joll (eds) *Anarchism Today* (London and Basingstoke: The Macmillan, 1971)

Ward, Colin, *Tenants Take Over* (London: The Architectural Press, 1974)

—, *Utopia* (Harmondsworth: Penguin, 1974)

—, *Housing. An Anarchist Approach* (London: Freedom Press, 1976)

—, *Anarchy in Action* (London: Freedom Press, 1982, first published George Allen and Unwin Ltd, 1973)

—, 'Big Brother Drives a Bulldozer', in Paul Chilton and Crispin Aubrey (eds), *Nineteen Eighty-Four in 1984* (London: Comedia Publishing Group, 1984)

—, *When We Build Again, Lets Have Housing that Works* (London: Pluto Press, 1985)

—, 'Anarchism and the Informal Economy' in *The Raven*, 1, 1986, pp. 25–37

—, 'Cheer Up!', *New Society*, June 1987

—, *The Child in the City* (London: Bedford Square Press, 1990)

—, *The Child in the Country* (London: Bedford Square Press, 1990)

—, *Influences. Voices of Creative Dissent* (Devon: Green Books, 1991)

—, *Education for Resourcefulness*, Lecture to annual Human Scale Education Conference at Dartington, April 1992, (Bath: Human Scale Education, 1993)

—, *New Town, Home Town* (London: Calouste Gulbenkian Foundation, 1993).

—, 'Witness for the Prosecution' *The Raven Anarchist Quarterly*, 29, 8, (1), Spring, 1995

—, *Social Policy. An Anarchist Response* (London: Freedom Press, 2000, first published London School of Economics, 1996)

—, *Reflected in Water. A Crisis of Social Responsibility* (London and Washington: Cassell, 1997)

—, 'Orwell and Anarchism' (1955), printed in *George Orwell at Home* (London: Freedom Press, 1998)

—, 'The Unofficial Countryside', in Anthony Barnett and Roger Scruton (eds), *Town and Country* (UK: Vintage, Random House, 1999)

—, *Anarchism. A Very Short Introduction* (Oxford: Oxford University Press, 2004)

Ward, Colin (ed.), *A Decade of Anarchy (1961–1970)* (London: Freedom Press, 1987)

Ward, Colin, and Anthony Fyson, *Streetwork: The Exploding School* (London: Routledge and Kegan Paul, 1973)

Ward, Colin, and David Goodway, *Talking Anarchy* (Nottingham: Five Leaves Publications, 2003)

Ward, Colin, and Dennis Hardy, *Arcadia for All. The Legacy of a Makeshift Landscape* (London and New York: Mansell Publishing Ltd, 1984)

Ward, Colin, and Eileen Adams, *Art and the Built Environment. A Teachers Approach* (Essex: Longman, 1982)

Weir, David, *Anarchy and Culture. The Aesthetic Politics of Modernism* (Amherst: University of Massachusetts Press, 1997)

White, Stuart, 'Making anarchism respectable? The Social Philosophy of Colin Ward', *Journal of Political Ideologies*, 12 (1), 2007, pp. 11–28

Widgery, David, *The Left in Britain 1956–1968* (Harmondsworth: Penguin, 1976)

Wieck, David, 'Anarchist Justice', pp. 215–38, in J. Roland Pennock and John W. Chapman (eds), *Anarchism*, Nomos XIX (New York: New York University Press, 1978)

Williams, Leonard, 'Anarchism Revived', *New Political Science*, 29(3), 2007, pp. 297–312

Woodcock, George, *Anarchism* (Harmondsworth: Penguin, 1962)

—, *Herbert Read: The Stream and the Source* (London: Faber and Faber, 1972)

— (ed.), *The Anarchist Reader* (London: Fontana, 1977)

—, *Letter to the Past: An Autobiography* (Canada: Fitzhenry and Whiteside Ltd, 1982)

Woodcock, George, and I. Avakumovic, *The Anarchist Prince* (New York: Schocken Books, 1971)

Worpole, Ken (ed.), *Richer Futures. Fashioning a New Politics* (London: Earthscan Publications, 1999)

Young, Nigel, *An Infantile Disorder? The Crisis and Decline of the New Left* (London: Routledge and Kegan Paul, 1977)

Zaslove, Jerald, 'Herbert Read and Essential Modernism: Or the Loss of an Image of the World', pp. 287–308, in David Goodway (ed.) *Herbert Read Reassessed* (Liverpool: Liverpool University Press, 1988)

Index

Lightning Source UK Ltd.
Milton Keynes UK
UKOW031524210513

211044UK00005B/68/P